PENETRATIONS
&
(s)PERMUTATIONS
A Psychological Exploration
of Modernity, Islam
& Fundamentalisms

Dr. D. Latifa

PENETRATIONS & (S)PERMUTATIONS
A PSYCHOLOGICAL EXPLORATION OF
MODERNITY, ISLAM & FUNDAMENTALISMS
Dr. D. Latifa

*

A
Yunus Publishing
Punkademics
Publication

*

Toronto, Canada
Lahore, Pakistan
Ghent, Belgium
2017

*

Version 1.0

*

ISBN (print): 978-90-814-9967-5
ISBN (ebook): 978-94-926-8902-3
ASIN (kindle): B0742JZBTV
D/2015/12.808/2
NUR: 717, 775

*

To the Ulemama's, Saeenjee
and the Silsilah of Bhangees (SOB).

Battle not with monsters
lest ye become a monster,
and if you gaze into the abyss,
the abyss also gazes into you.

(Friedrich Nietzsche)

TABLE OF CONTENTS

Part IV: Psychological Explorations of Global Paranoia..... 239

Preface from the Publisher

When I met Dr. D. Latifa for the first time in 2012, we were supposed to meet for a short interview, as part of a series of conversations with influential Muslim scholars, artists and activists. I eventually ended up staying three days at her home in Pakistan.

D. had a long history in Pakistani and international academia and as such had already written several articles and books. Yet, when we met, she felt the need to keep a low profile. She was very well aware of the fact that her ideas and propositions may evoke some aggressive opposition in certain circles. She therefore decided to use a pseudonym in the eventual publication of our interview. That's how the name 'Dr. D. Latifa' was born. It carries a double meaning. *Al-latif* (pronounced: *al lateef*) is one of the 99 names of God which can mean 'The Most Subtle'. The word also has connotations of pleasant, pleasing, gentle, knowledgeable, kind, in a subtle way. In Urdu, for example, the words *funoon-i-latifa* refer to the fine arts, while, at the same time, *latifa* means 'a joke', because, perhaps, the essence of good jokes resides in its subtle twists.

Dr. D. and I kept in touch and meet occasionally. At one of our encounters in Europe, I explained my idea of creating punkademics publications. This would be a series of independently published books with an interdisciplinary approach that breach the boundaries of mainstream research and that are somewhat dissident in an academic sense. That is, the author would be pushing against many constraints imposed by academia. At the same time, such books would still be aimed at readers with a thorough background in particular topics and thus would not exactly be meant for a more 'general' public. But the texts would not get mired within the navel-gazing discussions of a particular in-crowd of supposed experts, rather, they would offer genuinely fresh and useful perspectives which can help inform contemporary social debates. In short: the intellectual analysis would be there, but as a whole, the text would be a little edgy.

D. liked the idea and mentioned a text she had written but which had been lying around for a couple of years. After reading her manuscript, it quickly became clear to me that, whatever the considerations of academia and publishers might be, this text was a much needed one. As such, it finally saw the light of day in the form of this book—an independently published work on the psychology of fundamentalisms in our modern world, the first of the Punkademics publications.

One needs to keep in mind, of course, that the book was originally written in 2010. Therefore, certain aspects of contemporary history and world politics are not taken up into the wider analysis. The emergence of Daesh/ISIL/ISIS/IS (however you want to name the phenomenon that started rampaging Iraq and Syria since 2014) is one example. Where appropriate, some extra small references have been added during the final redaction, but the ideology, behavior and *psychology* of such groups is not discussed in depth since these groups had not arisen at the time of these writings. The reader will thus notice that groups like the Taliban and al-Qaeda—which used to occupy the media headlines more in the last decades of the 20th Century and the first decade of the 21st Century—are more consistently used as examples.

I am convinced however, that this is not a shortcoming of the book. On the contrary, this is its strength. The text is not narrowly focused on the geo-political hype of the moment. Instead, it goes much deeper and reveals certain larger, long-lasting and constantly recurring psychological patterns which underlie current geo-political events. As such, it is up to the reader to apply the concepts described in this work to other modern 'penetrations' and '(s)permutations' like Daesh or drones. In other words, the news of today and the events of tomorrow form an immediate test for the theses proposed in this book.

I'm confident that Dr. D.'s theses will not only easily stand the test, but will also offer the reader a much deeper understanding of current conflicts. Precisely because the book does not lose itself in elaborations on whatever is the most recent event in the shifting geo-political spectrum, it makes it amply clear that there is nothing 'new' or 'unseen' but rather that these events are predictable expressions of deeper (psychological) patterns that repeatedly affect all of us all over the world.

Jonas Slaats
Ghent, June 2017

INTRODUCTION

He alone is modern who is fully conscious of the present.
(C.G. Jung[1])

Islam, Modernity and Fundamentalisms

Beyond economics and international geo-politics, two common explanations for the rise of Islamist fundamentalism* or Islamism,† have to do with concepts related to the project of modernity. The first, usually put forth by writers from within the Muslim world, concerns itself with low levels of education, particularly modern science, which is then prescribed as the requisite antidote to potential fanaticism.[2] In short, it sees an insufficient 'modernization'. The second type sees Islamism as a reaction to the social changes brought in the wake of rapid modernization.[3] While there is much truth to both perspectives, on closer scrutiny they raise more questions than answers. By now, many studies show that

---

* While recognizing that the term 'fundamentalism' is propagandist and misleading, one is also in agreement with Karen Armstrong that "like it or not, the word 'fundamentalism' is here to stay... the term is not perfect but it is a useful label for movements that despite their differences, bear a strong family resemblance." (Armstrong Karen, *The Battle for God*, 2000. p. x.)

† The term 'Islamism' could also be problematized in more ways than one, but since its use has become so widespread and because of a lack of better words to describe the same concept, the word Islamism is used here in its general sense of 'ideologization' of Islam. It thus refers to the subjugation of a broad religion/ worldview/tradition/cultural matrix to socio-political means and ends.

religious fundamentalism is not restricted to Islam but is a powerful presence in all religions across the globe. In the Judeo-Christian world, its rank and file comprise non-Muslims, well-educated individuals living in, what are in many ways, postmodern societies.[4] One way or another, fundamentalism, as Habermas says, is 'an exclusively modern phenomenon'.[5]

After the events of September 11, 2001, it has become amply evident that a modern (scientific) education is no guarantee against the emergence of a violent, fundamentalist mindset in Islam. From Saudi Arabia to Egypt to Pakistan to Indonesia, increasingly the key figures in Islamist movements are highly trained in scientific disciplines such as engineering, medicine, even nuclear physics.* Clearly they cannot be considered in the same category as the barely literate, non-scientifically 'educated' Taliban, who are nevertheless also enamored of high-tech missiles and other modern weaponry. Given that people like Osama bin Laden and many of his contemporary 'colleagues' in places like Syria or Iraq, were and are well educated, professionally trained 'minds', the psychological links of modernity with Islamism cannot be ignored. To the extent that increasingly it is such high ideologues who provide the inspiration (and frequently financial and technical support) to their less well to do and less educated, low ideological brothers, modernity and its problems and prospects, not just in places such as Pakistan, remains a central issue.

The terms 'high' and 'low' Islam as used initially by Gellner in the context of modernity, referred to the urban-rural divide and correspondingly differing expressions of Islam.[6] 'High' Islam derives its authority from text and scholarship, emphasizing order and strict observance of rules, puritanism and

---

* To name a few: Osama (engineering), Atta (architecture), Zawehri (medicine) and Bashiruddin Mahmood (nuclear physics).

scripturalism. In contrast, 'low' or 'folk' Islam was more free-wheeling, mystical, emotional and deeply imprinted with the cult of saints and generally more inclined to 'wilder practices' such as 'drug use hysteria and possession'. While such conceptual distinctions may have been valid earlier, present circumstances indicate that much has changed especially in the domain of what constitutes 'low' or 'folk' Islam in Pakistan today. Whereas three to four decades ago this relatively relaxed form of Islam may have constituted the majority of the population, today it is perhaps no longer the case. Varying degrees of literacy and a relentless indoctrination from the 'priests' of 'high' Islam have created another category of Muslims of which the Taliban are just one example. Best termed as 'mass Islamism', it increasingly constitutes, I believe, the bulk of fundamentalists at the lower end of the socioeconomic spectrum in Pakistan today. Thus, in this context 'low' or mass Islamism does not refer to folk/popular Islam but to another pole of fundamentalism.

Folk or popular Islam is of course present across the demographic spectrum but is increasingly under siege from Islamists 'high' and 'low'. Given that it also actually has a highbrow dimension, and as a whole remains strongly anchored in regional culture, it is best referred to as indigenous, Sufi, or in the case of Pakistan, Indo-Persian Islam.

Modernity and Postmodernity

This book is a feminist exploration of the psychological underpinnings of both 'high' and 'low' Islamism and their relationship to issues such as gender, violence and sexuality. Both types of Islamism are not starkly separate categories/individuals, and are part of a wider spectrum with some common elements. Almost all Islamists tend to have repressive, even brutal attitudes towards women, so broadly speaking they are similar in their socio-political attitudes and impact. And above all, both of them are inextricably linked with the psychological underpinnings of modernity.

When I speak of modernity, I refer to the modes of social life which emerged from about the 17th Century onward, when, along with the Enlightenment, Western Europe underwent political and industrial revolutions. The latter, heavily subsidized by the colonialist project, initiated a process of change that steadily started transforming the entire world. As Karen Armstrong says "Western civilization has changed the world. Nothing—including religion—can ever be the same again."[7]

Some key features of modernity are economic production, urbanization, centralized bureaucratic states, the privileging of science and rationality over religious faith and a belief in progress based on science and technology. In the last century, it also includes women's rights and feminism. These features of course did not have a uniform impact on what we today call postcolonial societies, but collectively form an *idea* of what it means to be a modern person or state.

In the academic world today, it is fashionable to talk of post-modernity. Its features are the globalization of business and culture across national boundaries, fragmentation, and a general mistrust of 'grand narratives' and absolute truths. It asserts that all knowledge is subjective and relative, and here the feminist perspective in many disciplines has played a major role in challenging the modernist paradigm. However, while posing intellectual and philosophical challenges, postmodernity remains more of a debate within the global intellectual elite. In fact, some believe that it is better called 'high' modernity, in which through a process of reflexivity, social practices are constantly examined and, as new information comes in, transformed. This includes feminism, which is an ongoing evolving project.

As a contemporary intellectual and psychological 'condition', post or high modernity represents a still emerging threshold holding both positive and negative potentials. The prospects for the latter are evident, for example, in academic deconstruction which even as it theorizes the impossibility of shared meaning, ensures that the status quo of power relations remains intact. Additionally, given deconstructionism's espousal of socio-psychological atomization/alienation, suicide becomes the only logical option, which in fact, has been exercised as an intellectual 'statement' not only by Foucault, albeit indirectly, but more consciously by some of the French situationist theorists.[8] Are they and the Islamist suicide bombers two sides of the same coin? It is all too easy to play such postmodern mind-games in a framework that ultimately renders everything devoid of meaning.[*]

If modernity created what Sartre called the 'God shaped hole in human consciousness', deconstruction offers a nihilistic black hole. Collapsing all meaning of language into itself, it simply reinforces (post)modernity's impetus towards disconnectedness. Feminism itself can be seen as inherent to the emergence of postmodernism and continues to reflect its problems and potentials. At one level it was, and remains, a radical and liberating perspective exposing the underpinnings of extant views on not only women but also the anti-woman bias in disciplines spanning history and sociology to the sciences,[9] and of course religion. At the same time, it remains riven by internal differences, for example, the 'essence' versus 'diversity' dichotomy. The former position assumes that there is something essentially different between men and women, witness the body;

---

[*] Although, at the same time, it is notable that op-eds in eminent political journals report that suicide rates in the US are indicative of "national security crises." (See: Deboer Fredrik, *America's Suicide Epidemic Is a National Security Crisis*, 2016.)

the latter posits that gender is in fact a social construction.

Whereas the bulk of (academic) feminism remains entrenched in these debates, there are significant currents, particularly feminist spirituality and ecofeminism, that have, in turn, critiqued this dichotomy as yet another patriarchally inspired project, one that is deeply linked to Western knowledge systems.[10] From these feminist spiritual and ecological perspectives, an un(self)critical modernity or postmodernity are 'masculinist' philosophies alienating humans from life, woman, nature and the transcendent. As Spretnak points out, the Eurocentric machismo of modernity has simply been replaced by an equally masculinist, atomized notion of complete autonomy in postmodernity.[11]

At another level, the postmodern turn signifies a welcome counterbalance to the West centered biases of different types of modern knowledge, and has led to the emergence of new disciplines including postcolonial/cultural studies. Recognizing the relative nature of knowledge, it accepts a diversity of viewpoints, encouraging articulation of individual and cultural identity. It can be argued however, that this consciousness of what makes one distinct must also include a recognition of what it is that connects us, and meaningfully so. As the by now burgeoning literature on women, religion and spirituality indicates, these ideal(s) of meaning and interconnectedness are paramount in feminist reviewing of religion whether in the ancient traditions or contemporary variants such as the Goddess movement in the West.*

It is worth noting that in the new revised edition of a premier

---

* There are many radical scholars such as Mary Daly and Carol Christ giving the 'Goddess' movement some exceedingly sophisticated conceptual frameworks vis-à-vis Western women's spirituality and feminism. For the moment, much of this work remains marginalized by the 'malestream', but it is only a matter of time before these trends will become fully evident.

reference text, the *Encyclopedia of Religion*, the longest new addition (80.000 words) is the compound entry on 'Gender and Religion' and another long entry on 'Ecology and Religion'. As noted by Ursula King, this is the strongest evidence for the occurrence of a massive paradigm shift in the scholarship on religion.[12] This being so, the question is not only about changes (if any) in conceptions of Islam, gender, violence etc. but also how religion and gender have been constructed within Western psychological and religious discourse. Thus, while the post-colonial focus on the crisis in modernity may seem academically passé, the fact is that even in the West, in the context of the study of religion, 'postmodernism has not yet displaced modernism; the two compete for the current Western mindset'.[13]

About two decades ago, it seemed that postmodernity had firmly 'arrived' outside of the academy onto the world stage. Its hallmarks of ambiguity, doubt, and relativization of values had *Newsweek* describing Bill Clinton as a "post-modern president".[14] None of these terms could be used to describe the following president George Bush, or the mood of the current times. In both rhetoric and action, a very modern sense of certainty prevails regarding right/wrong, good/evil, for/against, us/them. This rhetoric finds an almost verbatim echo in many parts of the Muslim world and the uncanny similarity between the utterance of George Bush and Osama bin Laden have not gone unnoticed.[15] As the world is propelled towards greater violence, this language psychologically signals a set of pervasively *modern* attitudes within and between, Islam and the West. Thus, however well documented the critique of modernity, it is vital to revisit it in the present situation.

Muslims and Modernity

While we all can agree that sociologically all identities are constructed, the real issue is how, from what, by whom, and for what purpose? The human self and its sense of identity is dynamic, complicated, multidimensional, drawing from history, geography, biology, collective memory, power structures, media, religion, to name just a few. It becomes all the more complex in the context of globalization and communities in diaspora.[16] All these dimensions, and others, have been brought to analyses of Islam and Muslims and I don't dispute their relevance. Yet the times demand that Muslims (and non-Muslims) recognize how key dimensions of Islamism are deeply linked to the modern Western 'mind', which, from the feminist point of view, represents a violent and masculinist ethos.

Academic, theological and cultural discourse in Muslim societies such as Pakistan are overwhelmingly dominated by modern ideals either explicitly or implicitly via the media and in notions such as 'modernization and development'. As such, the critique of modernity needs to be restated in terms of the feminist view and especially in psychology in order to draw connections between it and contemporary issues/events as they relate to the psychology of Islamism, high and low. At the same time, many Muslims, who see themselves as 'secular' and/or 'moderate', and 'intellectual' and who are trying to cope with the present polarization have yet to seriously consider the psychological and political significance of feminism and the critique of modernity for these times.

Within those who see themselves as devout believers but not extremists, it is fashionable to condemn the West for its 'godlessness' and excessive materialism. Showing a lack of self-reflection, it is seldom recognized that actually what they share with the West is a peculiar, deeply misogynist view of oneself and religion. Given that a powerful critique of this type of Christianity exists within the West, along with a by now well established critique of the virulent dimensions of modernity, it is best to utilize these, if only in the interests of civilizational propriety. In short: apart from scrutinizing the Muslim psyche's engagement with Islam, one needs a psychological framework that is contemporary and critical, not only of (post)modernity but also of Christianity as critiqued from within the West.

The choice of such a framework is based on recognition of the globalization of knowledge as advanced by the idioms of the West. Being a product, however partial, of modernity oneself, the Muslim analyst should have no hesitation working within these idioms, albeit critically. Especially in view of an urgently needed civilizational dialogue, the effort should be to seek out common ground and to a great extent the onus is on the Muslims. This responsibility should include an acknowledgement of the more positive dimensions of (post)modernity foremost among which is the West's historically evident capacity for ruthless self-examination, as well as the capacity to assimilate knowledge regardless of 'origins', and, above all, the articulation and steady unfolding of the spectrum that is feminism.

Most Muslims will recognize these qualities, at least theoretically, as a quintessentially Islamic virtue when seen through the Prophet's tradition of urging Muslims to 'seek knowledge even if it is in China'. Given that the Prophet himself is seen as the fountain-head of spiritual knowledge, such a statement can only be construed as referring specifically to the significance of more 'worldly' types of knowledge and not just the scientific-technical. One can only be grateful for the 'appropriation' of Islamic philosophical frameworks by Western scholars since they offer Muslims a space to not only engage the West but more importantly, also analyze the contemporary

Muslim condition. Such a process, in turn, can become a catalyst for building bridges between Islam and the West. The current polarization, then, requires frameworks that are hybrid, not hidebound.

The Subjugated West

As I proceed to delineate the frameworks of this book, many readers will come across names of Western authors who usually do not constitute whatever is considered the mainstream of their discipline. For example, within psychology, it is quite evident that Freudian ideas and concepts such as 'id', 'ego' or 'superego' continue to be influential and are now part of popular culture and modern education. In contrast, relatively few are aware of the ideas of Jung, who was initially Freud's star pupil and subsequently his rival, but in any case an equally major foundational figure in psychology. Jungian terms such as 'enantrodromia', 'anima' or 'archetype' are certainly not as well known. Without going into numerous political, social and historical reasons as to why these thinkers remain eclipsed in Western academia, suffice it to say that they can be considered part of what a leading postcolonial scholar, Ashis Nandy, aptly called the 'subjugated West'.

As Nandy points out in his varied and incisive post-colonial critiques of the Enlightenment, and the implications on the West's dominance through the colonial project, any dialogue between the 'West and the 'rest' today cannot be fruitful if it does not include the 'disowned or repressed West'. That is, within modernity, there have been many thinkers in the West who were critical of colonization and the damage being done to other cultures. This is as true today as it was a century ago. There are indeed numerous academic and public intellectuals who speak truth to power in the West about its past and present, not only about its destructive impact on much of the world, but also its internal crises of meaning, values, war mongering, consumerism etc. But the question is: who is listening?

Nevertheless, given the tension-riven times, it is important not to abandon dialogue. In the words of Nandy:

> Any alternative form of dialogue between cultures cannot but attempt to rediscover the subjugated West and make it an ally. The attempt to do so could be an important marker of the new cosmopolitism that would use as its base the experience of suffering in Asia, Africa and South America during the last two hundred years.[17]

Similarly, Muslims too have their own share of 'disowned' and 'repressed' writers, thinkers, saints, 'heretics' etc. In short, in the interest of dialogue, and simply as a break from the usual hidebound academic analyses, the conceptual frameworks in this book are located from these lesser known dissident communities of the disowned.

An Interdisciplinary and Jungian Approach to Modernity

This book primarily draws on a hybrid critique, based on post analytic Jungian psychology, continental feminist philosophy, ecofeminist critiques of science and modernity, and post-colonial cultural studies of women's spiritualities. As such, it's an explicitly interdisciplinary examination of the relationship between patriarchal constructions of the modern self and their psychological impact on how the modern mind constructs religion. In so doing, it draws on critiques by C.G. Jung and James Hillman, who argued that a 'Cartesian' and 'Christianist' construction of religion has by now been globally internalized, thereby distorting the contemporary (self)understanding of all religions and precluding a realistic engagement by women (and men) with their subjectivities and spiritual-imaginative potentialities.

Between the widespread and well established critique of modern science[18] and the feminist critique of Judeo-Christian theology,[19] today different perspectives are converging to examine the (negative) role of Christianity in key aspects of modernity. This scrutiny is not just limited to the role of missionary Christianity in the colonization project, but has also considered its relationship to the environmental crisis and current geopolitical trends.[20]

Freud & Jung

Within psychology, which itself can be considered an inextricable and foundational aspect of modernity, the Freudian explication of personality/behavior was almost immediately followed by the ideas of Jung, whose work is a critique of Freud as well as Christianity and modernity. Referring to the differences between Freud and Jung, is not to deny the current presence of what can be called the therapy supermarket. But as distinct epistemological premises underlying the psychotherapeutic project, until today the Freud/Jung differences still form a tale of two cities, one of which all psychologists/psychiatrists eventually inhabit.[21]

In disagreeing with Freud about religion being an 'illusion' without a future, Jung was not a sentimental advocate of a pre-modern past. For him, the human psyche and its capacities for knowledge, including of oneself, was nature's greatest experiment. Taking a psycho-historical-cultural-spiritual view of individual/ collective consciousness as ongoing evolutionary phenomena, he saw both Christianity and scientific modernity as quantum leaps in this process, albeit with major provisos. Scientific rationalism's significance lies in the enabling of capacities that assist in an 'objective' understanding of what is mostly the material world. Recognizing the epistemological constraints of the individual human psyche, scientific knowledge, for Jung, is not rendered useless if this subjective aspect is acknowledged. In fact, recognizing this keeps one humble, and in a way, genuinely within the essence of science-as-fact(s).

For Jung, who saw his framework of depth-psychology within this conception of science, we are, as it were, programmed by nature towards knowledge, including of oneself, and to this extent, modernity and its ethos of 'objectivity' was/is vital. As a project aiming at understanding human (self)consciousness, modern psychology and its myriad schools reflect both the psyche's inherent diversity and its natural impetus towards understanding self and other(s). This includes the religious impulse, which for Jung, is inherently part of being human. Functioning like an instinct, it unfolds in stages within individual and collective existence, requiring a progressively conscious engagement/ understanding.

Jung & Modernity

A problematic controversial figure in the history of psychology, Jung can nevertheless be considered ahead of his time, in many ways even postmodern. Accordingly his use of the terms 'modern' and 'pseudo modern', can be read as postmodern and modern respectively. Deriving his data from decades of psychiatric practice, Jung was of the view that within the Judeo-Christian West, the Europeans, or rather, the 'white man in general', was/is essentially 'pseudo modern'.[22] That is, white people are unconscious about themselves as well as their religion. Protestant Christianity particularly, had been cut off from its ancient psycho-historical matrix and scientific rationalism has prevented the unfolding, maturing and assimilation of the religious impulse in the consciousness of its white adherents.

Psychologically, beyond the first half of life, any objective self-awareness must include not only personal history, but also one's collective, religious and cultural past, and which, inevitably means engaging with the eternal questions posed by religion. Locating oneself as a subject at all these levels and bringing them into consciousness in a rational and detached manner, is, according to Jung, the distinguishing feature of 'a modern individual'. That is, someone who can be objective about one's own subjectivity. Once the element of religious subjectivity comes into this equation, Jung's modern individual cannot but find himself in a tortuous situation.

In the light of the two World Wars and the large scale man-made catastrophes of the last century and till today, the truly (post)modern Western person would have a very humble attitude regarding the techno-triumphs of scientific rationalism, at the very least, skeptical regarding such 'progress' in human knowledge. An "honest admission of modernity means voluntarily declaring oneself bankrupt … renouncing the halo of sanctity which history bestows."[23]

Given the genesis and flowering of modernity in the Judeo-Christian West, Jung's criticism was primarily addressed to that audience and its attitudes towards religion. He was convinced that institutionalized Christianity, and Protestantism particularly, has been rendered spiritually invalid for the individual (Westerner). He based his criticism at two levels, namely, the place, or rather the absence, of the Feminine and the problem of evil. Whether in the rejection or acceptance of religion, from his point of view, it nevertheless remains an uncritical, that is, unconscious relationship. In the absence of a conscious engagement with religion, the psychological energy behind this universal instinct continues to impact behavior, and eventually turns onto itself. The Nietzschean 'death' of God is, at many levels, illusionary since the archetypal idea of the 'God-image' exists indelibly in the human psyche and this has to be engaged with consciously.

> When someone hits upon the idea that God is dead, or does not exist at all, the psychic God-image, which is a dynamic part of the psyche's structure, finds its way back into the subject and produces a condition of 'God-Almightiness', that is, all those qualities that are peculiar to fools and madmen and therefore lead to catastrophe.

> This, then is the great problem that faces the whole of Christianity: where now is the sanction for goodness and justice which was once anchored in metaphysics? Is it really only brute force that decides everything? Is the ultimate authority only the will of whatever man happens to be in power? ... God-Almightiness does not make man divine, it merely fills him with arrogance and arouses everything evil in him.[24]

The history of modernity shows the consequences of the (hu)man centered view of life engendered by scientific rationalism. It shows how we are equally ready to kill in the name of ideologies that have nothing to do with religion. "We can no longer deny that the dark stirrings of the unconscious are active powers ... forces exist... which cannot be fitted into our rational world order ... modern man has lost all the metaphysical certainties ... and set up in their place the ideals of material security, general welfare and humanitarianism."[25] However well meaning, they are not able to replace religion, the 'absence' of which will continue to negatively impact human existence.

Jung lived through both World Wars and his writings are as much about the collective and cultural as they are about individual psychology. A substantial part of his massive *Collected Works* focused on the role of the Judeo-Christian West and 'the white man in general' in creating the modern world. While acknowledging its achievements, Jung ruthlessly criticized the West and what he perceived as its ultimately enormous potential to destroy itself and the entire world. This could only be avoided through a heightened self-awareness of (self)destructive capacities—the 'shadow'—and acknowledgement of guilt, not just limited to the Holocaust. This is a painful process, requiring ruthless honesty and self-contemplation, and few individuals are willing to do this.

For Jung a (post)modern person, then, 'is often to be found among those who call themselves old fashioned'.[26] That is, those who can examine the existential self-awareness of one's own destructive potential and yet remain connected with the eternal dimensions of religion. Hence, the truly (post)modern person is a radical, since s/he interprets religion according to the context of the time and not official dogma, as lived experience not just faith. The emergent identity is not based on an inflated grandiosity about self, history, religion, but a tentative humility grounded in religious/universal values.

A rare occurrence as an ideal-type, this combination of existential self-awareness and a recognition of an inner, transcendent impulse, was becoming evident in the West, even during Jung's life time and especially towards the end of the Second World War. Since the 1960's this subjective current in the West is now fully visible not only in the steady acceptance of postmodern ideals in academia but also in the spectrum of New Age movements and the search for spiritual alternatives. Collectively, they signal the paradoxical problematics and potentials of what today, one calls a postmodern consciousness. However, when de-linked from religion, such a consciousness becomes an illustration of what Jung referred to as (post)"modern man in search of soul". Given its direct, historical understanding of the depth of violence within itself, such a consciousness demands, and rightly so, not just faith but also knowledge(s) about religion grounded in experience. (Post)"modern man abhors faith and the religions based on it ... he wants to *know*, to experience for himself."[27]

Noticing how Christianity was unable to deliver this need, Jung was scathingly critical of particularly Protestant Christianity, seeing it as a principal player in the dark side of modernity. Simultaneously, he remained firmly of the view that the European-Western drift towards 'eastern' ideas such as Theosophy were not the answer, which he insisted had to come from within, from a different vision and understanding of the Judeo-Christian monotheisms, especially Christianity.

Jung's engagement with Christianity was deeply complicated. Many of his psychological concepts were drawn from an exploration of Gnostic Christian texts, and especially the arcana of the European alchemists. Dismissed by modern science as a primitive precursor to chemistry, Jung showed how these texts were actually describing different psychological and spiritual processes. Having long disappeared as a living tradition within Christianity, the absence of Gnostic pathways—what in other religions is now called mysticism by modern academia—can be seen as a contributing factor to the rigidifying and shriveling of the soul of Christianity.

Recognizing the impossibility of reviving the Gnostic tradition within Christianity, Jung nevertheless remained convinced of the significance of its ideas. Unless the white man finds and values his 'soul', the Western world would wreak more psychological havoc on itself and continue being propelled towards destruction of self and the world at large. This is why, in the West, one way or another, humans continue to fall into the grip of seemingly non-religious ideologies (such as socialism, humanism, materialism, etc.) which exercise a power that is *psychologically* similar to religion.

Jung's Relevance in the Contemporary Debates on Islam

On the whole, Jung remains, in many ways a prescient and important figure, not only in depth-psychology, but also for his ideas about Christianity as transmuted into a key factor in the cultural crisis of modernity. For example, the existential crisis of the European psyche in search of its soul was, for Jung, the initial stage of an emergent *weltanschauung* (i.e. postmodernity) that had to do with a genuinely objective sense of a self-rooted in a more inward, contemplative attitude. As early as 1933, he sensed that this self-reflective awareness would be problematic for the West, since the U.S.A. culturally represented the antithesis of the requisite psychological qualities for self-awareness: "… we see as the Western world strikes up a more rapid tempo—the American tempo—the exact opposite of quietism … an unprecedented tension arises between objective and subjective reality. Perhaps it is a final race between aging Europe and young America".[28] The race, for Jung, was about a spiritual self-consciousness tempered by a profound recognition of one's inner capacity for destruction. This was the European experience. While leaving the winner to history, Jung was certain that until the West as a whole came to terms with its 'shadow' it would continue behaving like a:

> bird of prey with his insatiable lust to lord it in every land, even those that concern him not at all … that megalomania of ours which leads us to suppose, among other things, that Christianity is the only truth and the white Christ the only redeemer... To make matters worse, the enlightened European is of the opinion that religion and such things are good enough for the masses and for women, but of little consequence compared with immediate economic and political questions[29]

Whereas I will continue to use the term 'modern' in its usual contemporary sense, Jung's notion of the 'pseudo modern' nevertheless remains significant for those Muslims who are (in)directly educated in modern ways. Transposed within the modern/postmodern frame, here the questions around modernity have to do with the nature of (lack of) self-reflection undertaken by Muslims in modern times. Any discussion on the psychology of modern Islam must take into account these lesser known counter perspectives on modernity, particularly by those Muslims who are equally skeptical about a techno-scientific future as they are about the (im)possibility of returning to a 'glorious' past. Given the Jungian critique of both Cartesianism and Christian monotheism, the Muslim analyst is fortunate in being able to locate him/herself within such a psycho-religious critique, since, in a sense, s/he is relieved of having to initiate/adopt a negatively critical view of another religion. In any case, I'm relying on such a critique, not to demonstrate any inferiority/superiority of one religion over another, but to eventually adopt a more conscious and (self)critical view of Islam. That is, whereas comparisons with Christianity may be inevitable, they are made in the context of critiques of Christianity by Jung and post-Jungians such as James Hillman in order to show what Muslims themselves have 'done' to Islam in the modern world.

All of this is not to suggest an uncritical acceptance of Jungian ideas—particularly in light of Jung's own relative ignorance about Islam.[30] Additionally, he has also drawn criticism from various quarters including certain schools of feminism for being essentialist and conservative.[31] Simultaneously, there is a flourishing post-Jungian European-Anglo-American discourse and one which is not limited to the clinical context. In fact, it is more at the cultural level that Jung's ideas, reworked, expanded and deepened by post Jungian scholars, including feminists, continue to have a growing impact. This is true especially in the humanities and academic cultural studies,[32] and in certain men's movements regarding religion and spirituality.[33] To this extent, when utilized broadly, many of Jung's ideas remain useful in an arena in which the discourse on religion remains stultified at various levels.

Given the virtual nonexistence of *any* sort of (post)Jungian discourse within Muslim academia, this book utilizes Jungian ideas in a simplified manner since one aim, among others, is to offer the Muslim reader alternative ways of looking at himself and religion. While it locates itself in various academic discourses it assumes a degree of cultural and historical awareness of certain ideas, seeking to bring them into a more general dialogical frame and as such, not addressed to the 'expert'.

If Muslims know little of Jungian ideas, the vast majority of Jungians (and Westerners) remain equally ignorant of Islam. There is virtually no Jungian psycho-cultural analysis of what many see as an impending Third World War in which religion is a major factor. Given Jung's canvas of concerns spanning the individual to the collective, and particularly religion, the absence of Jungian voices needs to be redressed.

Academic Déjà Vu

In stating Jung's ideas about modernity and what he saw as the psycho-spiritual plight of the Christian West, one is neither decrying Christianity nor suggesting that Muslims/Islam are a superior species. Using Pakistan as an example, the attempt here is to locate some dominants of contemporary Muslim un/consciousness within the larger project of modernity and try to go beyond the idea that Islamism is a refuge against the Godless, materialist values of the West. As suggested in the brief review of Jung's ideas, and which will be amplified in the sections to follow, modernity carries within itself a specific psychological and religious consciousness, which, given the current focus on Islam, needs to be identified, articulated and examined. Thus, for example, my use of the term 'Cartesian-Christianism' is a combination of two terms used frequently, but separately, by the post-Jungian scholar James Hillman in his critiques of the distorted Christianity as 'Christianism' and scientism as 'Cartesianism'.

The very fact that this book allies itself with various streams in feminism should indicate that it does not advocate a wholesale rejection of the (post)modern. In its recursive style of writing, it does not aim to have a *consistent* view of modernity but rather an *insistent* one about key psychological themes within the modern psyche. Similarly, feminism itself has innumerable variants/ dimensions and feminist spirituality and theology are today well-established fields of inquiry, yet remain at the margins of the global discourse on religion.

Insisting on taking just one position regarding, for example, holism or the essentialism versus the deconstruction debate, only leads to more polarization within feminism. Ultimately, all scholarship, feminist or otherwise, falls victim to what the philosopher Jenny Teichman calls the 'peacock' or 'rooster factor' in academia. That is, rivalry between purportedly incommensurable theories is often only an illusion based on *rivalry between men* and the masculinist tendency of competitive castration. The present political climate of rising counter/terrorism and militarism obscures the fact that it is women who lose most rights in war. Feminism needs to focus less on questions of 'theoretical (in)consistency' and more on utilizing different perspectives to expose the androcentric biases underlying dominant ideas of both modernity and modern religion.

Over the last decades, the tensions and controversies around

Islam and the West have generated a huge number of analyses from within academia. While not denying its significance, as one scans this material, there is a certain sense of *déjà vu* reminiscent of the intellectual enterprise of 'Soviet Studies'. After the collapse of the Soviet Union *The American Scholar* asked the question 'Why Were We Surprised?'[34] One main answer was the academic tendency to view events/phenomena through the "thin slit of social science" which pays attention to only military forces, economics, the relationships among leaders, that is, politics etc. Issues related to ethnicity, religion, culture and the passions they evoke were ignored and those academics who focused on them were scorned as intellectually soft or unscientific. Similarly, other eminent publications point out that Soviet Studies had as much to do with various intellectual positions within academe (liberal, conservative etc.) as without in the real world of people and politics. Yet, despite "prodigious intellectual labors and the prodigious sums spent to make them possible" not a single academic or expert from different perspectives could even vaguely anticipate the events which led to the final collapse.[35]

The value of such postmodern postmortems notwithstanding, in view of the current literal postmortems of Iraq, Afghanistan, Libya and Syria one wonders whether the ghost of Soviet Studies has returned to haunt current scholarship on Islam. Yet again, economics and politics and military/security concerns dominate the flow of analyses.

But attempting to look at modernity and Islam from lesser known interdisciplinary perspectives can be a hazardous undertaking in contemporary academia. The multi-levelled expansion of academic disciplines and wide spectrum of variation in thought within and between them is a double edged sword. The present complexity within the social sciences, humanities and cultural studies, along with the globalization of knowledge has, on the one hand, led to more space within global academia in terms of creative and professional possibilities. But between the 'end' of disciplines ranging from art to history, to the 'death of the subject', the individual who may not be a specialist but who nevertheless wants to conceptually engage with issues that either directly impact or simply interest her, remains bewildered and at a loss.

Even as boundaries between disciplines blur, psychology itself becomes a borderline case especially in the academic-applied realm of psychotherapy. These dilemmas are most evident in depth- psychology for the person seeking assistance as well as the practitioner. That is, in the face of suffering and the enormous complexity of the human individual in a globalizing world, which explanatory theory does one turn to in a process of endless de-construction? As Jan Campbell has observed, psychotherapy today overvalues theory and language over experience and history. Jungian and intersubjective psychoanalysis are some of the few exceptions[36] but as noted earlier they too are academically growing, fragmenting fields.

No psychotherapeutic system always delivers from suffering. By and large, the psychotherapeutic project is in the business of selling optimism and then attempts to justify it with an inflated idea of what life is all about. Even though, more often than not, the issues are less about 'cure' and more about *coping* with life and questions of its meaning(s).

More than a decade ago, *The Economist* ran a detailed special report with images of a cross and crescent and the title *The Next War, They Say*.[37] Regardless of who 'they' are, and wherever the reader chooses to locate herself between 'them' and 'us' in this scenario, to demand that every discussion around these issues must adhere to what are by now infinite and fragmentary academic 'norms', borders on insanity. For these and other reasons that will shortly follow, whether Jungian or otherwise, one will not be getting into the academic nuances of key terms such as 'modernity', 'feminism, 'gender', 'the West', 'Islam' etc. Most readers will have some broad idea of them and this is enough to raise, and engage with, the more pressing questions facing us today. Since I'm simultaneously critical of both Islam and the West, the book implies alternatives in what are, in fact, innumerable 'feminisms', 'Wests' or, most importantly, 'Islams'.

Academia at the Margins: Publish *and* Perish

Academic or not, the human psyche is capable of relativizing any statement by an equally valid and opposite one, and to this extent there is no certainty. The only certainty, and something we all will face—death—is one we know nothing about. Given the reality of suicide bombings in many parts of the Muslim world and the sense of a lurking fear (of death) everywhere, an academic can choose to stay within the safe confines of the ivory tower and indulge in endless hairsplitting, pursuing theoretical somersaults on tightropes set up, to begin with, by other academics. And so, perhaps, can the practitioner. But for some academic-practitioners, particularly in parts of the Muslim world, including Pakistan, such options are themselves becoming increasingly theoretical and illusionary, particularly in the context of the discourses around Islam and even more so when it comes to issues related to the politics of gender and sexuality.

Critique implies alternative. To over ambitiously place 'the West' and 'Islam' in the same boat is to risk being crucified between one's coreligionists and academia, particularly when one draws from different disciplines. It is to invite accusation of either not being rigorous enough or an 'apologist' for Islam—or a heretic. To put it bluntly, apprehensions regarding the reactions of what is essentially a global academic/psychoanalytic elite driven by its own contingencies to publish or (professionally) perish, seem mildly absurd in a situation in which there is real risk of literally perishing (violently) *because* of being published. Apart from physical survival, writing under a pseudonym brings an additional bonus in (self)liberation from the personal and collective (academic) ego.

Without wishing violence on anyone, one can nevertheless invite colleagues to consider such an experiment: Faced with a personal prospect of violence and one's mortality, authorial anonymity leads one away from the disembodied treadmill of 'knowledge for the sake of knowledge' to the question 'knowledge to what end?' However much a cliché, in this case, it is to try and build bridges. Among the media images of war, the crumbling verticality of tall buildings has their horizontal counterpart in the twisted steel of blown up bridges and the breakdown of communication among communities.

Seeking to also bridge the particular and the general, the book aims to add a third dimension from depth-psychology. In a sense, it envisages a reader in the same generalist spirit of the early days of analytical psychology in which the analysand was not necessarily 'mentally sick' nor did the analyst pose as a guru or savior. Like (post)Jungian and intersubjective work today, it was and remains, a dialogue and conversation among various participants. In so far as, for the psychologist, all writing is ultimately autobiographical, the participants are as much within as there are readers out there. This book is therefore an inner/outer dialogue between the 'Muslim' and 'the Westerner', including the feminist, as I know and experience them.

At one level then, this book is also a diagnostic and therapeutic exercise of/for my academic 'self' and for which a brief personal catharsis is in order.

Apart from its conceptual academic framework, thE book is based on decades of clinical experience, global popular culture, personal observations and experiences. It locates itself in 'real life' and not in the (phallic) confines of the 'ivory tower'. The main focus is not Christianity, Islam or modernity per se, but rather, how moderns *think* about them. It aims to deconstruct some dominant patterns of thought and implies alternative frame works which an average, well educated person/student interested in the issues can understand.

Possibly, professional academics will find a lack of nuance from within their specific disciplines. Nuance is, of course, always welcome. But when the purpose is merely to add more references simply to bolster the argument or because one must demonstrate to the reader one's knowledge of 'the literature' in a given field, serves little purpose other than to confuse/overwhelm the non-academic reader. As a Muslim who remains sceptical about the project of hadith classifications according to 'authentic', 'good' or 'weak' chain of narrators, I have always been struck by the similarities with the modern academic norm of establishing credibility by citing 'lineages' of authority (or 'the literature').

Of course, I rely on the work of numerous academics, but also choose not to subscribe to sundry academic norms such as adhering to the typical standard, linear, discursive format and style of writing, or citing the 'latest' pros/cons in a given field. While I understand the intellectual constraints/expectations of 'high' academia, the inordinate attention to form over substance, to references over argument, to 'nuance' (the 'fine point') over simple good sense, is often disconcerting.

As most academics know but may not admit publicly, these compulsions are also related to the 'publish or perish' syndrome which ultimately has much to do with careers, jobs and money. The constant need for the 'latest' can also easily be linked with more general psychodynamics discussed throughout the book, about the modern obsession—including academia's—with heroic masculinist youthfulness ('always new') and the discarding/ denigrating of the 'old' as 'dated'. It belies an exhibitionist compulsion to dispute/contest, regardless of context or central relevance to a given discussion. This academic compulsion to show off in an arena of antagonistic 'credit'/'discredit', is yet again a manifestation of teenage mores and the 'rooster' or 'peacock factor'.

From politics and democracy, to the media, medicine or law, vested interests are an inextricable part of human individual and social functioning; and all professions, including academia, have vested interests. Whether we talk about economics, ecology, breast feeding or raising children, today we have come to rely on experts, usually sanctioned by academia, in every aspect of life. Despite the fact that we also know that there are frequent disagreements among most experts, we rarely challenge the professional persona for what s/he represents, namely, simply one opinion among others—and which are also subject to temporal fashion. In that sense, apart from alerting us to the possibility of the illusionary nature of 'objective' knowledge, the tyranny of 'experts' needs to be countered. Not with a blanket anti-intellectualism, but with a healthy dose of skepticism. The awareness of increasingly corporatized vested interests within academia is particularly important in the social sciences and even more so in psychiatry and psychology which, in terms of their relatively short history and scant knowledge, have an inordinate and disproportionate degree of power and influence over the general population.

For many decades then, I have consciously chosen to stay on the margins of academia, preferring the real world instead. Occasionally I return to a university/institution (when invited) and invariably discover that beyond text books, students hunger for meaningful knowledge with which they can connect at a personal level, especially regarding religion and psychology.

Nevertheless, they are principally encouraged to sharpen their disputational, that is, antagonistic skills, manifested as 'critical thinking'. Of course these are vital but they should not become the primary aim of every exchange of ideas. Given the enormous spectrum of views available on every subject, today, it is easy to give any number of counter responses to virtually any statement. Surely we need to move beyond such juvenile mental fencing games and stop perpetuating the 'rooster/peacock' syndrome. The aim of research and analysis should not be to 'win' but to understand. Knowledge is more about degree and depth and less about a 'position' of who is on 'top'.

In sum: within the social sciences and the humanities, examining any complex phenomenon, particularly in the initial stages, requires a broad and more general view. Such a macro approach is important because it enables us to discern specific patterns and to derive meaningful generalizations. Naturally, this will be at the expense of individual detail and nuance. Thus, as an interdisciplinary conceptual collage encompassing several related theme(s) that normally belong to different academic domains, this book explicitly takes a broad view. As a whole, it is a series of introductory explorations/meditations on certain themes and not about the state of the art of any discipline. As such, it seeks to generate fresh connections, provoking questions and future interrogations from both within and outside of academia.

PART I:
PSYCHOLOGICAL EXPLORATIONS OF MODERNITY

CHAPTER 1:
THEORETICAL BACKGROUND

Today has meaning only if it stands between yesterday and
tomorrow.
(C.G. Jung[1])

The Broad Framework

As was explained in the introduction, this book is an interdisciplinary exploration of the relationship between patriarchal constructions of the modern self and their psychological impact on how the modern 'mind' constructs religion. Apart from being based on Carl Jung's critique of Protestant Christianity and the writings of post-analytic scholar James Hillman, it also draws from various strands of feminism including continental feminist philosophy, ecofeminist critiques of science and modernity, and post-colonial cultural studies of women's spiritualities. These and other disciplinary strands converge into a broad overall framework of Archetypal Psychology, which, as Hillman explains, is:

...a style of thinking and a revisionist engagement on many fronts: education, criticism, medicine, philosophy, religion, therapy and science. In trying to delineate the structure of a postmodern consciousness, archetypal theory lends its terms and viewpoints to a variety of intellectual concerns, seeking to draw individuals from diverse geographic and intellectual areas into rapport with each other for the revisioning of their ideas and their worlds.[2]

Feminist Philosophy and the Modern Self

Given that religious fundamentalism today is not just restricted to Islam, modernity can be linked to a certain 'mindset' about how we think about self, others and the world at large. In many ways, the modern idea of the self has been a long standing and ongoing concern in feminism, which has extensively critiqued the construction of the self in Western moral and political philosophy in the 20th Century. The critique is important since the self is pivotal to issues concerning agency, personhood, identity, the body, and is thus one of the most significant issues in feminism.[3]

Existing dominant notions of the self are primarily based on the (neo-)Kantian notion of a freely choosing ethical subject, functioning on the basis of pure reason leading to pure moral truth which transcends culture. Thus, the self is identified with abstract rationality. Similarly, economic behavior is seen as the application of reason to prioritize desires and devising means for their satisfaction. In short, the self is either *homo rationalis* (rational man) or *homo economicus* (economic man). For decades, Western feminism has challenged this idealized and narrow conception of the self, claiming that Western philosophy and popular culture is derived from the experience of predominantly white, heterosexual, economically advantaged men who have wielded social, economic and political power, dominating the arts, literature, media and scholarship.[4] To this extent, in "law, customary practice and cultural stereotypes, women's selfhood has been systematically subordinated, diminished", even when it has not been seemingly denied. Cast as a lesser form of the masculine individual, woman is the Other and thus, is the non-person, non-agent, non-subject.[5]

Kant's free and rational self, according to feminism, is not raceless, sexless, ageless, classless or genderless. Whether as ethical subject or *homo economicus*, he is actually a "white, healthy, youthfully, middle aged, middle class, heterosexual Man",[6] playing two dominant roles: as an impartial judge/legislator or as a self-interested bargainer/contractor in the marketplace. Either way, he rules through politics and commerce, both domains in which women have been historically excluded. In short: "In Western culture, the mind and reason are coded masculine, whereas the body and emotion are coded feminine (...) To identify the self ('I think therefore I am'), with the rational mind is to privilege a narrow idea of reason and to masculinize the self."[7] The split between an emotional, nonverbal, 'feminine' body and a rational 'masculine' mind is of course simultaneously a critique of the Cartesian dic(k)tum about the self, leading to what innumerable feminists, in different disciplines, have called the 'logocentric', 'phallocratic', 'disembodied' mind in Western cultural and intellectual consciousness. This critique is not limited to feminists and is today part of a different emergent paradigm. However, in much of the *real* world, via the modernity project, regardless of where we come from or whatever our faith, vast numbers of people have internalized the legacy of the young, white male, manifest in questionable ideas about life, nature, human psychology and religion.

What does this mean in psychological terms?

Briefly, in the Freudian view of personality, our consciousness and self-awareness relies extensively on the notion of 'ego'. The principals and goals of ego consciousness are will power and reason. That is, a mentally healthy person has a well-developed capacity for rationality and the ability of will power to control that which is not amenable to logic and reason. This is the ego, the 'I', who must control and civilize the unconscious id. In short the ego/self is equated with *reason*. Once the rational ego is developed, religion seems irrational, leading to the common notion that 'those who think can't believe and those who believe can't think'. Thus, for Freud, religion was an 'infantile neurosis', an 'illusion' without a future.[8] Considering the global resurgence of religion however, apparently it did have a future.

In contrast, as was mentioned in the introduction, Jung disagreed with Freud about the significance and place of religion in human life. Exceedingly critical of Christianity and often called a heretic, Jung nevertheless claimed that the religious impulse was inherent to the psyche and should be taken seriously. Given that the main quarrel between Freud and Jung was around religion and the self, in light of present realities, one needs to have a basic idea of Jung's critique, which was not just about Freud's ideas but also Western civilization generally.

Archetypal Psychology and the 'Polytheistic' Self

Psychological Diversity

Although Jung agreed with Freud about the existence of the unconscious, his attitude towards the psyche was radically different. Based on many years of psychiatric practice, and drawing on a vast knowledge of comparative culture, Jung's model of human consciousness relied less upon theoretical assumptions (none of Freud's concepts have a biological base), and more on the structure of the psyche *as it exists in human experience*, which is one of inner multiplicity.

One can test this inner multiplicity when one is alone. Even at this moment, you, the reader, may be *pre*occupied with some other thoughts. Alone, or with others, there is nothing particularly rational about the inner streams of thoughts and emotions we experience daily. Entering and exiting randomly, they rove from desire, to ambition, betrayal, anger, sex and more. At times, we are 'haunted' by recurring ideas/emotions which refuse to submit to our logic/control. In short, to recognize the reality of this inner diversity is to understand the psyche as it *lives* in our daily experience, and not how we think it 'should' be.

Additionally, Jung recognized that all cultures have mythologies which were actually religious *and* psychological in substance, and as such, were the earliest models for both psychology and religion. Different gods, male and female, have different domains which constantly intermingle. The gods frequently behave in (in)human ways. Mars, ruling over war and bloodshed, has a secret affair with Venus, paradigm of love and beauty. Apollo rules over knowledge and reason but was capable of irrational cruelty. Individually and collectively, the gods/godesses were complex, multifaceted, at one level benevolent, presiding over agriculture, health, love, war, knowledge, death etc.; at another, capable of cruelty and caprice. Very much, in fact, like you and I, as we experience the self(s) daily.

In post/Jungian analytic psychology, the figures of mythology are symbolic *person*-ifications of different sides to us, which in turn, can have different genders and qualities. So the psyche is 'polytheistic', that is, polyvalent, containing masculine/feminine aspects having numerous variations in form and style. Pan of the flute also represents panic. Zeus and Apollo are different and both have to contend with the bisexual Hermes or Dionysus who express more psychologically ambivalent ideas of masculinity. Similarly, the female form is host to Demeter, Venus, Athena and so on. Artemis the huntress, is quite different from the mature Aphrodite. Each is an archetype, that is, a *style* of un/consciousness, a psychological *attitude*, suggesting different *perspectives* on life, its stages, events and relationships. These attitudes/qualities are evident in *both* sexes, yet uniquely *embodied*. Thus, male and female divinities are symbolic representations of different dimensions of the Divine and diverse *psychological capacities* within humans. That is, they were/are *simultaneously* a reflection *and* a projection, of both the transcendent realm and the psyche's inherent multifaceted, polyvalent diversity.

Similar to the *Yin/Yang* of Taoism, the monotheisms also contain this symbolic, internal, nuanced, multi-dimensionality. In their stories and descriptions of men, women and God, we see soft, tender 'feminine' dimensions, such as the Virgin Mary, and more awesome 'masculine' qualities. The Torah has hundreds of 'faces', one for each Jew in exile, and in Islam there are the proverbial 99 Names of God and many other Attributes in the Quran.

In view of our inherent inner multiplicity, the rational modern Cartesian-Freudian 'ego' with which we principally identify the self and our common sense, is modelled largely on a set of youthful heroic male gods, including Apollo.

Archetypal Experience(s)

If this sounds 'unscientific' and 'archaic', it confirms the triumph of Freud's ideas, which are even heralded as "universal common sense" by respected magazines such as Time and Newsweek.[9] It should alert us to how handicapped we are when it comes to words such as 'symbolic' or 'archetype' which we connect primarily with art/literature and not with our self. Starting with Jung, to by now many others in the West, there is a well-established corpus around the idea that the great tragedy for the West has been its loss of archetypal consciousness.

Building on the work of Jung, James Hillman considers archetypes as axiomatic first principles, similar to models which are found in other fields, like 'matter', 'energy', 'health', 'society' and 'art'. These ideas hold whole worlds together, and yet can never be pointed to, accounted for, or even adequately circumscribed. They are the deepest patterns of psychic functioning governing the perspectives we have of ourselves and the world, as axiomatic self-evident images to which psychic life and our theories about it ever return.[10]

In spite of technological progress, life, as we live and experience it, remains the same: security, love and its defeats and triumphs, confusion, despair, and death. In all their nuances and opposites, and more, the 'stuff of life' is unchanging. The archetypal is about this 'stuff', which because of its universality can be seen as stereotypical and banal. Nevertheless, when encountered by the individual, the impact is frequently profound. All of us have experienced being 'in the grip' of emotions such as love, grief, fear, or 'moved' by an event/situation. Psychologically, these are *archetypal* experiences and best understood/expressed symbolically. Thus, when we are emotionally impacted by idea or feeling, and the discourse of ordinary life is inadequate to express it, as was the case on September 11, 2001, it is an archetypal experience.

Structures of consciousness

In more contemporary images, myths and archetypes are programs, the software governing the way individuals perceive 'reality'. Like cultural DNA, they tell about who we are, where are we going and what are the various options about life. They help organize society, families, individuals in ways which are simultaneously creative and destructive, quietly maintaining a balance. As long as things don't change, they give stability. But in times of crisis or rapid change, the duality emerges in its fundamental polarities, frequently violently so. Constituting a kind of web of inner meaning often unavoidable to our direct inspection, archetypes are the foundations of our basic assumptions about life and are the controlling images which determine much of the course of our lives. It is from these inner predispositions, and the feeling and images clustered about them, that we form a sense of who we are, collectively and individually. In sum, myths and the archetypes therein, can be considered as attitudes, *perspectives* on life, events, relationships—or as Hillman calls them, "structures of consciousness".

From this perspective every theory whether in science, economics or psychology, rests on certain ideas/assumptions about human nature. Every discipline is a unique way in which the psyche seeks to describe and understand life. The original meaning of the word 'idea', is from the Greek *eidos*: not only that which one sees but also *by means* of which one sees. For example, the idea of science as objective, amoral and neutral has its archetypal premises in Apollo: detached, dispassionate, exclusive masculinity, clarity, formality, geometrical beauty, far-sighted aims and a certain elitism. Thus, theories reveal an archetypal and mythological basis. In trying to profile the nature of these assumptions from the archetypal perspective, one may then ask 'who' rather than 'what' impels us to think the way we do about ourselves, relationships, social policy, religion etc.

Of course, when I suggest that we should ask ourselves 'who' rather than 'what' determines our dominant structure of consciousness, one might wonder how literally or symbolically this 'who' should be taken. And indeed much depends on the literal or symbolic manner we deal with myths and archetypes.

For example, a common criticism of religious fundamentalism is that it interprets religious scripture and texts literally. Yet while this is indeed the case, the question arises, what exactly is a symbol? That is, if an implied antidote to literalist fundamentalism is the symbolic, then what does 'the symbolic' mean? The answer entails a closer look at modernity's relationship to myth and symbol.

Mythos and Logos

In a study of fundamentalism in Judaism, Christianity and Islam, Karen Armstrong distinguishes two ways of thinking, *mythos* and *logos,* both of which are essential to humans and serve as complements to each other in the search for knowledge and truth.[11] *Mythos* has to do with meaning, with 'making sense' of the complex, often emotional experience that is life. The strange stories of mythology—and every society has them—were not meant to be taken literally. They were imaginary, psychological; metaphors for situations and experiences which are simultaneously ubiquitous to humanity and have a powerful impact on the individual. For example, birth and death, love and its loss or betrayal, are myth themes which engage us at a different level than, say, the molecular structure of water. How we construct the meaning of *mythos* has a profound impact upon our behavior.

Equally important, *logos* concerns the rational, pragmatic and scientific, and enables us to function in the practical world. In the pre-modern world these two domains were kept separate but valued equally. According to Armstrong, in the last two centuries, the sense of *mythos* was steadily lost in the West; today it is regarded by many as false superstition. Those who regard scientific rationalism as the only truth try to turn *mythos* into

41

logos. Religious fundamentalism makes the same mistake the other way round.

As derived from the work of Johan Sloek, Armstrong's use of *logos* can be considered partial.[12] It is also problematic since the word simultaneously presents a *religious* association that can be traced from the Greek for 'word' in (Johanine) Christianity where Christ is the *Logos*, the incarnation of God's 'word'. Islam too is based on the idea of the 'word' as a Divine force as related to the creative and knowledge giving aspects of language, as for example, in the first verses of the Revelation to Muhammad (96:1-5) or in the reference to God's power to create simply on the basis of the word "'Be', and it is" (36:82). In Greek, *logos* meant both spoken word and pervading principle, not just about material knowledge but also about the idea of wisdom, which, while including materiality, functions at a larger connective level. For the Greeks, *logos* was the principle around which the universe is ordered and the wise person aims to live in harmony with it. In short, *logos* has strong Christian associations which in turn contain a strong parallel to the concept of wisdom in Hellenic and Jewish thought in which wisdom and word were associated.[13]

While Armstrong rightly locates the questions of fundamentalism within the context of modernity, to say that in the premodern world *mythos* and *logos* were separate but complementary itself reflects the modernist impulse to separate the two. In the context of Christ as the 'Word' made flesh, *logos* itself contains, a mythic/symbolic aspect with strong religious connotations. Perhaps James Joyce was alluding to this when he spoke of "in the virgin's womb of the imagination, the word is made flesh."[14] Taking a more nuanced view of *logos*, the questions around fundamentalism have as much to do with a circumscription of meaning in both *mythos/logos*, as with the attempt at imposing principles of one category to another.

Modernity's Loss of Mythos

Human existence functions as a unified whole but for heuristic purposes one talks of the 'mind-body' spectrum. That is, there is an awareness of body but there is also a complete inner world that we inhabit—consciousness—where body awareness recedes into the background. We say "Don't' kick me", rather than "Don't kick my legs." The first is symbolic, the second literal. To the extent that we are physical and psychological beings, what is literally so is at some level symbolically true and vice versa.

The collective/social aspect to us, in order to adequately express itself, requires the symbolic, that is, something which will unite and yet be transpersonal. Symbols, therefore, are flexible, that is, ambiguous and open-ended enough to receive and respect individual differences. At the same time, insofar as we are hostage to the physical, this symbolic expression cannot but be expressed through physical means. That is, there has to be an image (such as a flag), sound, movement or person which gives form to the symbol. The content, insofar as it pertains to the individual, is literal and can even be precise, the form reflecting the collective is more open ended, subject to variation and can never be totally circumscribed. If this circumscription, or pinning down occurs, the symbol loses its uniting 'power'; the individual (literal) becomes dominant, and diversity, with its requirement of *interpretation*, is excluded. But the power of the idea lives on in the individual in terms of affect, albeit literally.

The modern understanding of symbols, such as in anthropology and semiotics in which meaning can be categorically decoded is, more an interpretation of signs (such as the matchstick figures for male/female public restrooms). This is allegorical, not symbolic. True symbols, that is those which survive over a considerable period of time, have an affective element capable of 'holding' a particular emotion or idea such as the *Kaaba*, the *swastika* or the *mandala*. They can never be fully explained, and will always have an element of mystery, that is, an individually unknowable, transpersonal element. As Henry Corbin put it, symbols say that *which cannot be said in any other way*.[15]

Symbols then have a certain affective/emotional power and can never be fully explained in terms of what they evoke. The attendant aspect of mystery is what we call(ed) a 'sense of the sacred' and which is intimately connected to that ultimate mystery: death. As something we all will experience but know nothing about, death, by definition can only be 'known' in terms of the symbolic imagination. Insofar as it forms the bedrock of the enterprise of religion, our understanding of what life 'means' (or doesn't) is closely linked to how we understand death.

*

It was these notions of the symbolic and its virtual absence in modern sensibility that Norman O. Brown was referring to when he said "the thing to abolish is literalism … truth is always poetic in form, not literal but symbolic."[16] Brown's concern has been similarly echoed by many others who see the primary malaise of modernity as its loss of the sacred/symbolic/imagination. That is, modernity itself breeds a literalist mindset, religion or no religion. Thus, one way towards reclaiming the sense of the symbolic is to study human behavior, not only as it appears in mythology and religion, but also in all dimensions of culture (epic, drama, poetry, architecture, music, dance etc.) and which, in this context, functions both as an archetypal canvas and a diagnostic perspective. This analytic approach, then, is not located in ideas of brain physiology, but in what has been called a 'mythopoetic basis of mind'.[17]

Phenomenologically, the symbolic may be a physical (literal) reality as, for example, a nation's flag, or the *Kaaba* in Mecca. But in its encompassing the literal, the symbolic retains primacy in terms of psychological meaning and metaphysical significance. For something to be symbolically true, at some level, it has to be literally true. Death, for example, is literal fact. But from the perspective of many religions it is largely a symbolic affair, a stage in a 'journey', a transformation, rebirth, etc. To talk of the loss of the 'sense' of the symbolic, therefore, is not to say that symbols have ceased to exist. Given their primacy and trans-personality, they remain as such, but, given the times, are manifest and expressed, at increasingly *literal* levels. Which basically means a narrowing of the spectrum of their meaning till eventually all ambiguity, multiple possibilities of interpretations, are excluded in favour of just one—as in all types of fundamentalism. As suggested in the introduction to Jung's view of religion, when the symbolic is not consciously recognized, its power manifests itself not only at the literal level but is also destructive. 'Summoned or not, God will be there.'[*]

The consequences of circumscription of meaning and the importance of the symbolic finds its fullest amplification in the writings of, for example, C.G. Jung, James Hillman, Paul Ricouer, Karl Kerényi, Erich Neumann, Joseph Campbell, David Miller, Gilbert Durand, Ernst Cassirer, Northrop Frye, Henry Corbin, Georges Dumezil, Karen Armstrong, George Lakoff and

---

[*] "Vocatus atque non vocatus deus aderit" is "a statement that Jung discovered among the Latin writings of Desiderius Erasmus, who declared the statement had been an ancient Spartan proverb. Jung popularized it, having it inscribed over the doorway of his house, and upon his tomb. Jung carved this Latin inscription above the door of his house in Kusnacht, Switzerland. (...) In a letter of November 19, 1960, Jung explains the inscription: "I have put the inscription there to remind my patients and myself: Timor dei initium sapiente - the fear of the Lord is the beginning of wisdom. Here another not less important road begins, not the approach to 'Christianity' but to God himself and this seems to be the ultimate question." See https://en.wikiquote.org/wiki/Carl_Jung (last visited 03-07-2015)

Mircea Eliade. Collectively this body of ideas signals that

> We should not be surprised ... to find that, in the last century, developments ... resulting from Freudian psychoanalysis and Jungian depth psychology have converged with a new orientation of the old history of religion discipline. Thus, with Mircea Eliade, Henry Corbin and Georges Dumezil ... to cite only a few authors ... reflections on the phenomenon of religion have broken away from etiological reductions within purely historical, social ... contexts to enter the territory of a more anthropological field—one centered on the properly religious function of the creative imagination.[18]

In this context, the word 'imagination' does not refer to flights of fancy but to a complex epistemological framework. Whether in Corbin's usage of 'Creative Imagination', or Ricoeur's notion of a 'poetics of experience' and the dynamic centrality of metaphor, or in Eliade's view that the soul stifling aspects of modernity can only be countered through awakening the imagination which is innately predisposed to perceive the sacred/symbolic, the imagination is conceptualized in a manner that can enable an articulation and understanding of religion and religious experience—or the lack thereof.

In sum: deeply intertwined with culture and religion, the symbolic world of mythos is the world of the imagination, providing us emotional 'containers', enabling us to say what cannot be said in any other way when faced with extremes of horror, suffering, joy etc. Helping to cope with the inexpressible by giving it a name, image, ritual, place; mythos also points to a parallel, 'higher' plane of existence/transcendence. Functioning as a sort of cultural DNA, the symbolic also has a transformative potential, offering cues, options, guidelines through various individual life stages. Since its meanings are ambiguous, multiple and subjective, it will always contain a transpersonal element of mystery, which at times we refer to as a 'sense' of the sacred.

Literal and Symbolic, Fact and Meaning, Masculine and Feminine

From the Jungian perspective, gender does not have to do with just the literal, outer manifestations of genital sexuality; but is also, more importantly, a psychological symbolic construct. By definition, a symbol invariably communicates multiple layers of meaning. For example, in contrast to Freudian reductionism and its tendency to view dream images such as a dagger or a pointed object as symbols of 'nothing but' the male genitals, the Jungian may regard them also as certain *attitudes* of consciousness which could be normatively termed 'masculine' and these can be both sexual *and* spiritual.[19]

Thus, Christ as *Logos* is one symbol of the Divine creative 'spirit' which also 'enlightens'. As illustrated in the hero archetype of, for example, Apollo, such a masculinity could also refer to *logos* as reason/rationality, a 'penetrative', logical analysis/insight into a situation, mastery of concept, detachment, clarity of thought. As a spirit of knowledge at the most mundane level the Apollonian *logos* functions as what we call 'thinking', 'intellect' but which can have different styles. For example, there is 'intelligence' and there is 'wisdom'. Even theologically, this ostensibly purely masculine symbol always had a feminine dimension. As Jung has argued in his *Answer to Job*, for example, the God-figure of Yahweh was balanced by a Judaic notion of Wisdom, which Jung relates to the archetype of Sophia.[20] (In this respect it is also interesting that the Hebrew *'ruhach'* is similar to the Islamic *'ruh'*. Both refer to a 'divine spirit of wisdom' and both are feminine.)

As a symbolic image, *logos* is frequently represented by the Phallus or Lingam. These are not simply sexual images but refer primarily to the creative being, the power of healing, fertilization of ideas. Thus, in these contexts 'penetrating' becomes less of a sexual activity and more a psychological quality which can also be experienced as thinking, an 'in'-fluence or 'in'-flux of ideas. As Jung remarked only half in jest, actually it is the penis that is 'nothing but' a phallic symbol.[21]

Similarly, a hollow object may become a symbol of a different set of 'feminine' psychological qualities, such as receptivity, inwardness, more reflective and contemplative rather than an action oriented attitude. In its inward dimension, such an attitude encompasses the 'knower' with that which is known through *logos*. Linking as it does, the material and/or conceptual world to the human psyche, Jung referred to it as *eros* representing the function of relatedness. A fundamental postulate also in Freudian theory, *eros* is the psychological carrier of the energy behind life (libido) and stands in contrast to the death instinct, *thanatos*. In spite of ultimately reducing *eros* to the sex drive, its broader conception as Love can also be glimpsed in Freud's writings. Jungian psychology presents a reverse emphasis, which, while not denying the sexual, sees *eros* in its ancient sense of Pan-Eros as the creative and procreative force permeating all of nature.[22] In simple terms, it can be described as a state of relatedness/connectivity which we frequently call love and which, as one's own experience tells us, is not just limited to sex.

The symbolic is not just 'allegory' or a literary term but a *psychological reality*. Science/*logos* itself utilizes symbolic language but according to the specific law of non-contradiction, applying Cartesianist logic to *material* facts. By definition a fact can only have *one* meaning. Water will always be 2 parts of hydrogen and 1 part of oxygen, no two ways about it. But what water 'means' to each of us will depend on our *span of experience* of it: as rain, sea, drinking, swimming we don't think of it as H_2O, but as qualities which are *subjective*, *multiple* and *cannot* be communicated quantitatively. Similarly, when asked to describe 'depression', we say, I feel 'blue', 'black', 'heavy', 'down'. This is the psyche's *natural* symbolic/metaphoric capacity for conveying its meaning via inter/connection and relationship.* The most significant events of our lives, from love to despair etc., engage us at a different level than, say, the molecular structure of water. Life as such, including religion, was never meant to be made 'sense' of literally. The question about religious stories was never, 'are they factually true?' but 'do we need to know this?', if so, 'what do they *mean*?' In short, the span/spectrum of meaning in *mythos* is expansive, multiple (meaning-full), and is restricted (meaning-less) in *logos*.

In terms of broad analytic categories, then, Armstrong's framework of *mythos/logos*, is replaced in Jungian psychology by the principles of *eros* and *logos*, representing central psychological dynamics and values. The former has to do with relatedness and feelings while the latter with thinking and cognition. At one level representing masculine and feminine, both at the same time contain a contrasexual aspect. Given the human (and divine) diversity of the pantheon, masculine and feminine can in turn have many different styles and expressions. To the extent that men and women literally *embody* these genitally based metaphors, they may exhibit individual predispositions. But to consider this, as Freud did ('anatomy is destiny') exclusively as literal, is to fall into gender reductionism. For the masculine and feminine are also *attitudes,* potentially available to both sexes and as such, do not have to do just literally with man or woman.

Critiquing Freud in this manner is not to deny the significance of his contributions about the unconscious and the psychodynamics of adolescent males. Yet beyond the problems

---

* For example, George Lakoff's work on Conceptual Analysis and Cognitive Linguistics shows how it is virtually impossible to communicate without metaphor which is central to human thinking, society and political behaviour. See bibliography for references.

PART I: PSYCHOLOGICAL EXPLORATIONS OF MODERNITY

of imposing that template onto women (by now vigorously contested by feminism), what is called into question here is the Freudian medicalizing and literalizing of the male model of the self. One can even note in passing that like Jung, Freud too was actually deeply influenced by the power of mythology, as for example, his ideas of the Oedipus/Elektra complex. Also, it is important to keep in mind that while he was never given the Nobel Prize for medicine, he did receive the Goethe Prize for literature. As he says about himself:

> A man of letters by instinct, though a doctor by necessity, I conceived the idea of changing over a branch of medicine— psychiatry—into literature. Though I have the appearance of a scientist I was and am a poet and novelist. Psychoanalysis is no more than an interpretation of a literary vocation in terms of psychology and psychopathology.[23]

Modernity's Myth: the Myth of the Hero

The Story and Ritual of the Hero

Eventually, every culture and religion is rooted in myth. As Margaret Whitford has pointed out, mythology is a culture's self-image and has today "become more important than philosophy, perhaps for political reasons, since mythology is more readily accessible to a wider audience and more formative of the social unconscious."[24] Similarly, for Irigaray, mythology is "one of the principal expressions of what organizes society at a particular time."[25]

Even though the project of modernity has split *mythos* and *logos* and even though, in several ways, it sees myth as "an inferior mode of thought, which can be cast aside when humans have attained the age of reason"[26] it is ultimately still driven by a strong and quite virulent underlying myth/symbol/archetype.

The modern loss of the symbolic and the corresponding rise of the literal is closely related to the myth of the Hero. Given that it lies at the roots of so much contemporary violence, religious and secular, it is imperative to briefly review the frequently undetected influences of a masculinity, which in different guises, is a key determinant in modern behavior. Thus, the ancient yet ever-present myth of the hero can become a means of understanding 'who' rather than 'what' impels the behavior of not only bin Laden, but also George Bush—and the rhetoric of politicians everywhere.

The story of the hero is a universal one.[27] Despite myriad variations, typically it is about the birth of a boy in unusual circumstances such as missing a parent or extreme wealth, poverty etc. This is followed by a separation from origins, a difficult journey, confrontations and battles, which eventually lead to his return, being acknowledged as ruler, giver of laws, unifier and redeemer. Then, either through betrayal, or the sin of pride (*hubris*), or heroic self-sacrifice, or simply because the gods have decreed him mortal, there is his fall, decline and death. Well known examples include Hercules, Oedipus, Ulysses, Jason. For the moment, one can note in passing, that reflective of our age, modern heroes such as Superman, Rambo, the Terminator, follow the same thematic trajectory but the only difference is that they refuse to undergo any fall, decline or death.

Typically, symbols have multiple layers of meaning. At one level, the myth is a rite of passage, of transition from boyhood to becoming a man. The story/ritual is an enactment of psychological *attitudes* required for separation from familial protection, letting childhood 'die' and being 'reborn' an adult. It is still present in rituals of joining the army or college, and also in 'primitive' tribes in which, for example, teenage males are sent to the jungle, expected to survive on their own and then return to the community. This process involves the emergence of reason (*logos*) which is needed to survive natural forces, and/or planning complicated battles/campaigns. Similarly, the process includes the ability to withstand and inflict pain, leading to will power. Thus, the pain and fear involved in the separation from the familiar/comfortable, are transformed into reason and will power. The symbolic therefore psychologically transforms consciousness, identity and the self.

Implying an organic and interconnected movement from experience to knowledge, rites of passage, therefore aim to transform consciousness, that is, our sense of self, others, and the world. Historically, such early masculine 'consciousness raising' came, for example, through tough rituals, or in traditionally recounted stories, or the initiatic context of apprenticeship and similar socio-cultural mechanisms, whereby male identity and consciousness could unfold in an organic, monitored manner, so to speak. In the hero myth, whether as ritual or story, there are tests of physical endurance, the ability to withstand and inflict violence, and the planning of complex campaigns for survival and victory. All this marks the emergence of *logos* and the psychological faculties of will power and reason/rationality. Their instrumentalist dimension can thus be described as 'heroic' and 'masculine'.

Along with *logos* and the enlargement of consciousness through reason and willpower, the hero-rite simultaneously aims to engage with more complex levels of *eros*. In tandem with an emergent *logos*, the sexual impulse too makes itself known powerfully in adolescence. Even as the need to control it becomes evident, this aspect of *eros* becomes part of the process of an enlarging consciousness through the exercise of will and a move towards a deeper understanding of *eros*. The disconnection from mother and familial protection gives way to being connected with the larger community. As a whole then, the hero rite can be seen as encapsulating a developmental frame of *logos* for males. As both a literal and psychological experience it also contains an emergent conception of *eros*. That is, the sense of connectedness starts to move beyond the juvenile/infantile. At one level experienced as sexual desire, it eventually is also meant to embrace the community and a different asexual idea of love.

Female rites of passage involve a different, less action oriented style. For example, when girls start menstruating in 'primitive' tribes, they may be secluded in a hut for a while separated from the community. The aim is to initiate/encourage reflection and contemplation (e.g. about the processes of life, birth and death). The development of will power, for example, is processed through childbirth and the patience required when dealing with infants/children. All rites of passages can be seen, depending on age and culture, as aiming to integrate various dimensions of *logos/eros* into psychological awareness. As expressed in the symbols of the hero-rite/story, it is a potential move towards adulthood and a psychological sense of self/identity based on individual achievement, recognition of one's limitations, and the need to belong to a social group. The need for a specifically spiritual-religious community/identity comes *later*, and depending on the individual's context/inclinations had corresponding rituals. In the past, different spiritual communities and guilds had their own initiatic rites of passage, marking yet another stage in the evolution/unfolding of individual identity and consciousness.

It is important to keep in mind that in roughly the first half of life, the hero myth/archetype functions primarily in the service of the individual on the threshold of social integration. Essentially an adolescent archetype, it is frequently referred to as the myth of the child-hero. In short, myths and/or traditional rites of passage provided natural pathways for different stages and different dimensions of individual development. Needless to say, these traditions were simultaneously and deeply anchored in different spiritual/religious systems. Their absence at many levels from modern life leads to all sorts of conflations, confusions and distortions regarding both human developmental psychology and the meaning(s) of God. The sayings attributed to the Prophet of Islam, 'whosoever knows himself knows his Lord', 'man's knowledge of himself comes *before* knowledge of God', reflect the wisdom of understanding the self and its un/consciousness as an unfolding of natural developmental stages, from the simple to the more complex. The chapters on both high and low fundamentalism will show how the absence of these symbolic rites and ideas have contributed to the literalist and violent mindset.

Monotheism and the Hero

Interestingly, the hero archetype occupies a central place in all monotheistic religions. Many aspects of the lives of the central figures in these (and other) religions are clearly reflective of the myth: unusual circumstances of birth, humble, wealthy or a missing parent (Moses, David, Christ, Muhammad). There are the miracles of healing and teaching, the separation from origins, danger from powerful enemies, difficult ordeals, victorious returns and ultimately, for the vast majority, mortal death.

Neumann has discussed the roots of monotheism in the hero myths, viewing it as a major shift in the (pre)history of human consciousness from a matriarchal period of the God(esses) to a more abstract and patriarchal conception of the Divine.[28] The monotheistic archetype's concern is an individual, moral striving for perfection, including the ethics of relationships mediated by conscience, an idea located in the imagination. Through an abstract and symbolic ideal of Divine Unity, it aims for transcendence, towards an ideal transpersonal future.

The archetype of 'mono-Theos' (one God), does in fact have strong elements of the hero myth but primary as a psycho-symbolic concept. In resonance with heroic consciousness, the *external* dimensions of monotheism in fact also exhibit a similar, linear sense of history, a 'separative' (objectified) sense of self/identity, self-assertive will and an active, uncompromising attitude based in God given revelation. Following the hero's trajectory, this 'masculine' shift from matriarchy towards a transcendent ideal of 'Light, Height and Law', is positive only insofar as it moves (potentially) towards a more comprehensive, increasingly symbolic understanding of the Divine. In Jungian terms, this includes the re-cognition, re-connection with the Feminine, as the matrix of Life (and Death)—hence perhaps 're-ligio', to re-link. This re-connection is rendered impossible if the adolescent, hero archetype refuses to acknowledge the limitation of decay and death.

The Feminine

When speaking of 'the Feminine', as is done throughout this book in various contexts, it is important not to restrict its understanding to the individual male/female psyche, nor simply to an image of a goddess. Along with iconic religions such as Judaism and Islam, it also encompasses various collective dynamics. For example, one major current within modernity has been a steady ascendance, by now ubiquitous, presence of a 'women's perspective' in contemporary affairs. Even in contexts where women are disempowered, through poverty, custom or politics, the issues around them remain prominent. Acknowledged or not, the voice and presence of woman—as activist, scholar, cultural critic etc.—is today undeniable.*

---

* By using the singular 'woman' to denote a diversity of women, is to invite criticism and the label of essentialism. While this is not the place to get entangled in these debates, it must also be said that the linguistic underpinnings of such issues along with the dominance of English in academic discourse, remains to be examined in detail in order to separate the substantive from the trivial. In Finnish and Urdu, for example, 'woman'

Similarly, since the latter half of the 20th Century, there has been a steady stream of feminist scholarship questioning not only the construction of the idea of gender, but also the way it relates to the production of knowledges such as history, psychology, philosophy, ecology, and numerous other disciplines, including theology. Feminist theology, for example, is by now a fully established discipline. Taken as a whole these feminist contestations and re-viewings, along with the slow but steady empowerment of women, are part of a rising constellation of 'the Feminine' on the horizons of human consciousness and knowledge.

In short, as part of an emergent *zeitgeist* which includes a rising interest in spirituality by both men and women, the Feminine is essentially a constellation of a different consciousness. Today, it is all around us, rising again as an archetype. It is evident in feminism, the empowerment of women, women's scholarship, in the increasing sense of unity with the planet, in ecological awareness, in the widespread urge to reconnect with the body and emotions, in the broad popularity of the Gaia hypothesis, in scientific ideas about chaos, dissipative structures and holism. The list could go on and on. The main point is that it is not 'just' an image, but a *consciousness* and it is this consciousness which must be reclaimed within the religious traditions.

Psychological Polytheism and Monotheism

Even though we can see a certain rise of 'the Feminine', by and large, the religious traditions are still strongly today dominated by masculine consciousness. Even more so, the literal hero archetype dominates the more abstract monotheistic one. The

---

can be used as both singular and plural without necessarily evoking stereotypes or loss of nuance.

former is essentially about being human and the latter primarily about God. Among the monotheistic religions, perhaps the story of Christ most closely approximates the heroic archetype, which, as a consequence of being taken too exclusively and literally, has led to what Hillman calls "Christianism" (as opposed to Christianity).[29] Rather than letting the heroic 'ego' of individual, social and spiritual consciousness come down to earth, literalized monotheism offers the all too willing adolescent ego an endless, ever-upward trajectory. This fusion of the two archetypes, of hero and mono-theos, dominated as they have to be, by heroic masculine principles of exclusion and a literalized sense of 'unity', keep the hero constantly in a state of literalism, emotional and social separation, battle and rulership.

When referring to the term 'monotheism', it is important to bear in mind the difference between a religion and a psychology. The first is a *belief*, the second an *attitude*, and one can exist without the other. For example, Judaism can be seen as a monotheistic religion but less so in its psychology of an undefined God, and the myriad faces of Torah, one for each Jew in exile.[30] Similarly, in Islam, the proverbial Ninety-Nine names and even more Attributes,* and the historic existence of innumerable communities till today, indicate an attitude of multiplicity. Nevertheless, both religions remain monotheistic.

'Theos' in Greek means god, and theo-logy is a *logos*-of-(a)god. But *'theos'* also constitutes 'theory' as in the intellectual endeavor of theo-rizing, that is, constructing a framework for meaning/understanding. Psychologically, there is a 'god' behind any construction of meaning. As said earlier, the word 'idea' not only means 'to see' but also 'the *means* by which we see'. Or, as

---

* Often the 99 Names are also described as the 99 Attributes but the Quran attributes many more 'dimensions' to God that are not always taken up in the traditional list of 99 Names.

Einstein said, "it is the theory which decides what can be observed." Thus, rational logic can psychologically become God, functioning with the same force as a religious conviction. In its quest for 'facts' as answers, *logos* generates an attitude of *monism* of singularity and only one (literal) meaning, creating a psychological 'mono-theism' which may have nothing to do with one's religion. A secular Hindu can *psychologically* be a mono-theist if he believes that only *his* view of the world is real and true. Any god then, by whatever Name, is also a psychological phenomenon, an attitude, a perspective, a style of existence. Which is why most religions until just a few decades ago were frequently described as a 'way of life'. Specific creeds were secondary. As Jung put it: "A creed gives expression to a definite collective belief, whereas the word religion expresses a subjective relationship to certain metaphysical factors."[31] The exception, according to Jung and Hillman, is modern Christianity, which made creed into the dominant and defining aspect of its religiosity.*

---

* It should be noted that Jung's/Hillman's critique focused on Western Christianity and not the Eastern Orthodox churches. Nevertheless, with minor variations, the Nicene Creed has been normative to the Anglican Church, Assyrian Church of the East, Eastern Orthodox Church, Oriental Orthodox churches, the Roman Catholic Church including the Eastern Catholic Churches and the Old Catholic Church, the Lutheran Church and most Protestant denominations.

The Nicene Creed
We believe in one God, the Father, the Almighty
maker of heaven and earth, of all that is seen and unseen.
We believe in one Lord, Jesus Christ, the only Son of God,
eternally begotten of the Father,
God from God, Light from Light, true God from true God,
begotten, not made, one in Being with the Father.
Through him all things were made.
For us men and for our salvation he came down from heaven;
by the power of the Holy Spirit he was born of the Virgin Mary, and became man.
For our sake he was crucified under Pontius Pilate;

Accordingly, by accepting a set of, essentially, *mental* beliefs in a specific male-person-as-God as historical 'facts', evil cannot touch me, my salvation is assured. Anyone who does not 'believe' this, even a Buddhist saint, is damned. Thus, Christianity became the first religion *ever* to try and prove its claim through sciences such as archaeology, carbon dating etc. (No such efforts were made, however, to locate the devil.) This sort of unprecedented application of *logos* to *mythos* was a response to the post Enlightenment, secular ideal that 'those who think cannot believe and those who believe cannot think.' The splitting of faith and reason, good and evil, leads to the tendency to split all phenomena, literalize and *morally reduce* them to irreconcilable opposites.

It was in the context of these notions of the symbolic and literal, *logos/mythos/eros* and the hero's hijacking of Christian monotheism which led Jung to say that "our [i.e. the West's] true religion is a monotheism of consciousness."[32] The next chapter will detail some of the implications of this Western consciousness in the Twentieth Century and its global impact till today.

He suffered, died, and was buried.
On the third day he rose again in fulfillment of the Scriptures;
he ascended into heaven and is seated at the right hand of the Father.
He will come again in glory to judge the living and the dead,
and his kingdom will have no end.

CHAPTER 2:
RELIGION AND MODERNITY

An honest admission of modernity means voluntarily declaring
oneself bankrupt, and—what is still more painful—renouncing
the halo of sanctity that history bestows.
(C.G. Jung[1])

Modernity and 'The Ascent of Man'

Jung's claim that the West's 'true religion is a monotheism of consciousness', concerns the dual presence of Judeo-Christian monotheism and scientific rationalism as dominant ideologies within modern Western consciousness. It refers, on the one hand, to the hero myth manifest in Christ as exclusively representing literal Divinity at the expense of diverse manifestations including the Feminine, and on the other, the eventual literalizing of *Logos* into the *logos* of scientific rationalism. That is, the Christian splitting of good and evil is reinforced by Cartesian science that splits the mind from the body.[2] The combination has (had) serious psychological consequences for the individual self and society.

A psychoanalytic history of Western civilization, as mapped in archetypal terms by Hillman, shows how the cultural locus of the upward 'ascent of the hero' can be seen as a movement from South to North. Beginning in the Mediterranean and the dominant archetype of the Great Mother Goddess (the Feminine) and other deities, it moved through an initially gender-diverse pantheon into the Age of the Heroes. Eventually Zeus, who was just one of the Olympians, gave way to Judaism and an abstract consciousness about Divinity, associated—like Jason's quest to the mountain top—with Light, Height, and Law. Followed by Christ as a direct expression of the *Logos*, Christian monotheism in its Catholic and Orthodox expression, managed to vestigially retain the Feminine archetype in the form of the Virgin Mary. Mary in turn, can be regarded as the counterpart to the concept of Wisdom in the Old Testament—which, as already mentioned, can be related to the Greek Sophia. [3] Eventually, in the Protestant Christian rendering of Mary as mundane, this (Southern-Italian) aspect disappeared and was left 'below', so to speak.

Culminating in Northern Germany, the ascent of the Christian *Logos* found its ultimate expression in a determinedly heroic, scientific and material Lutheran Protestant Ethic. In short, the idea of 'God' and *Logos* was drastically circumscribed into exclusivist and narrow 'masculine' domains.[4] This final erasure of psycho-theological diversity and the Feminine was accompanied by the Inquisition and its primary target was tens of thousands of women who were branded 'heretics' and brutally tortured/killed by both Catholics and Protestants.

In terms of cultural history, the change from *Logos* to *logos* was symbolically/literally evident in Germany and the emergence of crucial, consciousness-changing technologies such as the Gutenberg printing press and the subsequent spreading of mass literacy in Europe. Similarly, the scientific enterprise primarily emerged from the Germanic milieu and language. Additionally, Protestantism became the paradigm of what constitutes a 'religion'.

The Protestant Paradigm of Religion

A prominent Western scholar on Islam states: "… for Muslims the word 'religion' does not have the same connotations as it has for Christians … for Muslims, Islam is not simply a system of faith and worship … [it] concerns the whole complex fabric of life."[5] This is entirely correct.* But as vast numbers of even nominal Hindus, Buddhists, Sikhs will tell you, their religions too concern the 'whole, complex fabric of life'. Nevertheless, the Protestant Christian *exception* has become the decisive *norm* for studying *all* religions. Only recently have leading scholars started admitting that it was an enormous mistake to have considered Protestantism as the paradigm of religion, indicating that the entire edifice of the academic study of religion merits serious reconsideration.[6] In short: the dominance of the Protestant lens has serious consequences for the academic study of religion and in turn how it is understood by the public imagination.[†]

As Bruce Lincoln points out, prior to the Enlightenment, religion in Western Europe could not be analytically or practically separated from all other aspects of culture, that is, it too was more a 'way of life'.[7] In Roman times, for example, 'religion' was not a doctrine or dogma of speculative interest but something one 'felt and did'. While early Christianity still

---

* In Urdu, two words are used interchangeably for religion. '*Mazhab*' means going in one direction, school of thought. Strictly speaking it refers to the four main legal schools of Islamic jurisprudence, and does not appear in the Quran. '*Deen*' refers to phenomena that are regular, predictable, the word for 'city' ('*madina*') is from the same roots denoting social norms that define city. It may also simply mean 'perspective'. As such, it has an inclusive range of meanings spanning ethics and worldview to eschatology and social order/norms. Its various meaning are reflected in different verses of the Quran. The closest word for 'culture' is '*tehzeeb*' which refers to pruning the tree, to make it look neat.

† As Bruce Lincoln acknowledges, this recognition has been driven primarily by religious historians and anthropologists working on Islam, particularly, W.C. Smith and Talal Asad. (Lincoln; *Holy Terrors*. op. cit. pp. 3-4.)

retained the all-inclusive view, it also developed a definite conception of itself and with regard to other faiths, became strongly exclusive and intolerant. In the Middle Ages the word 'faith' was far more important than the word 'religion', which was a special designation for monasticism. For Reformation thinkers such as Calvin, *religio* designated something personal, inner and transcendentally oriented.[8] The word 'faith' and 'religion' gradually converged. Similarly, the Protestant emphasis on the abstract idea of a 'mental belief' and the highlighting of 'creed' became stronger, along with a virtual abandoning of bodily rituals.

As such, the modern concept of 'religion' with its emphasis on mental/abstract schematizations of 'doctrine', 'dogma' and 'belief' is an outflow of the Protestant view on its own faith/religion. It fully took root during the Enlightenment and was used as a frame by the religious as well as the secular psyche. This process of 'objectification' and 'classification' of religions according to 'doctrines'/'dogmas'/'beliefs'/etc. was taken further through the colonial period and the ensuing contact with other religions/cultures. By the beginning of the 20th Century, Western scholars had labelled all the great religions as 'isms', such as Hinduism, Buddhism, Confucianism.[9] In so doing, the post-Enlightenment 'Protestant' Christianist view, with its split between 'faith' and 'reason' and its reduction of *mythos* to *logos,* effectively became the measure of all religions/cultures.

Psychology and the Cartesianist Self

Significantly, the invention of psychology as a scientific discipline was overwhelmingly the work of young males under 30, writing primarily in the German language.[10] By the turn of the 20th Century, almost as if in protest at suppression over millennia, the psyche 'erupted': Freud's classic *The Interpretation of Dreams* sensitized the modern mind to the inner richness of the psyche. However it was done within a masculine frame of 'pathology'. The first two 'dis-eases' to be discovered were schizophrenia (multiple personality disorder) and hysteria (the wandering uterus), by definition, a dis-ease only women can have. By 1952 there was 130 page booklet listing around 35 mental illnesses. Today, it is 900 pages, listing 374 and still counting.[11] In Jungian terms, "the god/desses have become diseases"[12] Thus, what we today call psychopathology is a secular term for 'heresy', which in the historic Western public imagination remains vividly linked to women and witches.

Psychology itself reflects the heroic 'ascent', especially in Freudian-Cartesian ideas of the strong, thinking/rational ego-mind exclusively 'in charge'—as the self—which must control the id and its strange irrational forces of the unconscious 'below': namely, all the psychological diversity including the feminine dimensions which must be 'repressed' since they are 'other' than the self. The Freudian model of a strong and rational ego fortified by various 'defense mechanisms' as it imperiously surveys the scene 'below' (feminine/diversity/difference) is a derivative of the Cartesian mind-body concept 'I *think* therefore I exist'. Again, the body is 'below', in contrast to the rational ego-self, it is inferior, subject to control. Mind over matter. North over South. 'South', thus, is a physical, cultural, ethnic and *psychological* place. It is as much 'out' there as it is 'within', inferior and colonized. Like Woman and Nature, the South is 'mindless', something to be tamed, owned and mastered. As Freud's classic description of the purpose of analysis states: "to strengthen the ego … widen the field of perception … (to) appropriate fresh portions of the id, where id was there ego shall be … it is a work of culture."[13]

This is not simply a historical exercise but about cultural

realities having serious consequences. For example, while hysteria was epidemic in the West till the 50's, today it is almost non-existent indicating the deep-rooted cultural dimension of what we call mental health and the 'self'. The emergence of feminism itself can be seen as part of this ongoing struggle of the psyche against the heroic, masculinized, self. In ancient Greece, the word 'psyche' was represented as a beautiful woman, or then in the natural and complex symbol of a butterfly. Originally, 'psyche' meant 'soul' and psych-ology, a logos-of-the-soul. Its battles are far from over. Today, the conception of the self has taken two established trajectories: the Cartesian-Kantian hero continues to rule in the development of medical psychiatry in which the self has been reduced to a 'mind' residing in the head/brain and its biochemistry of 'hard' facts. In tandem, is the 'soft' psychotherapeutic project in which, till last count, there are more than 350 schools of psychotherapy. Collectively, they point to the vast multiplicity of the human psyche, albeit in suffering, representing pluralistic and feminine defiance of modern patriarchal masculinity.

The secularization of 'heretical' tendencies into psycho-pathology shows that women still bear the brunt. Even as multibillion dollar global psycho-pharmaceuticals promote a masculine 'mind' as a model of the healthy 'self', WHO claims that gender disparities remain a crucial issue in mental health.[14] Worldwide more women suffer from depression than any other illness. Almost everywhere women are given more pills than men having the same condition. In the U.S., women receive *twice* as many prescriptions, more multiple and repeat prescriptions and more prescriptions of excessive dosages than men.[15] In short, whereas earlier women were religiously bad (witches/heretics), today they are simply mad.

The alarming fact is that, the current profusion of therapeutic methods notwithstanding, Freudian (that is, heroic) ideals of consciousness prevail, by now, globally, albeit invisibly, as "universal common sense".[16] The feminist critique of the 'Cartesian masculinization of thought'[17] refers to the dominance of this narrow and exclusivist notion of *logos* and which makes the modern self masculinist, phallocratic and/or logocentric. Cut off from the feminine domains of the psyche, and the body, it is a disembodied 'mind' which overvalues (will)power, detachment and a strong urge to control via instrumentalist notions of rationality. Exhibiting what Hillman similarly calls 'the monstrous ego of Cartesianism', such a mind is overwhelmingly masculine, positivistic, Apollonic, Protestant Christian, heroic/monotheistic. It is unable to deal with that which it considers different from itself, including that which is feminine, intermediate, ambiguous and symbolic/metaphorical.[18]

Beyond Jung and post-Jungians, by now, there is a huge body of work from within different disciplines that places these ego-attitudes at the heart of modernity and its psycho-cultural condition. Critiques of scientific rationalism, shows how its methods, priorities and values are embedded in male adolescent psychology and *its* sexual preoccupations, and this criticism is not just limited to feminism.

> The metaphors of science are, indeed, filled with the violence, voyeurism and tumescence of male adolescent fantasy. Scientists "wrestle" with an always female nature, to "wrest from her the truth" or to "reveal her hidden secrets". They make "war" on diseases and "conquer" them. Good science is "hard" science, bad science (like that refuge of so many women, psychology) is "soft" science, and molecular biology, like physics, is characterized by "hard inference".[19]

The feminist description of the modern 'self' as 'phallocratic' and 'logocentric' becomes understandable if one recalls that the hero archetype is about adolescent masculinity. An age when the sexual impulse is at its peak in males, *logos* and phallus can only be known in the literally 'hard' facts of an awakening sexuality.

Similarly, ecofeminist analyses of the environmental crisis suggest how woman/body/nature are, from the view of the Cartesian ego, psychologically synonymous, regarding as this ego does, both women and nature as objects to be owned, mastered and manipulated at will. Thus, the *logos* Armstrong refers to as dominating modernity is, from this feminist point of view, a machismo that permeates our ideas ranging from politics and health to science, development and progress. Alternatives are dismissed on the basis that they are not 'rational' and there is a singular, exclusive value on power and 'hard' facts.

Cartesian-Christianism

Jung's view of the West's 'true religion' being a monotheism of consciousness and what Hillman refers to as the unconscious 'Cartesian-Christianism' of the West, should not be simply dismissed as Christian fundamentalism. Rather, it has to do with a deeper, all pervading *psychological* attitude towards self, others, nature, in short, the way we think about life at large, including especially, religion. Typically, it is a one-dimensional attitude, reflecting the (masculinist) Cartesianist impulse, as in science, on a singularity of meaning. The same vision self-reflexively affirms itself in a literalized view of Christ and the message/meaning of his birth, life and death. In their insistence on singularity of meaning, both perspectives leave no room for interpretation which is only possible if one admits a notion such as ambiguity, that is, multiple possibilities of meaning.

Between the single-minded visions of Cartesian thought and Christianism, there is little room for anything else, including that which is 'negative', even though, as all mythologies tell us (and we know from our own experience), in our/their moods of irrationality, anger, violence, jealousy, etc.; the gods, whether male or female, are quite capable of being in-human. Similar to the split in Cartesianism, the dogmatic foundations of Christianity tend to irrevocably separate in equally dogmatic ways, the archetypal and mutually defining (hence interconnected) notions of good and evil.

According to Jung "Christianity has made the antinomy of good and evil into a world problem and by formulating the conflict dogmatically raised it into an absolute problem."[20] His critique urged the "white man (and woman) in general"[21] to recognize the evil *within* the psyche (the 'shadow'). Similarly, for Hillman also, Christianist dogma turns evil into a metaphysical notion of the devil, which is projected onto others and then endlessly philosophized about as 'The Problem of Evil'. It is axiomatic in depth-psychology that what we deny within comes forward to 'meet' us from without, that is, our own evil is projected onto others, who are then seen as exclusively evil. No other religion, including Islam, is based on these metaphysics of evil.

The view from Islam is quite different concerning notions of creed, evil etc. For example, in Islam, the closest to a 'creed' ('I believe...') is actually not the *Shahada*, but verse 2:285 of sura *Al Baqarah* in the Quran:

> The Apostle and the believers with him, believe in what has been bestowed upon him from on high by his Sustainer: they all believe in God, and His angels, and His revelations, and His apostles, making no distinction between any of His apostles; and they say: "We have heard, and we pay heed. Grant us Thy forgiveness, O our sustainer, for with Thee is all journey's end!"[22]

The *Shahada*—'There is no god but God and Muhammad is his Messenger'—is a 'witnessing', more like a Zen koan, not a gendered-historic-event-belief. And since the Quran insists that

Muslims must believe in *all* the Prophets, Books, etc., because it is the same message, there is no claim to any exclusive or uniquely Islamic insight on morality. As such the Judaic 'eye for an eye' is as valid as the Christian ideal of forgiveness, though the latter is encouraged.

Most importantly, it does not subscribe to the notion of 'original sin'. As McLain observes, "the Quran makes no effort to explain evil in the world in—and it has no patience at all with the Christian obsession with original sin. Islam *accepts* the world, without presuming to *explain* the world."[23]

Whereas Satan (*Iblis*) is very much around, it is also a prototype of all wicked persons (2:102; 38:41; 43:36) and he has no influence on those who "put their trust in their Lord" (16:99). Human nature is seen for what it is, capable of being good, yet weak, prone to ingratitude, arrogance and forgetful of its Creator, but as a whole, the Quran "never wavers on man's essential worth."[24] In this sense, the closest idea of evil is similar to the Greek notion of *hubris*, arrogance, the archetype of which is Pharaoh, hence submission (*islam*) to God as a path that leads us out of the evil we create ourselves.

Finally, while there are the categories of *halal* (permissible) and *haram* (forbidden), morality is a spectrum and everything is not salvation/damnation. There are numerous grey domains such as *makruh*, that which is undesirable or frowned upon, but not a sin, for example, divorce. Similarly, there is *mandub*, acts of piety worthy of praise, but again, carry no penalty if not done. These intermediate domains reflect an approach to notions of 'evil' and 'morality' which are more about *proportions* and requisite *balance*, than absolutes.

In short, at numerous psychological levels there is no theological-dogmatic split in Islam regarding God, self, evil or original sin equivalent to the Christianist mind, which, as Hillman states:

> ...can't admit, can't allow, a destructive possibility co-present or
> co-terminous with love and goodness and salvation.
> Christianism has to use defense mechanisms to deny and split
> and project the destructive aspect onto the enemy—the
> heathens, the Jews, the Catholics, the Reformers, the
> terrorists... then it tries to get the part it has split from, by
> converting it or loving the enemy ...turning the other cheek. It's
> trapped in its own defense mechanism. It made a dogma of
> splitting, which it then glorifies as 'the Problem of Evil'.[25]

The Christianist separation of good from evil leads at times to
an endearing innocence, but is ultimately naïve and simplistic,
rendering both conceptually meaningless. That these are not just
reified ideas but remain powerfully present at the mass level, is
evident, for example, when *Time* magazine did a cover story on
'Evil'. Reflecting the resurgent Western interest in religion
evident during the nineties, it opens with the juvenile
proposition "God is all powerful, God is all good; terrible things
happen."[26] The fact is that in no religion has God said that He is
a Guarantor of a permanent source of bliss. No Divinity tself has
ever proclaimed that it is *exclusively* kind, good, and fully
comprehensible to reason. In Islam, as in Judaism, Divinity has
also some pretty terrifying Names (and to which, it seems,
Islamists have similarly limited themselves). Similarly, in the
Indian and Chinese traditions the concept of Divinity is
'paradoxical', in which opposites exist *simultaneously* as part of a
mutually defining Unity. It was this sort of naïve and dogmatic
Christianity disconnected from the complex realities of the
human psyche (soul) and God as they exist in our *experience*,
that Jung tried to combat all his life, only to be called a heretic.

> None of us stands outside humanity's black collective shadow
> ... one would therefore do well to possess some "imagination
> for evil" for only the fool can permanently disregard the
> conditions of his own nature. In fact, this negligence is the best

means of making him an instrument of evil. Harmlessness and naiveté are … little helpful. On the contrary, they lead to projection of the unrecognized evil into the "other". This strengthens the opponents position in the most effective way, because the projection carries the *fear* which we … secretly feel for our own evil over to the other side and considerably increases the formidableness of his threat. What is even worse, our lack of insight deprives us of the *capacity to deal with evil*. Here, of course, we come up against one of the main prejudices of the Christian tradition, and one that is a great stumbling block to our policies.[27]

The stumbling block, for Jung, was that rather than recognizing the propensity for evil *within* us, that is within the self, Christian dogma posits it as a metaphysical principle, "the great advantage of this view is that it exonerates man's conscience and foists it off on the devil". In terms of the psychology of the 'Problem of Evil' faced by Christianism, it does not matter if one is a believing or practicing Christian. Particularly, in view of a general decline in Christianity, for Hillman, the concern is how utterly unaware most Westerners are about this unconscious religious sub-text:

> … I am more worried about the actual shadow of Christianity working in our mindsets… The Christian heritage is constantly at work, like a vaccine, like a toxin, invisibly inside our feelings and reactions and ideas, preventing us from seeing ourselves and our world … you and me, too, we can't help but be Christian. …our unconscious is primarily Christianity… I am afraid of the Christian unconscious because Christianism lives myths deliberately, insisting they are not myths, and this has dreadful paranoid consequences.[28]

The Literalization of Monotheism and History

Monotheism itself is not some simple objective entity which functions in an invariable manner. From within Islam, the Quran insists on a recognition and respect of all religions (2:285-286), and as such, monotheism can be understood as a religious perspective *about* religious perspectives, diverse expressions of a transcendent Unity. What one is attempting to describe here is more the *psychology* of monotheism, as mediated by Cartesian-Christianism, and its internalization in the life of a community; a consensus of the faithful, where this large Greek word denoting belief in one God (*Theos*) has become a complex of images, feelings, metaphors, expressing the beliefs and everyday feelings of billions of ordinary people.

In contrast to the reality of a 'polytheistic' psyche, psychological monotheism refers to a *literal* attitude towards psychological, that is, symbolic events, in which, through a self-reflexive and infantile moral reductionism, one vision overwhelms all others, swallowing them in an attempt to extend itself and create 'unity'.[29] The tendency towards literalization and moral reductionism is peculiar to Christianism in which, as Hillman says, "our monotheistic tradition literalizes history into facts ... everything comes with a date"[30] and, as said earlier, there have been consistently scientific attempts to (dis)prove the historicity of the Bible. This historicism bears directly on individual and collective consciousness which, in modern times, believes that historical facts determine us to the exclusion of everything else. It ranges from evolutionary psychology to genetics, to the 'case history' project of psychiatry/psychotherapy's reduction of the meaning(s) of life to biochemistry or what happened in childhood, to the creation of nation states based on historical claims and related ideas of individual/collective identity through the politics of nationalism, to rigid ethno-religious ideas about identity.

The emphasis on literal, concrete, historical facts as *the* determining factors in individual/collective life ensure that other, more meaningful perspectives are not considered important when it comes to 'making sense' of human existence. Even though, as I will argue in Chapter 4, the Quranic view of history can be considered very differently from the Christian one. Today it is evident that even beyond the Muslim world the literalist-historical view of religious and political identity dominates. Modern disciplines such as archaeology, inspired Hindu fundamentalists to destroy the Babri Mosque and there are similar pscyhodynamics in process regarding archaeological sites in Jerusalem. Hillman's view of Christianism can just as well be applied to Islamism and other religious fundamentalisms:

> I equate Christianism with moralistic fundamentalism ... you have to face this level of Christianism because that is where its world conquering force lies. It's not Christian love that's conquered the world ... not its sophisticated interpretations and theology. It's successful because it mobilizes the will, and the will needs fundamentalism or it does not know what to do ...[it is] utterly monotheistic ... there is only one meaning, one reading of the text, for instances, the one meaning of Christ's suffering.[31]

The insistence on psychological singularity is a kind of implicit ideology, supplying images and appropriate feelings about them, creating a fantasy of what it means to be 'a people'. And this major archetype, of an essentially one dimensional 'god' brings with it its compatible and fellow archetypes. For instance, One Lord is accompanied by One faith (orthodoxy/modernism), One Law (shariah/WTO), One State (dar-ul-Islam/globalization), served by One body of the faithful (ummah/consumers). A beautiful evocation of the ideal totalitarian (and paranoid) society.

This idealized unity *requires* for its earthly (Cartesian-

Christianist) realization, an ideal man, the Hero, who can receive the (divine) commands and overcome in his own person and at large, the obstacles that stand in the way. These obstacles must also have a mythic dimension. Whether the story is retold in an Islamic, Christian, Jewish or Hindu setting, some dragon of dangerous strength must have its head chopped off, traitors everywhere must be sought out and eliminated since, 'you are either with us, or against us'. The Marxists, therefore, require(d) the Capitalists, the Western Powers their Communist threat and more recently, Muslims, who in turn, require the Great Satan and their own heretics. In sum, the heroic requires problems and, by implication, Final Solutions.

Similarly, psychological monotheism tends to regard difference and diversity as irreconcilable opposites and reduces all psychological life to moral issues. Particularly in the light of the impossible-to-resolve 'Problem of Evil' in Christianism, this kind of moral reductionism and its fusion with the heroic archetype, provides the justification for all types of action and violence against whatever seems 'outside,' a prescribed idea of 'unity'. Thus, Jung's view of the West's 'monotheism of consciousness' is directly related to the internalizing of a particular type of Christianity. As both he and Hillman reiterate, it does not matter if one is a Christian or not, 'believer' or atheist. Rather, it is a particularly narrow psychological *attitude* towards self, others, religion, knowledge, in short, life itself.

The 'monotheism' of modern consciousness, being in this case Christian(ist) monotheism, makes most modern individuals today 'behaving Christians' who judge themselves and others, not necessarily according to the paradigmatic meaning of Christ's message of love and peace, but according to the consequences flowing from what happens when his life and death is reduced to literal historical fact and a single meaning, all of which are further reinforced through Cartesianist ideals:

> Hillman: 'It will take us ten hours ... just to go around the very outside of this huge issue of the effect of the Christian two thousand years on the individual case one meets in psychology. You and me, too, we can't help but be Christian.
>
> Interviewer: We are not practicing Christians...
>
> Hillman: Yes, we are, because we are behaving Christians ... we suffer in a Christian way, we judge in a Christian way, we regard ourselves in a Christian way. We have to see this or we remain unconscious and that means our unconsciousness is primarily Christianity. Psychotherapy can't move anything, anybody anywhere, it sees this Christianist unconsciousness and that is why Freud had to attack religion and Jung had to try to move Christianity ... we behave as Christians when we believe facts determine us...'[32]

In the West, a dominant literalist view of religion along with the ideals of will power and reason culminated in, ironically, a general skepticism about Christianity on the one hand, and which on the other, continues to live on, not only in Protestant Christian fundamentalism but more importantly in its 'ethic' of capitalism and heroic individualism. As the pinnacle of Cartesian-Christianism, the Weberian Protestant Ethic lived/lives on as the psychological driving force behind the projects of colonialism, modernity-progress, the rise of science/industry and global capitalism.[33] It produced missionaries and other single minded individuals prepared to go out and make the world safe for their particular colonial 'raj,' as similar recruits do now for their transnational corporations. Similarly, perhaps the steady post-war influx of European (German) intellectuals, only added to the already existing heroic ideals of the United States. It finds an embodiment not only in the current political dominance of right-wing Protestant Christianity, but also in its cult of the youthful, self-reflecting global 'vision,' a high degree of internal and external violence and its almost exclusive emphasis on a literal, outer (rather than also inner/spiritual) individualism.

The hero archetype and the urge toward monotheistic consciousness, both refine mental focus and mobilize inner resources to function strongly in the service of a singular vision. But like all religions, the ideal goals of monotheism have as much to do (if not more) with our inner, psychological and spiritual development as with the outer material world. It is important to remember that most of the Islamic world was colonized and even more importantly, that as a harbinger of modernity, colonialism was deeply linked to the missionary endeavour. Which is not to say that everything wrong in the Muslim world(s) has to do with Cartesian-Christianism. Here, one is trying to identify certain psycho-religious dynamics within *modernity* as modes of thought and construction of the self coming from a distorted vision of Christianity which fuels all sorts of extremism, including the way we relate to self, society and *any* religion. Religious or 'secular', as participants in a global modernity, we all are influenced by "this extraordinary religion, the religion that we are all in no matter how hard we try to deny it or escape it…"[34] In short, for Hillman, you and I (the modern person) 'can't help but be Christian'. Muslim, Hindu, Jew and non-believer, we are all in the same boat.

Cartesian-Christianism and Modern Terror

To reiterate, the point is not that Christianity as a religion/tradition is some sort of evil construction, rather it is that there's a psychological tendency within the religion that can become destructive when it gets dismembered from its traditional spiritual wellsprings.

The point also isn't to glorify Islam. As will become clear

throughout the book, for different reasons, similarly destructive psychological tendencies can be found within contemporary Islam. Finally, the point also isn't that our ancestors were better or worse than us. But today's human capacity for large-scale destruction is simply unprecedented and, as Jung remarked, the moral aspect of human nature has not progressed in proportion to technological progress/prowess.

> Quite apart from the barbarities and blood baths perpetrated by the Christian nations among themselves throughout European history, the European has also to answer for all the crimes he has committed against the coloured races during the process of colonization ... the white man carries a very heavy burden indeed ... the evil that comes to light in man and that undoubtedly dwells within him is of gigantic proportion, so for the Church to talk of original sin and to trace it back to Adam's relatively innocent slip-up with Eve is almost a euphemism, the case is graver and grossly underestimated.[35]

Cartesian-Christianism has cut itself off from its inner psychotheological diversity, including not just the feminine dimensions, but also all sorts of other unpalatable, dark and dreadful aspects that exist in us, irrespective of male and female. That is, an (un)conscious Cartesianism which exclusively claims the 'light' of reason and insists on facts-as-meaning colludes with a similarly (un)conscious Christianity which also absolves oneself of evil on the basis of a mental belief-as-fact. The consequence of this 'unholy' psychological alliance prevents one from seeing the evil within. Instead it is projected, as a child does, onto others. In short: the moral dimension remains heroic and, in many ways, childish/adolescent because of simplistically fusing exclusivist either/or ideas of both religion and reason.

The current popularity of mythical heroes such as Harry Potter and Tolkien's *Lord of the Rings*, at one level underscores the abiding power of archetypes and the continuing dominance of a 'monotheism of consciousness', that is, the literalizing of Christianity, and its internalization into the collective/individual psyche dominated by heroic, masculine ideals. These and many other films, reflect the reductionist vision of both God/religion and (hu)man. Apart from a heroic, 'thoroughgoing maleness,' there is an association of magical power with weapons of destruction, "with devices, not with deliberation and negotiation". Instead of philosophical wisdom there is "only one way of viewing the world, as a decisive battle between good and evil with the triumphant goals of destruction, extermination and annihilation."[36] Even though, there are actually other historical and mythical alternatives to conflict, such as, redemption and reconciliation, not to mention the quintessentially Christian ideals of love and forgiveness.

The move towards extermination as the only solution, is a cultural corollary of the Freudian 'ego', which must, through various 'mechanisms' be 'defended' from difference, and its supremacy retained at all costs. From the Jungian perspective, the supremacist viewpoint of the ego, is basically fundamentalist and its denial of differences itself pathological. Hence Jung's definition of neurosis as a 'one-sidedness in the presence of many'. Put another way, an exclusivist psychological or theological consciousness is inevitably a paranoid one. Given that inner and outer diversity is a fact of life, it is axiomatic in depth-psychology that what is not admitted into awareness, erupts in ungainly, obsessive, literalistic ways affecting us with precisely those qualities, which we try to exclude. Split off from consciousness, these many 'others' within and without, are thus experienced as "paranoid fears of invasion by enemies. On the one hand, we have individual insanity, on the other, insane collective projections upon other people, whole races and nations".[37]

In the absence of symbolic capacities, when confronted with the world of *mythos* including the meaning(s) of religion, the logocentric mind can only see it in two ways, namely, for/ against, either/or, right/wrong. Thus, religion has to be literally true, or then, irrational nonsense. This is what mostly happened in the post Enlightenment West which heralded the 'death of God', leaving what Sartre called the "God-shaped hole" in Western consciousness. But since then, something has filled that hole.

The fact is that people are as ready to kill in the name of God as they are to kill without It. In the 20th Century, between the two World Wars, the Gulag, Hiroshima and Nagasaki, more than a hundred million people died violent deaths for reasons that had *nothing* to do with religion, and all this occurred either in Europe or originated in the modern secular West. Besides Saddam and the determinedly secular Baath Party, there have been no non-Western equivalents to Stalinism, Fascism, the Holocaust, apartheid, or the inventions of chemical, nuclear and biological weapons. As Karen Armstrong notes, the sheer scale of the Holocaust, Gulag and Hiroshima/Nagasaki 'reveals their modern origins' and 'the germs of nihilism in modern culture'.[38] In this respect Jung aptly remarked:

> The destructive powers of our weapons has increased beyond all measure, and this forces a psychological question on mankind: Is the mental and moral condition of the men who decide on the use of these weapons equal to the enormity of the possible consequences?[39]

It is self-evident then, that a rational 'secular' education is no guarantee against barbarism. Whether the Holocaust, the Indian partition, Rwanda, the Balkans, not to mention the Oklahoma bombings and periodic massacres in universities in the U.S., or school kids in Britain and Norway, all indicate that there is something inherently self-destructive within the modern self and that fanaticism and fundamentalism lurks deep within the human psyche. Secular or religious, there is a Taliban within all of us.

From the Archetypal and Jungian perspective, Germany as the 'pinnacle' of the ascent of the hero, was simply the logical locus for something as *unimaginable* as the Holocaust. The disembodied, compartmentalized, super rational modern psyche could ensure that a concentration camp could exist in the same neighbourhood as a great university.[40] One should note that Jung's verdict on Germany's role in the war was to see that nation as simply carrying, what was actually, the darkness and shadow of the West as a whole, and which he saw as being deeply connected with the unacknowledged religious crisis of Europe.

> This is not the fate of Germany alone, but all Europe. We must all open our eyes to the shadow who looms behind contemporary man ... anyone who does not understand it is simply beyond help. It is no small matter to know of ones own guilt and evil and nothing to be gained by losing sight of ones shadow ... anything that remains unconscious is incorrigible.[41]

The paranoia created by an excessive valorization of a supremacist, masculinist vision of self and soul (psyche), God and 'other', leads to a sort of inner psycho-cultural terrorism against all that is different from the ego. Beyond the dehumanizing impact of technology, it is accomplished for example, through scientific systems of education, that rely on compartmentalizing knowledge, insist on specializing at a younger and younger age and do not value the more imaginative disciplines such as the arts and humanities. Similarly, the techno-scientifically induced speeding up of modern life is akin to a sort of mania in terms of a rapid, hyper movement in travel, text, image. Life is reduced to an experiential blur of manic activity, preventing a genuine experience of seeing depth or difference.

Psychologically, this compartmentalization is meant to be accomplished by the heroic (Freudian) norms of will power and a rigid, narrow Cartesian idea of reason. When faced with that which is uncontrollable and different, the solution is frequently mind numbing drugs, electric shocks or therapies which aim to strengthen the ego's 'defenses'. The (inevitable) invisible underside of the mania that is modernity is the burgeoning psycho-pharmacological and therapy industry catering to what are being called, in the West, new 'maladies of the soul'.[42] As a whole, modernity creates a condition of manic-depression (now clinically rendered innocuous as a bi-polar disorder). Some of the best selling prescription drugs today are for anxiety, depression and schizophrenia. Four out of five of the top selling drug categories have to do with illnesses directly or indirectly related to psychological conditions, with the largest proportion of sales in the US, Europe and Japan.

The psyche is big business. The combined sale of the psychopharmacological industry is more than 300 billion dollars a year. Just the top five psychotropic drugs make more money than the GNP of over half the countries on earth. In the US, since 2008, more antipsychotics are sold ($14.6 billion) than cholesterol lowering drugs and robust growth is anticipated worldwide for drugs dealing with schizophrenia, anxiety, depression and other mental ailments.[*]

This global 'bi-polarity', from the Jungian perspective, is symptomatic, not just of the Cartesian split, but of a deeper psychological malaise, a dis-ease of the psyche/soul and which is

---

[*] Since the 90's, best selling prescription drugs worldwide include Xanax and Zantac used to treat ulcers which are linked to anxiety. E. Lily's top global money spinner, is the anti-depressant Prozac. *IMS Drug Retail Monitor. January 2008*, reports that: The top five therapy classes at ATC3 level from Jan 2007-2008 were: Cholesterol and Triglyceride regulators, Anti-ulcerants, Anti-depressants and mood stabilizers, Anti-psychotics and Anti-epileptics. Since 2008, in the US, antipsychotic sales have overtaken those of cholesterol lowering medicines. See *IMS Press Release 2009*. www.imshealth.com

a symptomatically linked to the dogmatic split in Christianity. Having separated Evil, it does not recognize its own inner diversity including its darkness. Internally, the psyche is obliterated through drugs. Since evil exists only externally, it must be eliminated. As Armstrong points out in a different context, "ethnic cleansing is a by-product of modernity."[43]

In the last decade, the symbol that encapsulates the relationship of Cartesian-Christianism to modernity is the image of Radovan Karadicz, the man behind the massacres in Srebrenica and other atrocities in the name of ethnic cleansing in the Balkans. A *psychiatrist* by profession, he was well known for giving interviews always with a Bible close by.[44] Thus, Islamist or otherwise, terrorism and terrorists are inherent to modernity as an expression of a particular, psycho-theological consciousness. Long before 9/11, Hillman observed:

> A terrorist is the product of our education that says that aesthetics is just for artists, soul is only for priests ... A terrorist is the result of this whole long process of wiping out the psyche. Terrorism and nihilism are already in our Western worldview, terrorists are the incarnation of the nihilism that is inherent to our system of thinking... *its roots lie in our religious consciousness.*[45]

An Environ-mental Crisis

From a psychological perspective, fundamentalism may be expressed in a religious or non-religious idiom but is imbued with a Cartesianist-Christianist 'mind'. To reiterate, this should not be seen as contesting Christianity as a religion, so it is best to let Jung speak: "I do not combat Christian truth. I am only arguing with the modern mind."[46]

This 'mind' according to Armstrong, has made "'God' a wholly notional truth reached by the critical intellect", and thus, has itself 'killed' the life nourishing symbol central to the Christian *mythos* by literalizing it. What we call the 'sense of the sacred' points to a mystery, it requires not only myth and ritual but an ethical and moral dimension expressed and lived in daily life, a way of life. All sacred texts are less about correct 'beliefs' or 'creeds' and more about how to *cope* daily with this beautiful, painful, paradoxical, frequently confusing and difficult business called 'life'— and about how to die.

Every religion urges humans to try and live according to two core, related principles: do unto others as you would have others do unto you, which automatically leads to the idea of compassion. These are the challenges of religion and they have been marginalized today by either taking mythical symbols as literal facts and hence 'right', or simply denying them altogether. As we know, the 'dark epiphanies of the 20th Century' have revealed that secular humanism does not automatically evoke compassion and nor does religious belief per se. These failures tell us that the problem is not with one religion or another but with human nature. Thus, it is imperative to be aware of how we conceive of and understand the human self, particularly its relationship with religion.

An extreme heroic masculinist self leads to extreme logocentrism at the expense of the 'Other' in all its dimensions: as woman, body, nature, the feminine face(s) of God, the world of *mythos/eros* and the symbolic, and last but not least, Islam. The issue is not about male or female but about a particular consciousness, a mindset or *weltanschauung* which can be present in anyone, man or woman. So it is about the imbalance between various complementary psychological and/or theological factors, all of which are required for life. When the balance goes haywire, as it has with the natural environment, it indicates a sickness rooted in the psychology of a human self— secular or religious—that has become one sided and fundamentalist.

This environ-Mental imbalance is ecologically a relatively recent development. Psychologically too it was initiated within roughly the last three hundred years of a 5000 year known history. The major force behind it was the Western religious and intellectual 'mind' and its ideas of the self, Nature and human nature. As Armstrong puts it, Western modernity is a "child of logos founded on the technological replication of resources and constant reinvestment of capital",[47] and it is this 'child-hero' as *homo economicus* which has changed the world in a way that has had disastrous environ-mental consequences.

Soon after 9/11, the question "why do they hate us?" was raised in the US. One recurring answer was "they" were motivated by envy of the West's life style. At that time I found this answer absurd but on further reflection, there is much truth to it: the psychological bedrock of global capitalism is based on desire and its inevitable corollary, envy. Both are constantly generated by the global advertising industry, reinforcing the self as *homo economicus*. Our psychological relationship with spiritual heroes, the prophets, saints and sages of mythos have been forgotten in favour of the scientist/inventor/warrior/politician/economist in the mythic quests for 'progress'. Yet, as was already mentioned, there is absolutely no evidence that we are morally/ethically better persons than our ancestors. If anything, we are regressing.

Myths and symbols, because they speak of eternal truths, do not die but keep reappearing according to the times, which today is the Age of the Literal. For example, female hysteria has given way to anorexia nervosa which becomes a symbol of the present condition of the Feminine. Without the capacity to comprehend their message(s), the moral and ethical transformative potential of *mythos* remains dormant.

The price for 'progress' is becoming self-evident. I have already mentioned the global embrace of the massive and growing psycho-pharmacological industry. Similarly, the natural environment symbolically reflects the ravaged human psychological condition in a demythologized world. The pathologizing and erasing of inner diversity is reflected in the steady extinction of different species and an ecological imbalance which is reflected in erratic climates and breakdowns of numerous eco systems. Still mysteriously connected by a mutual reflection-projection, both psyche and Nature point to what is truly a *man* made, environ-*mental* crisis.*

Modern myths of scientific rationality, progress, power etc., fail because they do not meet the requirements of *mythos* in participatory symbolic ritual and the psychological lessons regarding ethical behaviour as urged by all prophets/sages about compassion, love, tolerance, patience, in short, genuine transformation. These may have nothing to do with rational 'facts' but are inextricably part of the meaning-full sustenance provided by *mythos* for living the symbolic life. Putting it another way, the question about mythical and religious stories, legends etc. is not if they are 'facts' or 'true'. Rather, the question is what do they *mean*?

Both Plato and Aristotle recognized this human need for meaning. Rationally opposed to *mythos*, both nevertheless realized its significance and the centrality of religion. As a result, Greek achievements in rationalism had no negative impact on

---

* By now there is a huge body of work from within different disciplines that place these ego-attitudes at the heart of modernity and its psycho-cultural condition. Deep ecology, critiques of science, feminist spirituality and ecofeminism particularly, have analyzed how these *attitudes* underpin the environmental crisis. They suggest how woman/body/nature/colonized are, from the view of the Cartesian ego, psychologically synonymous, regarding them, as this ego does, to be tamed, owned, civilized, mastered and manipulated at will. The mythic element of the Hero remains. Thus, from this feminist-post/Jungian perspective the logocentric worldview of modernity is, a heroic, confrontational, patriarchal, fundamentalist machismo that permeates our ideas ranging from politics and health, to science, development, progress, religion and nature.

Greek religion which was eventually forcibly suppressed by Justinian in 6th CE and replaced with the myth of Christianity.[48]

Again, as a universal archetype, the issue here is not Christ, rather it is the steady literalizing of this enormously powerful, and profound symbol into the Cartesian-Christianist mindset of modernity. Today, there is a consensus that climate change and related issues are primarily linked to the advanced industrial states of the West and which in turn can be linked to the modern Cartesian-Christianist mind.

Current Counterbalances

While as a whole the West's 'true' religion still remains dominant, the longstanding, widespread, and multidisciplinary nature of the critiques of "the subjugated West" I have mentioned, has also had a discernible impact. Today, there are numerous movements within the West attempting to counterbalance the excesses of Cartesian-Christianism within and beyond academia. Within feminism itself, the environmental movement, ecofeminism, feminist theology and spirituality, the search for alternative paradigms in physical and emotional health, and the psycho-spiritual lifestyles of the 'New Age'; these 'post-modern' movements as a whole, represent powerful, albeit still incipient and marginal counterweights to the dominant *weltanschauung*. This paradigm shift has yet to make even a minor impact in the Muslim academic world leave alone civil society, which remains largely hidebound in terms of various set positions regarding religion and other issues in a psychologically ultramodern style.

Increasingly, ecofeminists and other men and women have noted the psychological links of Christianity with the environmental crisis.[49] Additionally, there are numerous feminist theologians engaged with a critical re-viewing and attempts at rescuing Christianity from Christianism.[50] Most importantly, the maturing of feminist philosophy of religion as a distinct field (from feminist theology) today can be gauged by a chapter in a major reference text, *Handbook of Contemporary Philosophy of Religion*.[51] Theologizing or philosophizing about religion, women such as Mary Daly, Grace Jantzen, Luce Irigaray, Julia Kristeva, Sally McFague, Riane Eisler, Carol Christ, Elaine Pagels, Catherine Keller, to name just a few, are approaching religion from diverse disciplines and perspectives. Along with critiquing and posing radical challenges to Christianity, they simultaneously challenge the fundamentals of Western philosophy and its epistemological and moral premises. As such, their work has global relevance and at this critical juncture in time, offers fresh and urgently needed perspectives on religion and its place in human existence.

Muslims need to engage with these developments with a critical and open mind. It is in the nature of paradigm shifts to emerge slowly and steadily, and feminism, even in the West, still remains at the margins in many areas. Nevertheless, after fifty years, for example, today Women's Studies is an established field even though its influence has not been uniform or always strongly present. The crises in modernity did not develop overnight and nor can they be re-solved quickly. But even outside of academia, there are indicators that many counter currents are emerging, slowly but surely in the West.

Such counter currents are barely present in Muslim intellectual/academic or popular discourse which remains mostly mired in recycling centuries old texts some of which were no doubt radical in their days but remain to be recast for the modern Muslim psyche. The absence of debate/exploration is intensified in the face of internal terrorism which, by definition, cannot and will not permit this. Similarly, Muslim feminism's engagement with Islam or religion generally, remains wholly marginalized but this in no way becomes an indicator that it is therefore not relevant to Muslims. If anything given the misogyny of fundamentalist Islam, it becomes even more significant for Muslim women—and men.

*

Returning to the issue(s) of Western(ized) masculinity, it is notable that since the 90's there has been a 'boom' in masculinity studies particularly by male social scientists.[52] Both critique and response to feminism, and much like the development of feminism as a whole, masculinity studies is an arena of multiple differences intersecting with diverse contexts such as nationalism, identity, race, class, sex, etc.

Similar to the broad references to feminism, the idea in the present context is not to get entangled within these debates on masculinity, but rather, to draw attention (especially of Muslims) to these conceptual arenas as possible avenues of engagement and self-reflection. For example, while identifying different masculinities, Connell shows how, nevertheless, each is associated with different positions of power.[53] A similar wider canvas is considered by Pfeil's *White Guys: Studies in Postmodern Domination and Difference*.[54] These and many other texts, while at one level critiquing feminism, simultaneously agree with the violent political, cultural and historical legacy of straight white males.[55] Developing in tandem with early capitalism and imperialism, white males and empire went together and were positively identified with rationality, control, the suppression of emotion—and women. Connell terms this still widely prevalent masculinity in the West as "hegemonic masculinity" and it is based on domination of others. In short, the significance of masculinity studies is that while remaining basically pro-feminist, almost all authors/social scientists agree that a vast number of straight white Western males are in a situation of psycho-social crisis and urgently require new definitions of manhood.

In the context of religion, and relevant to our purpose, one expression of trying to cope with this crisis in masculinity is the Christian men's movement in the U.S. and Europe, such as the deeply conservative and widespread 'Promise Keepers'.[56] At the same time, there are numerous other men's movements attempting to review masculinity and religion. Within the U.S., for example, a spectrum of researchers find that one of the most notable of these new social movements is the 'mythopoetic men's movement' which derives its inspiration from Jungian psychology (and Islam): "Masculine identity work became popularly noticed in the early 1990's as middle class white men sought to redefine the concept of masculinity through the mythopoetic men's movement ... [it] heavily utilized Jungian psychology influenced by Muslim Sufism."[57]

One mentions these academic/social/cultural/spiritual developments in the West, not to recommend that they be mimicked but rather, that they indicate strong conceptual counter currents to the psychological and gender/ideological underpinnings of modern thought. A recognition of these discourses/movements may alert, even inspire some Muslims to initiate similar self-reflection regarding modernity, religion, Islam, women etc. By simply rejecting some of the superficial and obviously negative aspects to modernity, there is a tendency to self-righteously indulge in West bashing and then retreat into hidebound, or orthodox ideas of Islam. The real challenge is to be psychologically aware of the white man's legacy and decolonize the (Islamic) imagination. Recognizing that many in the West are also searching for salutary solutions and alternatives within different traditions, Muslims can only gain by examining these initiatives. The globalization of knowledge makes this eminently possible.

Concluding Part I: Penetrations & (S)Permutations

To summarize: from the post/Jungian perspective, the psycho-theological ruptures in the modern self have created a psychological and moral sickness in the Western psyche leading to a worldview which can be called Cartesian-Christianism, often referred to with the sanitized term 'secularism'. As the 'dark epiphanies of the 20th Century' such as its wars, genocides and mega weapons tell us, the problem is not with any religion but with the human psyche and how it theo-rizes its self and its relationship with religion.

For Jung, it was not that Westerners are more evil than their ancestors, rather, given the distortions and internalization of Cartesian-Christianism, and given the wars, genocides and invention of horrific chemical, nuclear weapons etc., in the West, their moral capacities have not evolved in proportion to their modern ability to destroy on a massive scale. "That is the great problem before us today. *Reason alone no longer suffices.*"[58]

All religions encompass notions of good and evil and other dialectical concepts. However, these are not to be seen literally, or existing separately in warring conflict, but rather, as symbolic, interconnected, contrasting, *mutually defining* complementary qualities. Thus, the Islamic ideal is of the 'middle way', of balance. It's not an ideal of obliteration of one by the other which results in an inflated ego (arrogance/*hubris*) and absence of humility.

Promoted and internalized via the universally 'civilizing' projects of colonialism, post/modernization/globalization, or what Derrida also called Christianist 'Globalatinization',[59] the nature of secular fundamentalisms today exhibit similar Cartesian-Christianist features. Its world of 'facts', that is, One meaning, dominates along with an exclusivist literalism, coupled with moral reductionism. As the foundational post-colonial scholar Ashis Nandy wrote: "The concept of the modern West is a psychological category. The West is now everywhere, within the West and outside; in structures and in minds."[60]

It should not be forgotten that the majority of colonized people were Muslims. From the perspective of the colonized 'native', the primary image heralding the colonial project was of white men carrying weapons and accompanied by priests/missionaries. This telescopes the twin image of the 'warrior priest' in the fusion of a distorted hyper-macho vision of religion (Christianism) and an instrumentalist-weaponized rationality/power (Cartesianism). It is this image of the 'warrior priest' that has been internalized in the colonized/modernized psyche. Today the top leadership of Al-Qaeda is highly trained in sciences such as engineering, medicine, physics etc. The psychology of the rational-warrior-priest fuels all sorts of extremism, including the way we relate to self, society and *any* religion. Religious or 'secular' (Cartesian-Christianist), as participants in a global modernity, we are all influenced by what Hillman calls "this extraordinary religion, the religion that we are all in no matter how hard we try to deny it or escape it."[61]

By now, Hinduism is increasingly Cartesian-Christianist-Hinduism, and similarly, we have Cartesian-Christianist-Judaism or Buddhism, and of course, as will be made amply clear in the following chapters, Cartesian-Christianist-Islamism. Religious or secular, these fundamentalisms are misogynist, hegemonic, hypermasculine expressions which (psychologically and theologically) artificially negate psychospiritual tendencies in favor of logocentric supremacist thought. As such, the terrorism of political Islam is one side of the symmetrical psychodynamics underlying post/modernity where there is only *one* 'choice': Whether in the Cold War of the last century, or Algeria in the 80's, when religious extremists killed unveiled women and secularists the veiled, or today in the War on Terror, "you are either with us or against us". In the psycho/theological absence of the Feminine, it is a mirror image response to various masculinist 'penetrations': psychologically, of Western Cartesian-Christianist modernity, and literally, the penetration of a homophobic, homoerotic dialogue/battle into a language of violence/war.

Ideas, like pills, are not gender sensitive and can be swallowed uncritically by men and women. Given the psychological power of archetypal ideas, simply being female is no prophylactic against these psychologically heroic (s)permutations, witness the many women who join religious fundamentalist movements, in different religions or, for example, former secretary of state Condoleezza Rice in the U.S or the politician Marie le Pen in France.

PART II:
PSYCHOLOGICAL EXPLORATIONS OF 'HIGH' ISLAMISM

Chapter 3:
Cartesian-Christianist-Islamism

To know where the other person makes a mistake is of little value. It only becomes interesting when you know where you make the mistake, for then you can do something about it.
(C.G. Jung[1])

Academia and Religion, North and South

The North and its Renewed Interest in Religion

As a graduate student in the U.S. during the nineteen eighties I realized that apart from departments of religious studies, not many intellectuals were interested in religion. Since it was generally considered a private matter, the few colleagues and friends who knew that I observed the daily prayer, saw it as a mild eccentricity and left it at that. Generally speaking, none of my non/Muslim peers were interested in religion. Today of course, it has become part of everyday conversation.

The fact is that, it is only in the last few decades that academia's disconnection, from what remains a significant dimension of the life of the vast majority of humanity, has begun to change. If religion is being given considerable attention today, this has as much to do with the *nuisance* which the widely imagined Muslim/Islam is becoming, as it has to do with the fact that religion had been basically eclipsed by the 20th Century global intellectual establishments. North and South, given the dominance of the Marxist-Freudian view of the 'self', it had become the norm to deride religion in terms of 'those who believe cannot think and those who think cannot believe.' In post-Enlightenment terms, religion had come to be seen as 'philosophy's shadow'; a sort of counterfeit compared to the genuine superiority of rationalist thought.[2]

However, by the 1990's, an increasingly self-critical academic trend in the North had begun commenting on the "unexpected emergence" and a "recently revived interest in religion ... that has surfaced within the new postmodernist ... intelligentsia."[3] By the end of the millennium, religion was "no longer a prerogative of narrow circles of Parisian intellectuals, marginalized New Age scholars or feminist goddess-worshippers to theorize new religious insights. By contrast, spirituality and mysticism seem to impose themselves with increasing power on the post-Marxist agendas of secularized Western intellectuals.[4] In short, these developments among Western intellectuals were to some extent catalysed by New Age scholars and feminists. To this extent, the Western intellectuals' interest in religion is a recent development. Yet all of this has been very different in the case of the Southern (and particularly the secularized Muslim) intellectual and his relationship with religion.

The South and its Absence of Self-critique

It is ironic, even poignant, that, whereas in the North, the intellectual's earlier attitude to religion can be justified as part of a historical process in which modernity and secularism overwhelmed and marginalized religion, in the South the situation had *always* been mostly the reverse. That is, while modernity certainly had an impact, nevertheless, for the vast majority of non-Western populations, it was secularism, espoused mostly by the intelligentsia that was marginal, not religion itself.

Although Southern intellectuals had for decades asserted themselves vis-à-vis the North via the project of postcolonial studies, the vast majority of Muslim intellectuals remained oblivious or contemptuous of the religious ground realities they actually physically inhabited. In Pakistan, for example, with the collapse of the Soviet Union by the early nineties, two broad directions emerged among its secular intellectuals. Either Marxism was abandoned in favour of environmentalism which had also become fashionable in the West, or then, especially post- 9/11, many belatedly 'discovered' Islam and went from one extreme to the other. That is, instead of critically assessing the core reasons for the short shrift and denial that was given to religion even while inhabiting overwhelmingly visible, and obviously religious contexts; many intellectuals have simply gone from being Marxists to insufferably hair splitting, observant Muslims obsessed with West bashing. Decades of analytic training are set aside in favour of an uncritical acceptance of what is frequently a narrow and ultra conservative, masculinist expression of religion, with faith becoming an overwhelming substitute for knowledge.

The idea of a 'chasm' between faith and knowledge which can only be 'leaped' across, is part of the intellectual heritage of Western civilization and the creedal contingencies which are central to fundamentalist Christianity and not necessarily endemic to all religious traditions.* The Southern intellectuals'

---

* The absence of a chasm between faith and knowledge in other religions is why, for example, there has historically been no equivalent to the creation/evolution debate. It used to be a non-issue, just like the question of abortion. But as with abortion and Islam, it was only a matter of time before the creation vs. evolution 'problem' was imported and the theological debates began. Until the Cairo conference on population,

reliance on faith to the exclusion of reason, not to mention the conceptual and investigative resources of modern knowledge as applied to his/her religion, at best is frequently a mental-analytic cop-out; at worst it borders on fundamentalism. In both instances it betrays a still colonized imagination vis-à-vis religion.

This absence of self-critique is unfortunate, reflecting a similar *hubris* and self-ignorance as before. A more ruthless self-analysis may have provided certain insights which would have been uncomfortable to say the least, since these may have little to do with colonialism and possibly more with, to put it bluntly, a failure of cognition; which in turn is related to the rather mundane human need to follow fashion, in this case, following whatever was/is fashionable in the West. Following fashions, of course, runs counter to the self-image of a 'thinking' person. Nevertheless, this tendency within many Muslim intellectuals must be confronted. Even if only to be liberated by irony and the capacity to laugh at oneself by 'seeing through' the intellectual ego and its need to be always taken seriously. Otherwise we will remain incapable of recognizing the modernist penetration if Islam and its ensuing Cartesian-Christianist-Islamism.

---

abortion had never been an issue in Islam and the strong presence of Muslim creationism is a phenomenon of only the last few decades. For more on the traditional relation between faith and knowledge in Islam, see: Nasr, Hossein; *Knowledge and the Sacred*. Edinburgh University Press. Edinburgh. 1981.

The Modernist Penetration of Islam

When a paranoid, monotheistic consciousness encounters yet another monotheism, Islam, the result is a sort of 'triple jeopardy': Cartesian-Christianist-Islamism. It is most evident in the high Islamists since apart from well-developed literacy, they are frequently trained in sciences such as engineering, medicine etc., or at the very least have had some advanced form of a higher modern education. The preceding chapter has discussed the implications of the psychological underpinnings of the mind-set engendered by modernity and its logocentric, violent, compartmentalized, literalist psyche. One can speculate how this came about in Islam through the (irretrievable) unfolding of modern history, particularly since, Cartesian-Christianism has, historically, not been a longstanding or major aspect of Islamic intellectual and theological consciousness.

Islam too arose from a mythical matrix, dominated by the goddesses of pre-Islamic Arabia. Whether in the biography of its founder or more importantly, in the reiterations of the Quran to 'observe', 'reflect', 'think' and 'ask more of knowledge', it also reflects the heroic-monotheistic archetype as a movement towards rational, abstract, consciousness in conceptions of both the material world and the Divine. If this had not been the case, Muslim achievements in sciences such as medicine, astronomy, mathematics, architecture, chemistry and the invention of algebra, would not have been possible. In these and other disciplines, their contributions formed the pre-modern foundations of many modern sciences. As Catherine Wilson points out, Islamic philosophy is not just by Arabs or in the Arabic language. Socratic rationalism and logocentrism which is supposed to characterize European thought, whether or not it sprang from Greek soil, acquired its characteristic intensity and precision in Muslim countries between the ninth and thirteenth centuries. Greek philosophy was adopted by the Arabs vis-à-vis monotheism thereby ensuring its relevance for Christianity. According to Wilson, one aspect of the Arabic contribution to European philosophy was the heightened standard of philosophical discourse.[5] Nevertheless, at a certain stage this flourishing of knowledge petered out. At its zenith in Spain and principal point of contact with the West, even as it passed on its own contributions and the West's ancient heritage, Islam simultaneously 'retreated'.[*]

In the light of existing critiques of modernity, development and science,[6] the idea here is not to get ensnarled into a socio-political discussion as to why Muslim consciousness did not evolve widespread, similar, counterparts to these projects.[†] Rather, the focus is on a particular understanding of Islam as it has come through the psychology of modernism and its links with the Christianist unconscious.

The point is that, in spite of a scientific vision pertaining to the material world, the Cartesian split has not had a widespread equivalent in the Islamic *logos*, and one will be discussing its implications in the next chapter. An absence of Cartesianism is

---

[*] As brilliantly 'mapped' by Corbin, this dual movement is intellectually telescoped in the Aristotelian philosophy of Averroes and the neo-Platonism of the Spanish Sufi Ibn al Arabi. If the former represented the earliest stages of modern scientism, which would culminate in the North and exclusivist literalizing of religion, the trajectory of Ibn al Arabi's life is a symbol of a more 'southward' movement, towards a more symbolic perspective, which, while incorporating reason was simultaneously based on an inner and outer vision of psychological, cultural and religious pluralism, alongwith an emphasis on different aspects of the Feminine. A near contemporary of the Persian poet-philosopher Jalaluddin Rumi, Ibn al Arabi's metaphysics can be considered the more rigorous, analytic counterpart to Rumi's psycho-spiritual poetics. See Corbin; *Creative Imagination in the Sufism of Ibn al Arabi*. 1975.

[†] Given the questions around the sustainability of the earth's resources and the relationship of modernity to consumerism, one could argue that if the presently one billion plus Islamic world had materially 'developed' in tandem with the West, matters would have been even more critical than they are at present.

not the same as saying that Islam did not partake of the hero archetype's impetus towards reason/rationality. By definition of its monotheistic features, it does, not only in the mythical hero motifs in the biographical narrative of the Prophet, but also as the 'youngest' of the monotheisms, evident in its early dynamism and energy in political conquest on the one hand, on the other, the many schools of rationalist philosophy that emerged across its geo-cultural spectrum. None of the latter however, can be considered as an all pervasive *weltanschauung*.

The acknowledgement of the steady presence of different rationalist philosophies, but which failed to have a transformative and unifying impact, is a refrain in the discussions around Islam and science in the Muslim world.[7] Overwhelmingly, these discussions do not consider this failure in terms of the implications of the crises of modernity and their links to Cartesianism. Neither is bin Ladenism/'high' Islamism linked to the exclusivist, violent and paranoid worldview inherent to the Christianist/religious roots of modernity, but solely to his view of Islam. Given the nearly century long dominance of the Freudian-Marxist paradigm which sees religion as an infantile-opiate, the Muslim intellectual's own disconnection from Islam prevents him from seriously contesting the ideas exemplified by bin Laden. Those who do are mostly unable to see how modernity (and hence their own psyche) is part of the problem. Thus, many (otherwise) well-educated Muslims are largely unable to conceptually contest 'high' Islamism from within such a dual critique. In fact as part of Islamic identity-crisis politics it was evident in the early 90's that more were steadily falling victim to extremist ideals.[8] Barring a few exceptions,[9] the central crisis of modern Muslims in relation to Islam, has been, until recently, a sort of complacent intellectual inertia.

Whatever the level of critique, the relationship of modernity with Christianism, which is by now fully evident in the ascendance of the political power of the religious right in the United States and Europe, is rarely discerned and remains an intellectual blind spot, which can also be related to a dismissal of Western feminism generally. The fact is that apart from Jung, Hillman, etc., it is from within especially feminism that the destructive relationship between Christianism and modernity has been severely criticized. From within Islamic theology, similar self-critiques would be able to distinguish, and appreciate, the nature of a less (self)destructive Christianity from Christianism. Similarly, instead of indulging in simple West bashing, it would also be able to view the genuinely positive dimensions of both modernity/postmodernity *and* Christianity. Recourse to different epistemologies and more inclusive psycho-theologies that are available both outside and within Islam, may have enabled such discernments. In the absence of alternative perspectives, the modern understanding of Islam has begun to manifest the psychology of Christianism which is, ironically, but also inevitably, virulently anti-Christian. Even prior to modernity, the Christianist influence on Islam is evident, for example, in the practice of veiling women, which, as Armstrong points out was taken from 'upper class Byzantine Christianity' and was initiated three to four generations *after* the death of the Prophet.[10]

Literalization of the Quran

In contrast to Christ as the pivot and miracle of Christianity, the miracle of Islam is not Muhammad but the Quran, and which becomes, therefore, the primary psychological core of Islamic consciousness. While both can be seen as manifestations of the Divine *Logos* ('The Word'), the differing forms suggest very different interpretive trajectories regarding *Logos* as both rational knowledge and spiritual 'presence'. Yet, the original structure of the of the Quran and the traditional approach to Its language starkly contrast with the literalized manner in which the Quran is increasingly read and interpreted. This contrast offers us a good example of the (psychological) dynamics behind Cartesian-Christianist-Islamism.

A Reminder

The Quran frequently refers to Itself as 'A Reminder' (15:6, 9; 3:58; 12:104; 16:44; 21:10; 38:87, etc.), thereby implying a certain historical/spiritual memory of the past. Even as a monotheism, in partaking from the narratives of its predecessors, it presents a polyvalent view of itself in form and content. Claiming no original morality, it accepts the Judaic 'eye-for-an-eye' but at the same time urges Christian forgiveness and restraint as the 'higher victory' (42:40, 43, 4:149, 3:134, 23:96, 90:10-17). This symbolic polyvalence towards a 'middle way' (2:143) makes the 'mono' contours of this 'theism' rather different. Simultaneously, its view of history extends further into the past, claiming that the Reminder is a reiteration/reconfirmation of all religions, which in turn, are expressions of the same, eternal Message.

Thus, whereas Abraham is a major touchstone in this historical/spiritual/religious consciousness there are also references to other, non-Biblical figures, hence outside of chronological time. In popular Muslim belief, there have been more than 100,000 prophets and thus, the Quran's consciousness of history has to do with a deeply primordial past aiming to engender a different psycho-religious identity. That is, beyond the overarching emphasis in Christianity regarding the concretization of Christ-as-God into historical fact, the Bible and Quran engender differing perspectives on history. These differences are clearly evident in the contrasts between Biblical and Quranic styles.

Orality and Literacy

As a product of literacy, the Bible is, in many ways, a modern text. It assumes literacy and has a linear, narrative structure, moving from Genesis ('in the beginning...') to the end-as-Apocalypse. Certainly in the New Testament such a linearity is reflected the stories around the birth, life and passion of Christ.

In contrast, the Quran was the product of an oral tradition which, even when 'written' reflects its original, essentially oral form. In its recursive style and absence of a central linear narrative(s), the Quran is more of a series meditations on different *themes* and less about history as we know it. For example, while it frequently refers to certain Biblical accounts around Moses, they are dispersed across the text. Stripped, as they are, to their bare essentials, the stories are basically illustrative of archetypal themes.

Thus, the Moses motif may appear in the context of Pharaoh whose arrogance makes him the archetype of Evil. Elsewhere, Moses may figure in the context of a different (esoteric) knowledge and its relationship with the (Written) Law (Sura 18). Similarly, other Biblical prophets, including Jesus, enter/exit in no particular historical order, the textual structure suggesting an indifference to the details of stories, which, from its (the Quran's) perspective were/are already known. What is important about a story is its *meaning*. In short, its form emphasizes archetypal theme(s), the Message, not the messenger(s). Which is also, perhaps, why its final form is de-linked from the chronology of the Prophet's life. Thus, a recursive meditation on themes, the structure of the Quran is less symphonic, so to speak, and more like a raga, or a jazz composition. As a whole, and this is the only way such texts can be taken—as a whole—it is not any Prophet/person, but the Divine to whom all themes return to proclaim Its Glory and Omnipotence.

Beyond aspects of style and form, the linguistic structure of

Arabic adds to the complex and layered meanings of the Quran. Similar to Hebrew, Arabic words are based on a tripartite root system whereby each word has many meanings, and which, in turn, depends almost entirely on varying contexts. As such, there are no translations of the Quran, only interpretations. From the psycholinguistic perspective, it has been suggested that literacy changes consciousness along principles of visual perception, functioning as it does, unidirectionally and analytically. Orality, by definition, is aural/auditory, simultaneous and synthesizing. As discussed in terms of the impact of 'the technologizing of the word',[11] these different styles of consciousness can be related to the Bible and Quran which, as Muslims believe, was revealed to an 'unlettered' Prophet.

An Avante-Garde Classic

The absence of a narrative/historical structure in the Quran has long confounded the modern Western(ized) reader. R.A. Nicholson's comments about the Prophet not being a great "raconteur … most of the stories … are narrated in a rather clumsy and incoherent fashion,"[12] is echoed even by Jung, who saw the Prophet having a "primitive cast of mind."[13] Thomas Carlyle's response can be considered typical "… a wearisome, confused jumble … endless iterations … long-windedness … incondite… Nothing but a sense of duty could carry a European through the Koran … one feels it difficult to see how any mortal could consider this … as a Book … as a well written book, or indeed as a *book* at all."[14]

Carlyle's comments can be considered a modern response to a literary style, which is more postmodern than modern and is exemplified in the writings of James Joyce who was a harbinger of this changing form of the novel/text-as-linear narrative into a more 'stream-of-consciousness' narration. Whether in fiction, film or art, this non-linearity is today a defining feature of the post-modern sensibility.

In 'The Poetics of the Open Work', Umberto Eco has discussed how the form of texts such as Joyce's *Ulysses*, can be both a 'closed' form in its "uniqueness as a balanced organic whole, while at the same time constituting an *open* product on account of its susceptibility to countless different interpretations which do not impinge on its unadulterable specificity."[15] That is, each reader brings to the text his/her own existential credentials, a defined culture, a set of tastes, personal inclinations and prejudices. As such, its validity lies precisely in proportion to the number of different perspectives from which it can be viewed and understood. The stream of consciousness form employed by Joyce, along with other emotional-semantic techniques such as using words having double meanings and other elements of ambiguity, ensure that "Joyce's world is always changing as it is perceived by different observers and by them at different times."[16] If one keeps in mind the non-linearity and other aspects of Quranic style discussed earlier, the following observations by Eco on Joyce's *Finnegan's Wake* may well be applied also to the Quran. And which is why perhaps, it tends to easily become part of a psychologically selective repertoire of quotations by so many Muslims for every conceivable context.

> The work is *finite* in one sense, but in another sense it is *unlimited*. Each occurrence, each word stands in possible relations with all others in the text. According to the semantic choice which we make in the case of one unit so goes the way we interpret all the other units in the text. This does not mean that the book lacks specific sense. If Joyce does introduce some keys into the text, it is precisely because he wants the work to be read in a certain sense. But this particular 'sense' has all the richness of the cosmos itself. Ambitiously, the author intends his book to imply the totality of space and time, of all spaces and all times that are possible...different etymological roots are combined in such a way that a single word can set up a knot of different submeanings each of which in turn coincides and

> interrelates with other local allusions, which are themselves
> 'open' to new configurations and probabilities of
> interpretation... *Here are no privileged points of view, and all*
> *available perspectives are equally valid and rich in potential.*[17]

The Quran can be seen as a quintessentially 'open' text and
necessarily so if it is to be considered (by Muslims) as both a
universal and eternal message. Rooted in the etymological
complexity and ensuing ambiguity which is inherent to the
Arabic language, its 'open' character is even more so since the
complete and transparent intention of its 'author', God, can
never be fully fathomed. It is precisely this 'open' nature of the
text which has enabled its message(s) to be interpreted variously.

Apart from the codification done by the Caliph Usman—
within years of the Prophets death—to this day, unlike the Bible,
there are no 'Standard', 'Revised' or 'King James' editions of the
Quran in Arabic or any given translations/interpretation.
Similarly, it is the open nature of the text which enables the
discerning of all manner of hidden 'wonders' by Muslims about
their Book. For example, thanks to modern computing power,
there is a stream of emails circulating on the internet, pointing
out various symmetries of words, phrases as they statistically
appear in the Quran, drawing attention to a (perceived) range of
mathematical structures underlying the text. Regardless of what
value other individual Muslims would ascribe to such
calculations, the fact is that in its own way the Quran continues
to be perceived subjectively by innumerable subjectivities and its
quantitative/qualitative interpretations remain works in progress
because of its 'open-endedness'. The existence of numerous
translations/interpretations of the Quran *within* a given
language is itself also an indication of its multiple possible
meanings.

Like a hologram in which every part reflects/contains the
whole, the meaning and significance of such open texts is similar

to what Umberto Eco calls 'simultaneous totality' and which ultimately has to do with an individual reader and his/her subjectivity. Long before Eco and semiotics, Hodgson noticed these dimensions of the Quran, "almost every element which goes to make up its message is somehow present in any given passage".[18] Interestingly, as a principal fore runner of postmodern literature, it is now established fact that Joyce drew directly from the Quran in terms of style and allusions.[19] Drawing parallels between this genre and the Quran have led to the observation that the generation which can appreciate Joyce and Eco in the West, is actually the first to be able to finally understand and appreciate the Quran in avant-garde terms.[20] In sum: It is best approached as a 'postmodern' text.

Fundamentalist Historization

All these features of an open text make the Quran a very different 'read' from any standard narrative (structure) to which the modern mind is attached, including the scriptural. Such a mind insists on certainty and hence, singularity of meaning, unambiguous clarity, wanting to 'get to the point' with a 'straight forward' (linear) story/message. Additionally, the meaning 'should' be clearly located in human-historical terms. All these are expectations of a modern mind which, when it turns to read a scripture, is frequently unaware that whereas the Bible is directly historical and indirectly doctrinal, the Quran is the reverse.

Taking the Quran on its own terms, and exhibiting as it does a holographic 'simultaneous totality', in fully developed Islamic theology only the moment is real. As Massignon observed, the Quran projects a transhistorical or metahistorical plane regarding historical events which makes their meaning eternally relevant. There is no necessary connection between cause and effect and time does not accumulate.[21] Koranic statements such as "... and the matter of the Hour is as the twinkling of an eye, or it is nearer still" (16:77) are typical of the meta-historical viewpoint. The Apocalypse *and* Creation are simultaneously and ever present, and as such, are primarily psychological phenomenon/'events'.

> The Koran backs off from that linear organization of time, revelation, and history which became the backbone of orthodox Christianity, and remains the backbone of Western culture after the death of God. Islam is wholly apocalyptic ... its eschatology is not theology... The Koran breaks decisively with that alliance between the prophetic tradition and materialist historicism—"what actually happened"—which set in with the materialistically historical triumph of Christianity.[22]

These central dimensions of Islamic psycho-theological consciousness, and its roots in the Quran, run counter to the psychology of modernity and its underlying Cartesian-Christianism. One has already noted Brown's and Hillman's views regarding the exclusivist, historicizing of Christ and its impact on the individual and collective psyche in terms of believing that we are determined by historical fact to the exclusion of everything else. Contact with modernity in the last two centuries and the impulse within Islamism to return to the days of the Prophet can be considered peculiarly modern. It has no widespread precedent in Islamic history and has led to peculiar ideas. For example, it is not uncommon in a city like Toronto to see some Muslims wearing the Middle-Eastern *abaya,* a loose robe-like garment ideal for the desert heat but not for sub-zero temperatures in Canada. Similarly, while it can be argued that many elements regarding the ever (psychological) presence of Creation/Apocalypse are evident in the phenomenon of suicide bombings, it is clearly the conflation of this psychology with politics and a modern sense of history that drives these acts.

In her study of fundamentalism, Armstrong has discussed how

in all three monotheisms, the desire to return to a pristine, historical past, can be seen as an understandable response to the de-humanizing, alienating aspects of modernity and globalization. The Islamic impetus can be additionally seen as an attempt to regain the self-esteem and counter the humiliation of being colonized. But however intense these feelings may be, unlike Judaism and Christianity, there are no textual-historical imperatives towards regressive literalism regarding time and place.

Given the centrality of the Quran in Islamic consciousness, there is little within it that may psychologically propel adherents towards an exclusivist mythical-historical literalism regarding its Messenger, or towards locating the wellsprings of individual/collective religious consciousness within a historically determined geographic territory. In increasingly demonstrating these features today, 'high' Islamism today is psychologically less inspired from within the Quran and more by Christianist-Cartesianist modernity.

Christianist-Islamist-Ulemasculinization

The Quranic stress on the human dimension of prophecy is evident in the reiteration that Jesus, even while having been conceived miraculously, was nevertheless, the 'son of Mary' (3:34, 9:19, 19:35, 3:58), and that Mohammad a man 'just like yourselves' (18:110). As the only prophet of the monotheisms who lived in the 'glare of history',[23] at one level, high regard and emulation of his 'way' is of course integral to the practice of Islam. At the same time, however, the corpus of *hadith* on which it is based remains historically contested by many different theological schools, sects and scholars.

Deriving laws from this domain, as in Pakistan, is to give

hadiths precedence over the Quran, of *logos* over *Logos*, of the word of man over God's Word. Similarly, organizations have sprung up with a focus on the Prophet comparable to the Christianist extreme dehumanizing/deification of Jesus and the tendency of damning/heretecizing all who do not subscribe to it. Seen through the Quran, such veneration verges on blasphemy. Variously named as the 'army' or 'defenders' of the Prophet and/or his disciples, these sectarian organizations are also the most violently anti-Christian. One can note in passing that the colonial legacy of Cartesian-Christianism lives on in postcolonial India as well where there is also a resurgent Hindu fundamentalism and anti-Christian sentiment. The destruction of the Babri Masjid can directly be linked to modern scholarship which relies on constructing linear histories and singular origins. A claim on origin-ality implicitly entails a claim of exclusivity. The Babri Mosque episode was fueled and justified on the basis of a modern approach to archaeological and historical scholarship. Once the literal truth of the historicity (dates) of certain bricks was 'established' by experts, the edifice was reduced to rubble.*

Beyond the Christianist influence of exclusivist literalism, there is, by now, the entrenchment of the *ulema* as a politically and financially powerful priesthood in Pakistan. The identity-crisis politics of the nation-state has encouraged the modern ideal of 'specialization' as applied to religion, facilitating the emergence of a priestly class in Pakistan and elsewhere, giving it

---

* Critics have made "... a defence of archaelogy against political misuse. The archaelogical discoveries which are supposed to prove the demolition of a Rama temple by Babur actually show no more than the logic of a politics which destroyed Babri Masjid on 6-12-1992." Manadal, *Ayodhya Archaelogy after Demolition*. On *Resurgence Online*. 1993. See also: World Archaeological Congress; *A Closer Look at Ayodhya' Issue World Archaeological Congress: Papers in Session7* / Coningham & Lewer; *Archaelogy and Identity in South Asia: Interpretations and Consequences*. 2000.

a power it has rarely enjoyed in Islam. Its rise was accompanied by a parallel loss of interest (and understanding) of Islam by a postcolonial elite dazzled by modernity's Marxist-Freudian ideals of self and other.[24]

While the *ulema* have always been around in Islam and its politics, they are not inherently essential to the religion as the priest is to Christianity, in for example, the administering of the sacraments. In fact, from within Islam, it can be argued that its genesis coincided with the, by then, enthronement of a Church and related institutions which had proceeded to become sole arbiters between Christians and God. As a reaction to the pitfalls of institutionalized religion and its consequences on the individual psyche/soul, the notion of a 'professional' or religious 'priesthood' or any intermediary institution/person, is rejected by the Quran which brooks no intercessors, except by God's permission. Consequently, even while retaining many bonds with Christianity it can be said that Islam aimed to re-empower the individual. Thus, any Muslim can conduct *all* rites associated with birth, death, marriage, and worship. Until the mid-sixties, this was the self-evident norm in homes across the Muslim world, in which such rituals were done by family elders or revered elders from within the community. The increasing influence of *mullahs* and the *ulema* as a mediating force between Muslims and God, along with a vision of women as inferior, belies an attitude that is more Christianist and patriarchal rather than Islamic and has come about because the intelligentsia itself abdicated its God-given rights in favor of the religious 'professional' or 'expert'.

Alienation and Internalization

As pointed out earlier, in spite of being part of the heroic-monotheistic archetype, until the advent of colonialism, Islam as a whole did not have a strong internally dogmatic or theologically overwhelming disposition to a 'monotheism of consciousness'. Its presence today in 'high' Islamism has come about primarily through contact with the *psychology* of modernity via colonialism, whereby: "...most importantly, Western cultural symbols, modes of production and social values aggressively penetrated the Muslim world, seriously challenging inherited values and practices and adding to a profound sense of alienation".[25] What one would add to this diagnosis is that a religiously alienated modernity, along with its (unconscious) psycho-theological attitudes, was also *internalized*, albeit un(self)critically. Not only in the creation of the nation state through the 'secular' ideals of nationalism, but also in the states' cooptation of religious identity, as for example, Pakistan.

The hero motif, of an 'outward' journey/ascent followed by victorious return and death, is about the development of a rational consciousness which eventually re-connects with its origins in the sacred imagination through, being one way or another, humbled, rendered mortal, so to speak. The modern Muslim world is replete with figures who in varying degrees did intellectually, culturally or literally undertake this ascent/journey into the 'north', only to return and preside over massive destruction of existing structures of the indigenous and Islamic imagination, either in the name of Islam, nationalism/progress, or socialism. Khomeini, Zulfiqar Ali Bhutto, even Jinnah, closely approximate the heroic archetype and its modern largely negative manifestations in the Muslim world.

They represent a 'secular'-religious spectrum of the relationship of highly educated Muslims with modernity, the internalizing of which, has been more of a swallowing whole, rather than steady critical assimilation. Lawrence has noted that fundamentalists are simultaneously the consequences of modernity and the antithesis of modernism. That is, while accepting and exploiting the techno-scientific aspect, they do not subscribe to what are actually modern ideals of pluralism, relativism and autonomy.[26] Given the postcolonial critique of modernity/modernism, it is not clear whether Lawrence is speaking of (post)modern or 'high' modernity which, as one has argued from the outset, has not established itself firmly in the West either. And in any case, from other perspectives, including feminism, hegemonic masculinity prevails globally. Basically, modernism/modernity remain undigested, hence, the psychological presence of a Cartesianist-Christianism on the one hand, including now wholly externalized ideas such as free will and determinism, while on the other, a *sense* of alienation and suspicions about (post)modernity. There is a difference between 'making sense' of an experience and having a suspicious 'sense' of something, which is more akin to paranoia.

With few exceptions, these suspicions have not been 'worked through' via a subjective engagement with one's inner, psychological condition, including one's religion. Or any form of psychological engagement with alterity and the 'other'(s). Those who attempted this in South Asia during the colonial period, were attacked by orthodoxy even then and actually owed their safety to the colonial state.* As will be discussed shortly, it was other modern views of Islam, dominated by literalism and power, that became ascendant.

In the West, the suspicions/experience of modernity have, over

---

* For example, Sayyid Ahmad Khan or the founder of the Ahmadi sect, Mirza Ghulam Ahmad.

more than two centuries, been 'worked' through at numerous levels of individual and collective intellectual and cultural discourses. The current situation notwithstanding, modernity is still nevertheless being 'worked through' including the breakthrough into postmodern ideas, feminism, ecology etc.; and the moral challenges they, in turn, pose. Post or high modernity's extreme and dominant masculinist *weltanschauung* notwithstanding, the struggle with moral issues remains evident in initiatives about the environment, or feminism, or a generally greater tolerance for each other. While it remains to be seen how far these gains in individual and collective consciousness will be sustained in the future, presently the West's greater capacity for self-critique cannot be doubted. In Jungian terms, this self-critique can only be possible if the individual can see beyond the ego, into the multiple facets of the psyche, warts and all. This means being aware of one's shadow and not harboring, what Jung called the "unwholesome delusion that we should be at peace within ourselves".[27] A genuine political democracy contains different oppositions within itself and this also holds for the individual. "True democracy is a highly psychological institution which takes account of human nature as it is and makes allowances for the necessity of conflict within its own national boundaries".[28] In Islamic terms this means that while there is a need for an inner *jihad*, this cannot be without recognition of an inner *ijtehad* which is about taking into account a diversity of viewpoints. The widely prevalent idea that *ijtehad* is no longer necessary regarding different dimensions of theology, jurisprudence etc. in Islam is a reflection of the inner, psychological ignorance and arrogance of Muslims today. Not only regarding Islam, but also their uncritical internalizing of modernity, including Cartesian-Christianism.

In contrast, many well educated and moderate Muslims *and* high fundamentalists remain handicapped and hamstrung between a fascination and desire for 'hard' science, and just a strong 'sense' of suspicion about modernity. Ironically, the refuge from it becomes a literalist, regressive, yet peculiarly modern view of religion/Islam towards what has been called "contramodernity".[29] In a situation that largely still remains an intellectually/psychologically undigested experience of self and history, the primary response to the present is a paranoid, visceral one: a violent attempt to purge/disgorge the *externalities* of modernity, albeit selectively. Thus, the 'ideal' Islamic garment are the Saudi style of *hijab* and *abaya*. Visible women and their bodies frequently become the arenas of 'islamization' and a rejection of modern 'values'. Given the hero archetype at work, the 'contramodern' process of course does not include aspects of weapons and related power-technologies. This theme of 'lets-take-science/technology/weapons-but-not-the-rest' is a longstanding one in modern times.[30]

Many of the 'high' fundamentalist Islamist movements today had their genesis in the contact of an experience of modernity via colonialism. The desire to 'modernize' Islam was thus primarily driven by psychodynamics related to subjugation and power, not knowledge per se or as it may relate to a revitalizing of numerous Islams existing in the colonized lands. Instead, given the emphasis on the external, visible aspects of power, most of these revivalist movements were basically imitative and ideologically macho in nature, or then a rejectionist retreat into an equally macho yearning to the 'glorious' past of conquests. But most of all, the premium was/is on 'scientific' modernization and whereas this may be understandable in the context of power politics, the same psyche when it turns to religion has a similar attitude of *logos* over *mythos* and *eros*, of literal *jihad* over *ijtehad*. Apart from an extreme literalism and misogyny such a heroic attitude is rabidly anti-imaginal, reducing as it does the imaginal to a caricature of rational discourse. Hence *houris* are literally women and *jihad* is literal battle, rather than its primary psychological sense of inner struggle. In sum: the triple jeopardy of Cartesian-Christianist-Islamism in the high fundamentalism of the Muslim world is even *more* 'holy' than Christianism, and thus, more paranoid and self-destructive than its Western political and psycho-cultural-theological counterpart.

Saudi Money-theism and the Cultural Politics of Paranoia

Literalization of Tawhid and Jihad

Wahhabism emerged in Arabia when the project of modernity was at its zenith. Wahhabi thought is often conflated with Salafism in general, yet the original Salafism was an Islamist perspective that arose in the late 19th Century. It was formed by Muslim nationalists "who were eager to read the values of *modernism* into the original sources of Islam. Hence Salafism was not necessarily anti-Western."[31] Various strands of Salafism started to mingle, however, and from the early decades of the 20th Century onwards particular forms of Salafism also fused with the Wahhabism of the new Saudi Kingdom, which had stabilized itself by the early thirties. Eventually Salafism and Wahhabism became rather indistinguishable creeds. That isn't to say that Salafism is a monolithic branch of Islam/Islamism. Many contradictions, tensions and oppositions arose between different Salafi groups and ideas (not in the least because of their particular relation with Wahhabism and the Saudi monarchy). But whatever the internal variations of particular groups, on the whole, the Wahhabi-Salafi matrix got infested with a kind of "*supremacist* thinking that prevails until today... the prime and nearly singular concern is power and its *symbols*."[32] Literally.

Thus, while externally Wahhabism may be seemingly anti-modern, and today, apart from Saudi state policy, elsewhere anti-West, in psychological terms it has deeply modern ties with the West. In more ways than one, Saudi Arabia has become the nemesis of Western consciousness, in Jungian terms, the West's 'shadow'. Visually reflecting the either/or psychological impulse of a 'monotheism of consciousness', Saudi sartorial culture—the garments of men and women—is overwhelmingly of a literal black and white canvas. A literalization of the cult of (heroic) masculinist power, it is perhaps the only country in the world that chose to name *itself* after a *man*. His relationship of Islam with the Feminine is self-evident in the invisibility and status of women in that country.

The materialist, anti-feminine/literalist, hyper-masculinity of modernity, when internalized within the Muslim psyche, leads to an intensification of its pathologies as they strongly resonate within the powerfully symbolic essentials of Islam, except that they (symbols) are now utterly literalized (pathologized). Take for example, the monotheistic ideal of Unity (*Tawhid*), which can be considered Islam's defining feature. Concerning the underlying unity of creation, religions, humanity and God, *tawhid* is above all, a meta-psycho-theological perspective affirming the underlying unity of earthly and spiritual diversity. Given its enormous scope of an all-inclusive embrace (as opposed to obliterative denial) of diversity, *tawhid* is primarily an inner, psychological perception in which difference/diversity is consciously contained as part of an overall unity through *inner ijtehad*. When processed via Cartesianist-Christianity, *tawhid* is wholly externalized and expressed literally, aiming to enforce a 'unity' of *one* religious expression, ranging from politics to clothing, driven by notions of a pan-Islamic state and an idealized unified *ummah*.

Related to this, the idea of *jihad* in Islamic theology clearly also has a psychological primacy, that is, the *inner* struggle in terms of the ethics of relationships and human conscience which is considered the 'greater' struggle. As pointed out by Armstrong, *jihad* as an external, literal project ceased to exist within a hundred years of the Prophet's death which is when Islam had reached its pre-modern geographic boundaries.[33] Its wholly externalized expression in Islamist discourse today is not only antithetical to Islamic doctrine but has only resurfaced on a large scale in the last two centuries, subsequent to the colonial and missionary experience. As an Islamist version of a 'monotheism of consciousness', it is eventually self-destructive.

Massive oil revenues during the 20th Century have enabled Saudi Islam to participate in what, by now, can be globally better termed as money-theistic consciousness.[34] By virtue of the literal presence of the symbolic center of Islam, the Kaaba, Saudi money-theism has over the last decades, steadily promoted its modernity inspired vision of Islam. This vision can succeed only if all differences are obliterated leading to a false ideal of the 'unity' of the *Ummah*.

Culture, power and Islam

Like all religions, throughout its history, Islam has had its share of violent and theological/philosophical debates between different schools. And while it has occasionally found a power 'center' which had the support of a particular theological school, in its rejection of the professional cleric, his violence has rarely been widespread through a centralized 'church'.

The counter-monolithic message of the Quran is evident in the significance it gives to human, social, spiritual, racial and cultural diversity (99:14-15, 5:48; 30:21-28) and one has already referred to an inherent attitude of psycho-spiritual diversity, witness the 99 Names. This anti-monolithic current was further strengthened by the fact of Islam's vast spiritual and geo-cultural diversity, which can be considered its greatest strength since it has ensured that no single vision of the religion prevails over all others. In the real world of cultural decay, change, and the inevitable rise and fall of civilizations, (itself commented upon in the Quran), such diversity prevented the religion from becoming a monolith and ensured the continuation of its trans-historical vitality. Putting it differently, in the light of Jung's critique, the Inquisition was perhaps inevitable in Chrisitanist institutions/dogmas, but not, as such, inevitable in the monotheisms per se as for example in Judaism and Islam.

Origins and Cultural Austerity

From within Islam, it can be argued that the claim to a global religion could succeed precisely because it originated in the specific geo-cultural situation of the desert nomads. Given the peculiarities of climate, terrain etc., in contrast to other more material and visible expressions of human cultural endeavor(s), nomadic culture remains starkly austere. As Burkhardt has rightly pointed out, the single greatest cultural treasure of nomadic consciousness generally, and especially the Arab-Semitic, was the Arabic language.[35] One can argue that it was these culturally austere origins and absence of visible, material-cultural baggage that enabled the early Muslims to integrate across a vast spectrum of geo-cultures. Absorbed in turn, the culturally unhindered psycho-spiritual core of Islamic religiosity could not only survive but globally flourish, finding a myriad expressions through the cultures it encountered.

The modern Saudi impetus to become the sole arbiter of Islam, is psychologically understandable when seen in the context of Saudi Arabia's own historical and current cultural contours. If one turns to view the world from what was originally a materially minimalist cultural canvas, apart from prayer and Quranic calligraphy and recitation (and now high rise buildings), almost *everything* will seem 'un-Islamic'—when actually it is simply different from nomadic desert culture.

Retaining the symbolic significance of the Kaaba as a spiritual, primarily *symbolic* center to which all face during prayer in the

Islamic world, is not to say that Mecca was/is the same as the Roman papacy. Through the liturgical prayer in Arabic and in the facing towards the Kaaba, a sense of unified community and 'center' is indeed present. But this sacred geometry is essentially of a psychological, trans-geographic/historical/symbolic nature, having little to do with the literal, geographical existence of a modern nation-state. As mentioned earlier, the anchoring in different counter-monolithic features such as anyone being an imam etc., has ensured that beyond the spiritual-geometric center that is the Kaaba, the other, living 'center' of Islam is the *individual,* as such, everywhere, but always a part of his/her continuously transformed and transforming cultural environment.

Language as Presence

Historically, the main Arabist dimension to these diverse and multiple expressions of Islam was Arabic, principally through the liturgical prayer and the Quran. While Arabic may have had a linguistic, that is literal impact on some cultures, this was variable and secondary in comparison to its symbolic/spiritual and cultural role, but indirectly so. Regarded as the word of God, *Logos,* the enormous diversity in the Quranic arts of calligraphy and recitation are themselves testament to the strong influence of culture and its relationship to this sacred text.

All this is evident when one considers that, first, Quranic Arabic is by now an archaic form of the language but is nevertheless recited and memorized by millions who, otherwise, may remain illiterate in their native language and hence may never understand the Arabic recitation. This 'reading' of the Quran and the liturgical prayer is related to the psychological and 'mantric' notion of the power of the Divine word of sound-as-sacred-presence. This idea prevalent in almost all traditions including Christianity until the 1960's when, after Vatican II, Latin was no longer seen as crucial to the Mass which could henceforth be conducted in the vernacular. The idea of sound-as-sacred-presence is evident in the tradition of the Sikhs, for example, who refer to their Book as the *Guru Granth Sahib* and devotionally fan it, *Sahib* itself suggesting a High 'Presence'. Secondly, outside of these cultural-psycho-spiritual contexts, the significance of Arabic per se in the Muslim world can be gauged from the fact that in a population of more than a billion strong, four out of five Muslims today are *not* Arabs, yet thousands of millions can 'read' the Quran and respond with emotion even though they may not understand a word of what is recited.

The culturally adaptive/rooted strength of Islam lies, above all, in the evidence of history and the fact that over more than a millennium, the religion gave birth to five great civilizations spanning North Africa, Spain, Turkey, Iran and India, such as the Umayyads, the Mughals, the Ottomans, the Safavids etc. Indicating its inherent cultural adaptivity and fecundity, each was a distinct civilization of the highest order and at the same time uniquely Islamic.[*]

One can draw similar parallels with 'Christendom' as different from 'Christianity' the crucial difference being, however, the presence of an institutionalized Church(es) and other centralizing features. Thus, whereas one could say that Quranic Arabic and the arts related to it (calligraphy and recitation) were

---

[*] They are civilizations in the sense of different and highly developed languages and literature, cuisine apparel, architecture, to name a few. Architecturally, an Ottoman mosque is very different from a Persian one. Yet, both are instantly identifiable as 'Islamic. As part of the Indian subcontinent, Pakistani culture and hence its Islam, is primarily Indo-Persian Islam which subsumes the rich *mythos* of two ancient civilizations, not to mention the multi layered world of *mythos* which is the Quran. I was raised in a modern environment in which English literature, the Arabic Quran, the Persian poetry of Rumi (13th Century), the Punjabi poetry of Bulleh Shah (16th Century) and others, were intermingled in conversations on religion. Apart from literature, this intermeshing of culture and religion, in particular of Persian/Central Asian Islam and Hinduism, is fully visible in the exquisite beauty of Mughal architecture (and its colonial expressions), in the classical music and the performing arts of India even today.

major connective seams running through these civilizational fabrics, this is not the same as claiming supremacy of, or inspiration from, Saudi Arabia as a central authority, simply on the basis of its linguistic and geographical links to the origins of Islam or by virtue of the Kaaba. The present contramodern scenario suggests that having assisted in 'official-izing' Islam through the creation of a professionalized 'clergy', the attempt is now to create a Saudi inspired Church/Rome. Just how recent these developments are, in contrast to more than a thousand years of a different dynamic, is evident from the title the Saudi King has given himself vis-à-vis the Kaaba: 'The Servant and the Custodian of the Two Holy Mosques' came into existence only in the late sixties.

Cultural Vandalism (Part 1)

A singular, literalist, dogmatic interpretation of religion goes hand in hand with the Wahhabi attitude of suspicion towards its more freewheeling imaginative expressions present in both Shiite and Sunni Islam. The modernity-inspired, literalist and (self) destructive tendency propels the Wahhabi vision towards a violence which is both inner and outer except that it is even more paranoid and literal than its Western counterpart. Having forgotten its personal and profoundly simple and austere psychological and cultural ethos, Wahhabism projects it literally onto the Muslim world. Inwardly (and reflecting its own psyche), its efforts are to destroy all historic-cultural vestiges of earliest Islam in the name of 'idolatory'. It has obliterated, for example, the Prophet's house and the tombs/graves of his relatives and companions and destroyed the famous old mosque of Abu Bakr. The sites of the battles of Uhud and Badr have been turned into a parking lot and empty tarmac, as was the house in which the Prophet lived with Khadija and a public toilet has been erected nearby.[36] As always there is an obsessional focus on women. Recently attempts were made to restrict women from closer proximity to the Prophet's grave and a possibility being considered of keeping them at a 'safe' distance from the Kaaba.[37]

This utterly self-destructive and self-mutilatory and misogynist vision is not limited to religion but extends to all cultural manifestation different from itself. In the last few years, an Ottoman structure has been demolished near Mecca to make way for a 'development' project for five star hotels and other opulent structures. A similar pattern of destruction was followed by Saudi funded 'charities' and 'aid' organizations in the Balkans which in substance, style and support is the same as the destruction of the Budhhas in Afghanistan. Such cultural vandalism and erasure of the past aims to obliterate the cultural and psycho-religious diversity of the Muslim world, replacing the cultural-mnemonic void it creates with Wahhabism as the *only*, legitimate Islam.[38]

In lieu of financial support to states such as Afghanistan and Pakistan, there has been an ascendance of state sponsored, 'official', basically, Wahhabist Islam. Setting aside the Saudi contributions towards establishing Islamic universities and supporting different extremist religio-political movements in Pakistan, one can gauge the attempt at cultural coercion through the media. From 1990 till 2005, the Pakistani state-run television station broadcasts nation-wide, a daily news bulletin in *Arabic*. In a population of 150 million, it is unlikely that more than a handful of Pakistanis can understand a word of this daily 'news'. Along with such cultural strategies aimed at erasing the unique Indo-Persian consciousness of Islam in Pakistan, there has been a corresponding control/neglect of the Sufi traditions, the Wahhabi abhorrence of which is well known since they too are regarded as 'idolatrous'.

Within its exceedingly broad psychological spectrum, Sufi Islam can be said to have (had) a strong relationship with the imagination not just in poetry, dance and music but also in its myriad philosophical perspectives and spiritual practices. Their neglect/repression/cooptation through various state mechanisms, and the encouraging/strengthening of Wahhabist and similar regressive perspectives, along with a general decay in the traditions themselves, have all contributed to the creation of vast psycho-cultural voids. It was this sort of 'idolatry' and destruction of 'images' that Corbin referred to when he said: "what is wrong with the Islamic world is that it has destroyed its images and without these images that are so rich and so full in its tradition, they are going crazy because they have no containers for their extraordinary imaginative power."[39]

'High' Islamism and Modern Heretics: the Case of the Ahmadis

Science, Religion and Heresy

All this is not to suggest a wholesale rejection of modernity, science and rationality. Muslim feminism in particular owes a great deal to modernity and, one is certainly not advocating a sentimental return to the past. As stated at the outset, the ability to think rationally, logically and objectively are essential qualities, crucial in the development of the individual and valuable to all societies. However, they can become self-destructive, witness the links of Cartesian-Christianist modernity with environmental degradation or the obsession with weapons that wreak mass destruction on an unimaginable scale. These crises are a consequence of a mindset that exclusively values reason-as-science manifest in technical control. Excessively valorized through a process of a religiously inspired moral reductionism, it becomes an end in itself. Applied to the individual, it cuts off the pluralism of the human imagination and its diverse psycho-spiritual psyche, including significant feminine aspects.

Pakistan is a prime example of these various aspects of modern Islamist 'monotheism of consciousness'. Like Israel, Pakistan is the only other literalized embodiment of a monotheism. Its name means 'Land of the Pure' and it was envisioned as an Islamic country for the Muslims of India. Much of its history has been dominated by a heroic consciousness in the guise of a militarist machismo and misogynist interpretations of Islam. Even though intensely repressive/regressive and biased against women and the imagination, they are nevertheless regarded as 'modern', for example, the writings of Abul 'ala Maududi as analyzed by contemporary scholars based in the West.[40]

Similarly, discussing the connections between modern science and Islam as they exist in the psychology of 'high' Islamism, is not to suggest that they are antithetical and that it is not possible to value a scientific ethos which is simultaneously intensely, but not violently, religious. The history of science within Islam shows that they are not incompatible. The split between faith and reason, the so-called 'chasm' which has to be crossed by a heroic 'leap of faith' is peculiar to Cartesian Christianism.[41] Nor are Inquisitions necessarily endemic to the religious psyche. Similarly, issues such as creationism versus evolution, or abortion, have not had the same emotional/intellectual significance elsewhere in the world, as they do in the West, particularly the United States. But after fifteen hundred years of an absence of conflict on these matters, in the Muslim world, that is, these were seen as non-issues by Muslim scientists/theologians and ordinary people, today there are the seeds and arenas of future conflict: "The debate over creation and evolution, once most conspicuous in America, is fast going global."[42] Kepel has noted that since the 1970's, rational (high) fundamentalism in Islam has less to do with clergy attempting reform and more with the scientific/technical intelligentsia.[43] Once science is applied to theology, it can only produce a caricature of rational discourse. This sort of spurious religious *logos* is widely popular with Muslims in Pakistan as expressed, for example, in the lectures of televangelists such as Zakir Naik who speaks in English and relies on logic to convince his audience of the ultimate superiority of Islam. In short, given the psychological momentum of a globalized, hegemonic masculinity, Muslims are moving deeper into a Cartesian-Christianist-Islamism.

Hairsplitting and Heresy

A major example of the consequences of the steady convergence of a scientific mindset and its modern theological counterpart is the case of the Ahmadi Muslim community in Pakistan. Soon after partition, in 1953 there were widespread riots and violence demanding that the Ahmadis be constitutionally declared non-Muslims. Indirectly illustrating the inherently non-monolithic nature of the essence of Islam including its Indo-Persian expression, the investigations of the Official Court of Inquiry showed the untenable nature of the demand since it found *no consensus* among the spectrum of concerned *ulema* as to the *definition* of a Muslim.[44] This was inevitable, given the culturally and theologically fluid and infinitely varied nature of a tradition, which, as I have been stressing and any serious scholar would recognize, is not even easily encompassed within the (Western imposed) category of 'religion'.[45] More importantly, as Wilson observes, while Islam is a monotheistic creator religion, unlike Christianity whose doctrines were formulated in Patristic writings, Islam is without official creeds and dogmas which facilitate the definition of heresy.[46] Definitions—by definition—impose limits of interpretation, by providing "an explanation of the *exact*

129

meaning of a word, term or phrase."[47] The impossibility of this in Islam as it has existed—self-evidently -- for fifteen hundred years across the world notwithstanding, in 1973 the Pakistani state succeeded in defining a Muslim.[*]

To define is to confine. The eventually successful efforts of modernists inspired by Maududi to apostatize the Ahmadi community by getting it constitutionally declared 'non-Muslim', were financially and morally supported by the Saudis.[48] Significantly, this landmark change in Pakistan's Constitution was sanctioned by an elected government and presided over by a Berkeley educated Prime Minister whose election manifesto was (ostensibly) modern, secular and liberal. The implications of such a Constitutional amendment, for issues spanning democracy, citizenship and human rights, not to mention Islam and its relationship to these and a host of other matters such as identity, religious interpretation and the role of the state in matters of religion, have rarely been addressed by Muslim intellectuals in Pakistan or elsewhere in the Muslim world. Whereas human rights activists and the rare journalist did indeed take up the issue, and continue to do so, such activism or condemnation cannot be considered a substitute for widespread public debate in the media or any in-depth analysis or discourse at the more conceptual/analytic level, particularly in the context of how Islam was being (ab)used and 'interpreted'. Post-9/11 and the recognition of the need to be more 'self-critical', the Muslim academic/intellectual continues to avoid the subject.[†]

---

[*] According to *The Constitution of the Islamic Republic of Pakistan* p. 86 (article 260[3]: 'A person who does not believe in the absolute and unqualified finality of the Prophethood of Muhammad (peace be upon him), the last of the Prophets, or claims to be a Prophet, in any sense of the word or of any description whatsoever, after Muhammad (peace be upon him), or recognizes such a claimant as a Prophet or a religious reformer, is not a Muslim for the purposes of the Constitution of Law'.

[†] There are of course some exceptions, see for example the work of Ali Qadir; *When*

Overwhelmingly, analysis and commentators trace the rise of fundamentalism in Pakistan to the military dictatorship of Zia-ul-Haq instead of its genesis in the secular regime of Z.A. Bhutto. The absence of debate is even more intriguing, given the present significance of issues related to identity and Islam.

Modern Heresies

Ironically, the image of high-rational fundamentalism in Islam has a different counterpart in the Muslim world's first Nobel Prize winner in the sciences and that too in the highly abstract domain of theoretical physics. Abdus Salam (1926-1996) was at the same time, a devout Ahmadi Muslim, simultaneously well versed in the imaginative world of poetry and literature. An interview in a leading science magazine describes him as "deeply compassionate", having "the heart of a poet and the mind of a scientist", who loved "beauty and looks for it in his science." Whereas at one level, Islam was a "very personal thing" for Salam, at another, in the Quranic emphasis on knowledge "Islam plays a large role in my view of science."* Similarly, as described by the archives of the Nobel Foundation, "Abdus Salam is known to be a devout Muslim, whose religion does not occupy a separative compartment of his life; it is inseparable from his work and family life."[49]

The preceding descriptions of Salam suggest that the issue here

---

Heterodoxy Becomes Heresy. 2015 and *Parliamentary hereticization of the Ahmadiyya: The modern world implicated in Islamic crises*. 2014. For full references see endnote 51 in this chapter and bibliography.

* As described in the interview, Salam had "the heart of a poet and the mind of a scientist ... He loves beauty and looks for it in his science ... a deeply compassionate man ... direct, disarming, humourous, deeply serious... Salam's Moslem upbringing gave him the mores of Islam, the moral code of the Koran. 'Islam to me is a very personal thing', he says. 'The Koran places a lot of emphasis on natural law. Thus Islam plays a large role in my view of science...'" New Scientist; *An Interview with Dr. Abdus Salam*. 26-08-1976.

is not about the brain, 'mind' or IQ, but also of a 'heart' which responds to beauty, poetry and the imagination, and that for him both these dimensions were equally important and interconnected. His statements present a very different view of the modernist idea that there is a 'chasm' between faith and knowledge and hence, that 'those who believe cannot think and those who think cannot believe'.

Even though the prevalent modern view of the heart is simply as a pump, its symbolic significance is still evident in language pointing to crucial human psychological dimensions. In numerous languages, including English, it remains an unsurpassed metaphor for powerful emotional expressions such as 'heart and soul', 'all my heart', 'heart-throb', 'heartening', 'heart-rending', etc. To make something a part of oneself is to learn it 'by heart' and the deepest level of what we truthfully think or feel about something is in our 'heart of hearts'.

Salaam's 'heart of a poet' illustrates the deep bonds between knowledge, culture and religion all of which have to do with something more than just 'mind' or rational cognition and that heart and mind are not mutually exclusive. In the language of Jungian and Archetypal Psychology, this domain of the heart— in culture and spirituality—is the domain of the feminine and the symbolic imagination and is not inherently opposed to what we call (masculine) rationality. There is a world of facts and a world of meaning(s), and in Salaam's case both reinforce each other: '… his religion is inseparable from his work…'

However defined, the roots of heresy lie in a particular subjectivity whereby the individual insists on locating him/herself within a given religion, but is not accepted by the (mostly) 'malestream' of that religion. The prevalence of a high fundamentalist mindset in modern Pakistan, not only in the state, but also in institutions of 'higher' learning can be gauged by the fact that in spite of being honored by universities across the world, Salam's achievements were barely acknowledged in Pakistan, simply because he was considered a 'heretic/apostate' and 'non-Muslim'.

From within Islam, I have suggested that the impulse to marginalize/hereticize certain perspectives can be related to their emphasis on the more feminine dimension of the religion.[50] As such, Abdus Salam remains an important symbol around which Muslims may reflect on issues surrounding the problems and prospects of modernity, and its relationship to science, knowledge, culture and Islam.

Similarly, the marginalizing of the Ahmadis, the manner in which it occurred, as well as the (non)response of the secular or 'moderate' Muslim, presents a particular syndrome which, if not addressed, ensures that the current efforts of moderate Muslims to reclaim their faith from extremism, will bear scant fruit. Given the constitutional/theoretical/political/historical significance of the Ahmadi 'problem' and the failure of the intelligentsia to openly come to intellectual grips with it from *within* Islam, also indicates an intellectual and cultural amnesia at multiple levels. An inertia and amnesia not only about Islam, but also in a largely uncritical view of Islam as engaged with democracy and modernity (not to mention science, women and other significant issues). As summed up by Friedmann (commenting here on a period of secular democracy):

> The National Assembly of Pakistan thus arrogated to itself the authority of an assembly of theologians, competent to decide on matters of *faiths* and *fidelity*, and to pronounce judgments on the religious affiliation of individual citizens. If the secret deliberations of the Assembly are ever made public, they should become one of the more fascinating documents concerning the relationship between religion and state. The minutes of the secret sessions will describe how a group of politicians, elected through a secular process, debate a *subtle*

133

issue of Islamic theology. One may venture to say that a great number of them were ill equipped for such a debate, and easily succumbed to the arguments ... of the Jamat i Islami and of the various groups of *ulama*.[51]

As Friedmann proceeds to point out, it was not so much the caliber of arguments of the *ulema* and others that impressed the National Assembly or Parliament. Rather, it was their ability to rally the masses and this was what had given rise to the issue in the first place.

> The action taken by the National Assembly is rather extraordinary when we consider the fact that *Islamic history never knew assemblies convened for a similar purpose* ... [it] revealed again the dilemmas facing countries that try and govern themselves according to *modern liberal principles,* yet feel attachment to a medieval civilization that recognized no separation between religion and state. The way in which Zulfikar Ali Bhutto addressed the National Assembly after it adopted the constitutional amendments is an excellent reflection of these dilemmas.[52]

Bhutto's dilemmas can be summed up in his boast that his government had finally "solved ... an issue that defied solution for ninety years" on the one hand, while on the other, simultaneously disenfranchising and criminalizing the beliefs of an entire community but still proclaiming that "every Pakistani has the right to profess his religion, proudly, with confidence and without fear."[53]

More than forty years later, Bhutto's dilemmas have been internalized by the Pakistani body politic and have literally become a part of the identity (crisis) of every citizen. Thus, in order to apply for a passport, citizens must state their religion. Those who—like the overwhelming majority—call themselves Muslim, must *prove* this, not by reciting the *Kalima* but by signing a declaration stating that s/he believes that the Ahmadis are *not* Muslims.

Following is the text of the declaration required by the Pakistani State for getting a passport. It is also required documentation for the Identity card:

Declaration in Case of Muslims
I, ... S/o .... Age ....years, adult Muslim, Resident of ....
hereby solemnly declare that:

(1) I am Muslim and believe in the absolute and unqualified finality of the prophethood of Muhammad (peace be upon him) the last of the prophets.
(2) I do not recognize any person who claims to be a prophet in any sense of the word or any description whatsoever after Muhammad (peace be upon him) or recognize such claimant as prophet or a religious reformer as a Muslim.
(3) I consider Mirza Ghulam Ahmad Quadiani to be an imposter Nabi and also consider his followers whether belonging to the Lahore or Quadiani Group to be Non-muslim.

Meanwhile, national and international Human Rights groups continue to document the persecution of the Ahmadis pointing out that the greatest number of human rights violations in Pakistan are against them.[54] For example, Ahmadis are forbidden to use the basic Muslim greeting 'as-salamu-alykum' or calling their places of worship 'mosques'. Simply printing the common phrase 'bismillah ar-rahman ar-rahim' on a wedding invitation is regarded as blasphemy and carries a range of punishments from three years imprisonment and whipping to the death sentence.

Interesting to note as well is that among other issues, the Ahmadi community is committed to nonviolence and a different, nonphysical conception of *jihad*.[55]

CHAPTER 4:
CARTESIAN-CHRISTIANISM
& CARTESIAN-CHRISTIANIST-ISLAMISM

The body lays claim to equal recognition. We are still
caught in the old idea of an antithesis between
mind and matter.
(C.G. Jung[1])

Absence vs. Presence of Death

Whereas up to now one has referred to the deep connections between 'high' Islamism, modernity and Cartesian-Christianism, there are nevertheless certain intriguing differences which need to be considered. Foremost, is the seemingly greater propensity towards a particular sort of *self*-violence on the part of Islamists, high and low, and related to this, their attitude towards death. Such suicidal violence seems to confound particularly the modern(ized) observer. As discussed earlier (see Chapter 2), a key variant of the (modern) heroic archetype is its denial of death. What is notable are the differing *attitudes* of Cartesian-Christianism and its Islamist manifestation towards death, especially in the graphic image of the suicide bomber.

Part of the intensity of horror it evokes is, of course, due to the relativization of the observers' own experience and exposure to the phenomenon of death, which, in the case of the West is more distant and disembodied than in much of the rest of the world. This disconnection and distancing is fully evident during modern war and new weapons and technologies enabling long distance destruction of a basically invisible enemy. Making the individual physically and psychologically 'blind' to the experience, an illusion is created by veiling this as progress in 'advanced' weaponry/ methods. Meanwhile, regardless if the bomb is dropped from a plane or strapped to a body, on the ground, it is as it has always been (or perhaps worse): blood, gore and carnage. The only difference is of scale.

As handled even in times of peace, death in the West is largely from a distance. Obviously, one is not referring to media generated violence/death images. If anything, their prevalence simply numbs the psyche further to its (death) reality and their widespread presence becomes a symptom of a basic fear and denial of this fact of life. As lived experience, a certain de-humanization prevails when it comes to death: remote, removed from life and view, confined to hospitals, mortuaries and funeral homes.

> ... the developed countries have increasingly hidden death away. Three quarters of all deaths occur in hospitals behind screens or in separate rooms. A quarter occur with no close relatives present ... mourning has been abbreviated, and the bereaved no longer mark themselves out with black clothes. Each man is an island, it seems, whose death is largely his own affair.'[2]

As a heroic attitude, this distancing/denial is similarly visible in socio-cultural indicators such as an inordinate glorification of youthfulness and a corresponding denigration and virtual absence of the elderly in media and public life. The youth-hero archetype is also evident in medicine, whether in the emphasis on prolonging life at all costs (quantity versus quality), the enormous popularity of plastic surgery and other related anti-ageing multibillion dollar industries, or the inordinate research emphasis on genetics, indicating a pre-occupation with origins rather than end/destination. Collectively all this signifies a fear and denial of bodily decay and death, a symptom of what Hillman calls the West's "life-fanaticism".[3]

It is interesting that the obsession with youth and health as well as a general distancing from old age and death arises in Western culture. Fear of death is often cited as *the* (irrational) reason for religion by those who cynically dismiss 'the package' as a whole.* In the intermediate field of ever-shifting perspectives called life, death is the only certainty. As said at the outset, though we will all experience it, we can know nothing about it, except through the symbolic imagination. As such, to the extent that religion ultimately has to do with death, 'high' Islamism differs from, and raises questions about, modernity and Cartesian-Christianism's (self) destructive tendencies in terms of a reduced capacity for suffering and an abnormal fear of death—this in-spite of Christ's Passion.

---

* As John P. Sisk once remarked in The Georgia Review: "[A society's] fear of sacred space, which is a fear of life lived by what always appears to be the long odds of faith, goes with its reluctance to commit itself to the burden of distinguishing between re-vitalizing fresh perspectives and faithless subversions. For lack of something worthy of reverential attention it must worship life in its precarious time bound condition—it must worship youthfulness." (*The Georgia Review*. Fall 1989.)

Absence vs. Presence of Body

Chapter 2 detailed how the hero's 'ascent' can be symbolically understood in psycho-physical, religious, spiritual, as well as cultural/geographical terms. The Freudian model of consciousness as a fortified (defended) ego based on rationality and will-power, surveying the scene 'below' (unconscious/feminine) is the logical counterpart to the Cartesian mind-body split in which the body is 'below'. The body is thus associated with the feminine inferiority of emotions/feelings as opposed to the masculine head (thinking). Underlying the ideal of 'mind over matter' is of course the Christianist myth of Eve, 'the abysmal side of bodily man', that is, the body is imagined as female. This schemata is also symbolically and literally symptomatic of the cultural geopolitics of North and South whereby, via colonialism, the South was/is regarded as something to be tamed, civilized and controlled. We can repeat Freud's classic description of the purpose of analysis here and emphasize other aspects: As *a civilizational project*, the task of psychoanalysis is "to enlarge its (ego's) organization so that it can appropriate fresh portions of the id, where id was, there ego shall be. *It is a work of culture.*"[4]

In the postcolonial present, these psycho-cultural dynamics continue in the steady enlargement of a globalizing, hegemonic masculinity and its materialist 'ego' of a culture of consumerism, including the consumption of other cultures. One should keep in mind that the feminine/'body' of the colonized South consisted substantially, if not overwhelmingly, of Muslim societies. The West's Cartesian-Christianist disconnect from its own feminine/body may partly explain its fear and horror of death and simultaneous preoccupation with a youthful body. This 'absence' (unconsciousness) of its own body may also be a projected factor in the longstanding fascination of Orientalist perceptions regarding sexuality and women in Islam.[5]

Returning to the differences between Cartesian-Christianist consciousness and 'high' Islamism, however deeply the former may have 'penetrated' the Muslim psyche, certain key elements of Islamic monotheism may render the expression of the Cartesian split differently. To begin with, as represented by Christ and Mohammad, there are the differing attitudes towards body and sexuality. As Armstrong puts it, "Christian misogyny is potentially neurotic because it was based on a rejection of sexuality which is unique among the world's religions."[6] This is not to say that all is well in the Islamic psycho-sexual universe and one will examine this in the section on low or mass Islamism. (See part III.) But to continue in terms of the mind-body split, and more importantly, for the ritually observant Muslim, the steady rhythm of the prescribed daily prayers underscores the necessity of bodily commitment/connection to the religious impulse. Anything else is hypocrisy, which is an abiding theme in the Quran. In the context of Islamic practice, this ideally means to worship fully as a human being, surrendering one's mind *and* body.

The involvement of the body in daily life and religious practice is a hallmark of not only Islam, but many other traditions. While, at one level present also in Christianity, as for example, the *Eucharist*, Islamic worship is different insofar as it does not have to be mediated by a priest/cleric. The exception of Friday and other congregational prayers, can be, strictly speaking, led by any Muslim. Additionally, the *Eucharist* is not available as a ubiquitous and consistent experience like the five-times-a-day prayer. Furthermore, the daily prayers are grounded in, and preceded by, body rituals which must be performed every time. As a whole then, Islamic practice requires that the body actively participate in religious expression at an intense, daily, mostly individual but also collective, level. Thus, even when affected by

Cartesianism, Islamic religiosity retains a profound connection to the body. That this connection is internalized at a very early stage in life, principally through bodily mimesis, ensures that it is powerfully always present, consciously and unconsciously.

However, since other dimensions of the 'feminine', in terms of sexuality, women and related dimensions of psycho-spiritual femininity have been repressed by an uncritical (unconscious) internalizing of the Cartesian split, the rational fundamentalist psyche remains beset by a sense of an unconscious, (psychological) hypocrisy, and which, therefore, cannot find fulfillment only in the literal participation of the body in prayer. This spiritual-cognitive dissonance is expressed in intense accusations of the perceived hypocrisy in Western policies regarding the Muslim world. That is, it is projected onto the West. Simultaneously, in the context of a generally un(self)critical view of a literalist Islam, it takes the form of an obsessional-compulsive religiosity, frequently around bodily taboos and, above all, with the bodies of women and how they are (not) to be seen and heard. These obsessional preoccupations with one's body or bodies of women are evident in the nature of questions posed by readers in newspapers and call-in television shows, which have become widely popular in Pakistan, and also on websites offering information and advice.

The preoccupation with *halal* and *haram* is paramount, even though there are the subcategories of grey which give enormous leeway for individual inclinations, human desires and limitations. But once the field is reduced to black and white, every part of the body is subjected to close scrutiny: Applying nail polish, removal of hair around the genitals, brushing of teeth during fasting, not to mention the intricacies of positions and moves during sex, the most trivial and innocuous of physical activities are questioned and categorized as *halal/haram* and compulsively lived out. In short, the disembodied manic-depressive 'mind' of the West finds its Muslim counterpart in obsessive-compulsive ideas/behavior around the body.

Given the logical severity of Cartesian-Christianist Islam and its internal split in which the feminine/body remains present, the high Islamist ultimately regresses into a compulsive, purely visceral and bodily 'worship', the suicide bomber being the most extreme type. The final instructions to the September 11 hijackers and their own desires regarding their funeral rites vividly illustrate this bodily preoccupation.[7] This modern version of a pre-monotheistic human (self)sacrifice indicates how deeply the mythic and terrifying goddesses of pre-Islamic Arabia continue to exert their power in the Arab and Muslim psyche. Thus, whereas modern Christianism has surrendered the body to Cartesianism and is inclined to worship primarily (in) the 'mind,' at the global level, the Islamist suicide bomber (re)presents Cartesian-Christianism with its own shadow of the forgotten body/feminine, an incarnation of its own horror/terror. Together, they represent the Cartesianized condition of modern religiosity. Experienced psychologically but expressed literally, the Islamist sacrifice of the (feminine) body is rationalized by, and propelled towards, an equally literal vision of the Feminine: The *houris* of paradise.

The *houris* of paradise, are indeed feminine in 'form'. However, according to tradition, they wear seventy dresses which are, at the same time, transparent, and the marrow flowing in their bones will be visible 'like liquid and luminous honey'. Clearly, these images cannot be taken literally and are best understood in the symbolic-experiential framework of mysticism, for example, divine veiling and plenitude as symbolized by 'beings of lights'.[8] To this extent *houris* hint at a strong undercurrent in the spiritual journey to the Feminine within Islam. This 'feminine undercurrent' is also present in the mystical dimensions of Buddhism, Hinduism and other religions.[9]

The complex and basically unconsciously driven relationship of both literalist Islamism and literalist modernity with the Feminine, as manifest through women's bodies, is best illustrated in Algeria, where, at one stage, fundamentalists threatened to kill unveiled women and secularists (fundamentalists) the veiled ones. Outside of Islam, in the modern West, and in direct contrast to the image of the veiled woman, is the ubiquitous image of the naked female, anorexic body. In short, woman's body has become the arena in which the machismo underlying modernity is a mirror image of the misogyny of fundamentalism.

Absence vs. Presence of Mind

The differing attitudes towards death as mediated by the mind-body split in 'high' Islamism and Cartesian-Christianism, telescopes some intriguing issues: The strong presence of the body in Islam, at one level, compounds the problematics of its relationship with the modern, masculinist, disembodied gaze of the West, as well as with many modernized Muslims, practicing or otherwise. The psychodynamics of the mind-body hierarchy in the gaze of the Western ego in some ways does indeed perceive Islam as inferior. This gaze is evident even in someone like Jung, who saw the ritual prayer as evidence of a "very showy religion",[10] one that has "no mind to it".[11]

As a detailed study of *The Collected Works of C.G. Jung* shows, unfortunately his understanding of Islam can be considered, at best minimal, and biased at worse.[12] Ironically, when seen in the light of his (self)critique of Cartesian-Christianism, Jung's statement unwittingly points at precisely those areas, the absence of which have contributed to the malaise(s) of modernity, but which remain a powerful presence within Islamic monotheism. Given his overall ignorance of Islam and its multiple intellectual traditions, his perception of the prayer as 'showy' is in terms of what can only be an assumed absence of 'mind', rather than actual *presence* of body.

Nevertheless, at another level, Jung's statement is very valid. But his general ignorance of Islam and a lack of any substantive discussion by him on the topic precludes one from granting him any significant insight about the Muslim mind. The lack of (self)critique in high or 'low' Islamism, does in fact indicate an absence of 'mind' at many psycho-theological levels. Insofar as the human need for meaning is indelible, the high Islamist by now cut off from his indigenous spiritual roots and his own imagination, uses the logocentric mind as a sort of religious *particle* physicist: setting great store and significance to theological trivia based primarily on words of what the Prophet purportedly *said*, not what he did/did not *do*, nor taking into account the contextual, temporal and therefore, the variable.

Rather than engage directly with a vast spectrum of knowledge and information now available, thanks in part to modernity itself, many highly educated Muslims remain content to let the *ulema* tell them how Islam as a way of life is the *sunnah*, that is, the Prophet's way-of-life. As processed by the adolescent (heroic) 'mind', this 'way' becomes that of the Prophet but overwhelmingly in his dimension of a warrior in his forties, not as the multifaceted, enormously complex, deeply spiritual and compassionate individual that he *developed* into during a *process* of six decades.[13] Since it is impossible to 'get' a life other than one's own, the Prophet's (inner) *attitudes* and their changing/ unfolding, according to age, situation, circumstance are not part of this picture of his *sunnah*-as-way-of-life. Programmed, as it seems humans are by nature, to desire meaning, the otherwise well-educated Islamist mind finds meaning primarily in the compulsive-obsessive following of literal and physical Traditions irrespective of age. Apart from indoctrinating young males into these 'norms', the generally mindless attitude of a great many well- educated Muslims is evident not only in the widespread absence of self-critique but reflected most at the micro level of personal prayer.

Similar to many other traditions such as the Jewish, Hindu and Buddhist, liturgical prayer is not always in the native language of the majority of adherents. That is, not all Buddhist, Jews and Hindus understand or speak Pali, Hebrew or Sanskrit. Nevertheless, these languages remain crucial to what are vibrant and living religions. Similarly, the language of the Islamic prayer is Arabic in spite of the fact that, as was mentioned before, four out of five among a billion Muslims are not speakers of Arabic. The prayer itself is actually rather brief and includes repetitive phrases and as a whole is about twice as long as the Lord's Prayer in Christianity. Given the brevity, it is remarkable how many well-educated, practicing Muslims, do not take the trouble to know the meaning of this brief collection of Arabic phrases. Thus, whether in terms of self-critique, the abdication of basic religious knowledge/functions to the *ulema* or the personal level of meaning-full prayer, the 'mind' is indeed 'missing' in much of the practice of Islam today.

One variation on the connections between need for meaning, the relationship with the body, and suicide, occurs in situations of extreme conflict and dehumanization and when daily life, even at the most basic level, is rendered futile and meaningless, as in Palestine. Suicidal violence, in such a situation, becomes a dehumanized act in a dehumanized environment. But even here, one can see the adolescent archetype at work in all its literal violence and one-dimensionality. At one level, it illustrates the consequences of a cognitive-developmental-spiritual split in young Muslim males, which makes these acts peculiarly 'logical'.

What is more disturbing is their adult male mentors and their hero-mentality, who encourage and nurture these acts.

To conclude this discussion: As related to self-knowledge/reflection and violence, the lack of a (mature) 'mind' in Islamism indicates an essentially unconscious 'understanding' of Islam. The (unconscious) significance of the body, further complicates the situation, not just for Muslims but also for the West. A consideration of the role of the body in Islam and its expression in Islamism simultaneously raises questions about the impact of the mind-body split in modern consciousness. "…if we can reconcile ourselves to the mysterious truth that the spirit is the life of the body … and the body the outward manifestation of the life of the spirit—the two being really one … they may signify a rejuvenation…"[14]

Pope Benedict's much debated statements about Islam and Christianity are perhaps actually unwittingly correct at the symbolic level and symptomatic of these issues. Like Jung, in a way he is correct about seeing fundamentalist Islam as irrational. He is also on record for saying that the problem for Christianity is 'reason without faith' and for Islam 'faith without reason' (in fundamentalism).[15] The solution proposed by the Germanic Pope, is of course dialogue, which inherently can only be a heroic, theoretically endless boxing match. It would be more fruitful to cast the debate in terms of the mind-body split and see what each faith can give/take from the other. This requires less heroism and more humility from both sides.

Absence vs. Presence of 'Solutions'

More of the same

To date, this interfaith dialogue or rapprochement is not very evident. As discussed in this chapter, modern Islamism exhibits distinctly Cartesian-Christianist features. They include an insistence on a Cartesian literalist reading of the Quran in which only One meaning is 'correct' even though its linguistic and cognitive structure is drastically different from the Bible. Similarly, in spite of the Quranic critique of the Christian deification of Jesus, and the Quranic insistence that Muhammad is simply a mortal human; by now in places like Pakistan, the Prophet is increasingly being deified. Not just in the indiscriminate and violent understanding of blasphemy laws which have the Prophet, not God, as the target of any alleged blasphemy, but also in the various sectarian groups which exist to 'protect the honour of the Prophet'—invariably through violence.

Christianizing of Islam is also evident in the steady ascent of the *ulema* and other religious professionals who, till just fifty years ago or less, were largely economically, socially, culturally and spiritually marginal to most Muslim societies. As I have discussed, in Islam the equivalents of the Christian sacraments for birth, death, marriage etc. are so simple that any Muslim who knows the basic prayer can perform them, which is why there has been no organized 'priesthood' as such in Islam. Those who did adopt religion as a profession remained on the social margins of most Muslim societies for almost 1500 years. However, I have personally lived through a transformation whereby, thanks to national and international geopolitics and Saudi money-theism, by now, a priesthood has been firmly established within Islam and should be confronted, contested and delegitimized by Muslims everywhere.

In the Muslim diaspora in Europe and elsewhere in the West, I have perceived another closely linked and equally disturbing evolution. There is an increasing tendency to create and consolidate an Islamic 'clergy', not just by Muslims but more importantly, also by the State. These countries have belatedly recognized the virulent influence of Salafist inspired *imams* educated in Saudi funded seminaries in different countries, who then come to Europe as religious professionals to 'serve' various Muslim communities/congregations. The recognition that this influx of radicalizing *imams* must stop, is laudable. However, the alternative 'solution', as is presently being implemented in many European states, is exceedingly problematic and not without danger since various issues can be raised on the policy of training young European born Muslim males as *imams* and teachers of Islam in schools (along with young women).

To begin with, such policies ignore the debates within Muslim communities regarding the role of women leading prayers as *imams* and implicitly reinforces the patriarchal status quo. As such, Europe endorses and reinforces orthodoxy, and what is for many, a regressive Islam. Secondly, and more importantly, Islam is being viewed, 'understood' and 'managed' through a Christianist template in which religion is the domain of a professional priest who, usually as young man, has decided on this as a career and must spend time in a seminary studying the religion. Setting aside the many issues bedeviling the Catholic Church regarding child abuse by priests, the question here is about what may happen psychologically when young Muslim males are granted the license to hold forth as experts on Islam, not just in mosques but also schools.

One does not need a degree in psychology to know that starting in our teenage years and well into our twenties at least, it is not religion but *sex* and other relational concerns which are *the* major socio-psychological preoccupation for young men and women. Simply put: youngsters and adolescents have something else on their minds, primarily friends and sexual insecurities, and are not interested in the spiritual wisdom of religion. It has taken more than fifteen years for Western scholars on terrorism to recognize this simple human reality apart from a few such as Olivier Roy. Describing jihadism in France as primarily a "youth movement" he said in a speech: "The main motivation of young men for joining jihad seems to be the fascination for a narrative: 'the small brotherhood of super-heroes who avenge the Muslim Ummah.'"[16]

Recognizing these human realities, over the centuries most non-Christian cultures did not have the religious equivalents of 'Sunday school' for children. Generally speaking, in most societies, religion was transmitted in families. Young persons were not particularly encouraged to make it an exclusive career in the modern sense, particularly not in Islam. This is not to deny the existence of young, basically mendicant (beggar) monks in, for example, Buddhism, but that is a different order of debate. In the context of European policies about teaching Islam in schools and training of young male *imams*, the question is first, of imposing a Christianist template and creating a 'qualified priesthood', that is, graduates from sundry state or Islamic institution, who will not just lead congregational prayer which is actually only compulsory once a week on Friday. Rather, they would also explicitly or implicitly teach some version of Islam to not only their peers, but by default, also exercise a certain degree of authority over those much older than themselves.

"Don't Ask Questions"

Young or old, foreign or locally trained, the power of *imams* was evident in the numerous conversations I have had with Muslim women in Europe over many years. Many were aware that their children were unduly influenced by *imams* to the extent that youngsters would tell their parents that they (their parents) were not 'good' or 'correct' muslims. When I would urge them to question *imams* on various subjects, one common answer was that when they questioned the *imams*, they were frequently told not to ask too many questions because "this is the way the Christians destroyed their own religion. They asked the priests too many questions and now look: the churches are empty! So if you don't want to destroy Islam, don't keep asking questions." It was difficult to convince the women that if the churches were empty, it may have had more to do with people resisting the inordinate power of priests and the institutions they represented, rather than people asking questions in order to better understand their religion.

The fact that vast numbers of Muslims are 'technically' equipped to be *imams*, enables for example, any group of Muslims anywhere to say congregational prayers whether in a family or any other context. However, this does not mean that a prayer leader (*imam*) has any spiritual authority over anyone. By turning this simple and basic function into a full time salaried job paid for by the State, is to ensure that these young (heroic) males are invested with an authority and stature which is disproportionate with their psychological and spiritual capacities at that age/stage of life.

The same perils are there in the policy of training young Muslims to teach Islam at the primary and secondary school levels. Wittingly or unwittingly they also become role models for the students, as for example a hijabbed female teacher. While this may be her personal right, it does not mean that all visions of Islam subscribe to it as a compulsory requirement for woman, witness the tens of millions of women across the Muslim world who do not wear the hijab.

Such policies are yet another example of the heroic tendency to perceive what are routine difficulties as 'problems' which therefore require 'solutions' and which only exponentially generate more serious problems than before. Routine difficulties require methods of *coping*, not absolutist 'solutions'. Thus for example, instead of institutionalizing and creating a growing cadre of locally trained young *imams*, older, retired persons could be interviewed and selected to lead congregational prayers. Nominal fees, rather than full time salaries could be given. In short, there are other, less perilous, different creative possibilities that can be explored, developed and implemented. Generally, no religion should be taught in school. The transfer of tradition does not belong in a heavily logocentric environment.

As Kenan Malik has pointed out:

> Social policies in Belgium, France, and the United Kingdom aimed at fostering integration are all different. What they have in common, though, is that all have helped created a more fractured society, and all have helped entrench narrower visions of belongingness and identity. Neither assimilationist nor multicultural policies have created Islamism or jihadism. What they have done is helped create the space for Islamism to flourish, and to funnel disaffection into jihadism.[17]

CHAPTER 5:
THE UPHEAVAL OF OUR WORLD

The upheaval of our world and the upheaval of our
consciousness
are one and the same.
(C.G. Jung[1])

The Case of Mohamed Atta

Because of the general political support from the U.S. and its allies (often via Pakistan) to the Taliban and groups like al-Qaeda, Osama bin Laden can be considered, in many ways, a literal (and symbolic) creation of the U.S. However, Mohamed Atta, the leader of the 9/11 airplane suicide attacks, is even more the archetype par excellence of the various themes I have tried to interrelate. Flashed across the world, his face has become associated with evil incarnate. In keeping with the archetypal nature of what he embodied, for the first few months after 9/11, the only other full 'image' of him was a blurred, video frame: a Western attired (Muslim) male slinging a bag across his shoulder moments before embarking on an upward journey. A complete and visible figure, Atta as an *individual* with distinct features, nevertheless remained basically unrecognizable. The image was literally full/complete, yet remained 'empty', its ambiguity suggesting the presence of a true symbol (see Chapter 1). Without disclosing a distinct identity, it was, archetypally, simply a modern man striding towards (a) flight.

As psychologically described by Jung in *Modern Man in Search of a Soul*,[2] this 'every man' is the modern Western(ized) individual, whose heroic journey began in the mists of a monotheist history. As observed by many,* along the way he made a terrible mistake and somewhere lost his soul/psyche. The consequences of what have become by now a global and (self)destructive journey of what Jung would call his 'shadow', include the Cartesian-Christianist impact on almost every culture and tradition including especially the Muslim (wo)man and her/his soul. In his shadowy image and distinctly archetypal 'features', Atta offers an Islamist twist to the 21st Century profile of Jung's modern man in search of (his) soul.

*

It needs to be reiterated that the descriptions of Atta'a life to follow are not meant to illustrate the power of an individual, but rather the trans-historical power of symbols. Nor should the symbolic nature of archetypes be seen here as a literacy device. As clinically observed, they are impersonal, having a powerful, affective, transpersonal existence which can overpower the individual psyche at any time. Details of the hero myth and its psychodynamics have been discussed in Chapters 2 and 3 and need to be kept in mind for a Jungian reading of the archetype of Mohamed Atta and the images/events of 11th September 2001.

As an appropriate 'container' of an archetypal manifestation,

---

* Jung, Campbell, Hillman, Eliade, Corbin, Cassirer, Ricouer to name a few.

accounts of Atta's life suggest that in reality he was not so much himself a heroic or mysterious figure, as a mundane person. While not himself a man of epic scale, he eventually became part of an epic. Interpreted archetypally, elements of a biographical portrait[3] closely approximate key features of the psychological stages of the hero's journey and parallel to an uncanny extent the geographical and psycho-theological stages of the 'ascent' of heroic hegemonic, masculinist modernity. From the Jungian perspective, it does not matter how accurate these descriptions are. True or false, they are the product of how Atta is/was *imagined* by various people, including the biographer, and should be seen as an extension of that collective archetypal 'moment' that was 9/11.

*

Atta came from a middle-class moderate Egyptian Muslim family. Significantly, he was "neither politically active *nor particularly religious*"[4] during the time he lived in Egypt. His embrace of Islamism came many years later in Germany, *after* his mind had been trained scientifically, that is, it had in many ways become, quintessentially masculine and modern: Rational, concretistic (literal), controlled/controlling (will power), single minded, emotionally separative (in terms of relationships) unable to deal with the feminine and the realm of the imagination. In short, key elements which would lead to a 'monotheism of consciousness'.

Trained as an architect at an *engineering* university, the "utterly ordinary" Atta was a "*meticulous*" student, "an exceptionally *resolute, disciplined, stoic* man ... having *will* and *steadfastness*." The curriculum of the prestigious university he attended in Egypt was based on a vision of architecture that was both pragmatic/scientific and imaginative/artistic but with greater stress on the latter. Atta found this difficult. "A very clever person", he excelled in *"concrete"* subjects such as "mathematics, physical structures," but was "less good in *design* and the more *artistic* aspects, to which he couldn't adjust himself."

The delayed, but archetypally inevitable rite of passage/journey of 'self' discovery occurred when he left for Germany at the age of twenty-four. By now a qualified architect, he wanted to do a master's degree in urban *planning*. Psychologically, the choice can be seen as an attempt at controlling his psyche's (natural) inner diversity which, from the point of view of a by now already narrowly defined sense of self(ego), is experienced/perceived as a disorder/chaos that must be contained, ordered, controlled. (The outer reflections of Atta's psyche are fully visible in the chaos and terror that is a fact of daily modern life in numerous cities of the South, including Cairo.)

Roommates and companions in both cultures recall him as *"taciturn,"* *"self-contained"* "didn't like food or films or music...generally *reluctant to any pleasure*." Attempts to help him negotiate German social and state systems were mostly spurned, in a manner typical of an adolescent male. As he put it, "I am *grown up now*; I can take care of myself..." According to one of his hosts he said that a lot: "I am abroad now, I am grown up. Now I can decide on my own."

Exhibiting the deeply complicated relationship of modernity and Islamist high fundamentalism with the Feminine/body, Atta was noticeably uncomfortable with women. This may have had to do with the cognitive-spiritual split discussed in the previous chapter. As mediated by the body, the (unconscious) experience of hypocrisy vis-à-vis the (inner) feminine is expressed in bodily compulsions and/or extremely negative attitudes towards women and *their* bodies. While numerous commentators have picked up the misogyny underlying fundamentalism, rarely is it linked to male psychosexual dynamics: "...A kind of religion motivates the Taliban, but the religion in question, I'd say, is not Islam but insecure masculinity. These men are terrified of women."[5] Beyond such a discomfort around women, the anti-feminine attitude was symbolically apparent in his academic difficulty with the arts/imagination, and literally so in his will, written, it seems while still in Germany. It stated that no women should be allowed near his body and funeral!

In keeping with the hero myth, Atta had every intention of returning to his origins "to help build neighborhoods where people could live better lives." But also in keeping with disembodied Cartesianist-Christianist versions of the hero myth, other than leaving Germany briefly for some research projects in Egypt and Syria, he stayed on for almost a decade and basically *never returned* to serve his people. Somewhere along the way in *Germany*, he began to 'understand' Islam, it seems, for the first time and went to perform the *hajj*.

A consideration of the injunctions around the *hajj* and the requisite inner spirit of this major rite of passage for Islamic theological and spiritual consciousness, suggests that it should be undertaken in the second half of life. Thus, in contrast to the four other 'pillars of Islam' - the *Shahada* (witnessing), 5 prayers, fasting and charity (*zakat*) - the *hajj* is not a duty but an 'obligatory' act. That is, it should not be done with borrowed money and is to be undertaken only if the pilgrim can afford it, when worldly duties are done, families provided for etc. For most people, this would occur beyond the age of 40, at least. As evident in Atta's life (and many Muslims), the 'speed' and conflations of modernity lead to premature, rapid 'condensing' of many rites of passage and the negative psychological consequences of this have been discussed in part I.

After performing *hajj*, Atta's desire to return to Egypt was subsumed by a larger, literally transcendent, vision. From

Germany, he embarked on a journey, the culminating images of which, graphically illustrate the symbolic and literal dimensions of the hyper-masculinized, twin archetypes of modern (Cartesian-Christianist) consciousnesses filtered through Islamism, all mirroring each other in Atta's psyche at multiple levels of (self)destruction.

In Atta's life history, one can glimpse what Jung referred to as the "higher continuity of history"[6] or what Corbin meant about how, in archetypal situations, life events which come through as autobiographical data, at the same time become "charged with transhistorical meaning."[7] Strangely then, Atta's journey becomes a microcosm of the monotheistic hero's endless 'upward' quest. Not just in the image of an airplane in the sky and the earth/body left below, but as a cameo/instant-replay of the earthly trajectory of the hero's historical 'ascent': From its origins in (Judaic) Egypt, to (Protestant) Germany, and culminating in, on the one hand, literally in the (youthful/heroic) USA, and on the other, in the globalizing of modernity including the modern Muslim psyche. Many Americans were confounded by the fact that 9/11 occurred from 'within'. That is, the hijackers trained as pilots in the U.S and used American planes as weapons. Unrecognized psychologically was the 'shadow' re-enactment of an inner, collective and cultural narrative-condition. As a whole, officially it was regarded as a failure of a literal 'intelligence'.

An Invisible Woman's Voice

The rather phallic and identical twin towers were not only a symbol of material wealth but also a triumph of science in architecture and engineering. It is ironic therefore, that the man who led the assault on them was trained as an architect, and whose mentor (Osama), was an engineer. The psychodynamics of this irony are linked to what Heraclitus, and subsequently Jung, called the rule of *enantiodromia*,[8] that is, the tendency of phenomena when taken to extremes, to turn into the opposite. In the contemporary context of modernity's loss of the symbolic and the presence of overwhelming literalism, the literal *becomes* the symbolic and all is metaphor. The ultimate irony of course is that in spite of a psyche dominated by literalism, Atta and his companions responded to the, by now literalized, but still essentially symbolic features of what was/is psychologically as much *within* their own consciousness as it is in the modern West's; namely (phallic) dominance and power and its ultimately self-destructive tendencies. Thus, the targets of 9/11, particularly the twin towers representing the triumph of masculinist materialism in which the literalizing of life becomes manifest in the symbolism of death.

But perhaps, in this act of multiple levels of (self) destruction are the seeds of a (self) renewal for both Christians and Muslims and those who see through the icon(s) of modernity. Hillman suggests, for example, how the hero's obsession with upward vertically—what feminists call phallogocentricism—points to a corresponding lack of depth in attitudes to life.[9] The widespread prevalence of depression and the ubiquity of Prozac becomes symbolic of the psyche's need for depth as a relief from a persistently manic, outer oriented lifestyle. Accordingly, the psychological impact of the images of the *inwardly* collapsing towers, and their final fragmenting/dispersing, can be said to have had a powerful archetypal quality. The sheer scale, the intense emotions and the inner/outer connections between victims/perpetrators are so dense and layered that no single discourse was/is sufficient. Either there was the futile redundancy of words and being rendered 'speechless' and 'dumbfounded'. Or, there was a global echo of the words uttered by the voice of a (coincidentally?) *unknown* woman as it accompanied the first television images: an incredulous, horrified 'Oh my God!'. *Logos* evoked.

Deprived of language, one is returned to a more ancient, preverbal, psychological domain, closer to the body and mother. Collectively, it is a consciousness similar to the infancy of humanity and its strong bond with the Feminine matrix of life. In this sense, of being rendered speechless, vulnerable, almost everyone who witnessed it was 'feminized'. Not only in terms of silence but in the shattering and dispersal of phallic images, millions were 'impregnated', and its *meanings* will continue to be 'born' as repercussions reverberate across the globe into the present.

The 'feminizing' of consciousness suggests an inner process of contemplative reflection. Action seeks position, that is hierarchical dominance; whereas knowledge seeks degree, that is depth. In the aftermath, the position(s) adopted by our protagonists is to simply highlight the 'evil' of the other, exhorting him to repent before God's own vengeance strikes.[10] Such a singularly masculine missionary position, so to speak, in its hypermasculine absence of contemplative (self)knowledge and/of the Feminine, can give birth to nothing but more apocalyptic violence, terror and paranoia—hence the chaos we are presently witnessing in Iraq and Syria.

A reflective/contemplative approach towards the images of 9/11 may show the many meanings encapsulated in them. "The image of death is the beginning of mythology"[11] and the imagination and its indelible bonds with the sacred can still sensitize us to our different connections with that day, "for it is the imagination which is at all times capable of transmuting sensory data into symbols and external events into symbolic histories."[12] Even as defensive or aggressive explanations emanate from the Muslim world, Cartesian-Christianism continues its (un)conscious, now global, domination. The almost complete silence and/or marginalizing of a feminist and/or Christian (as opposed to Christianist) voice in the aftermath of September 11, namely of forgiveness and non-violence, is indicative of its own crises and absence from public consciousness.

*

To the West's credit, there are nevertheless numerous voices, postmodern and otherwise that have been engaged in requisite reflection. Long before 9/11, apprehensions/suspicions about modernity have been expressed by many, including Jung, Hillman, Corbin and numerous others, whose ideas form the theoretical underpinnings of this discourse. In spite of present attempts to muffle and marginalize similar voices, there is a continuing effort to engage the larger culture, trying to present a more balanced and (self)critical view of events. Given the transpersonal realities of psyche and history, Muslims can only be grateful for the presence of these voices, holding up, as they do, a mirror for mutual reflection.

Almost two decades ago, a critique/analysis of the modern Pakistani intellectual noted how, after unreflectively internalizing modernity and basically discarding religion in favor of Marxist ideals, many of them had started turning to Islam. This impetus gained momentum especially after the collapse of the Soviet Union and the steady demonizing of Islam by the West and the events in the Balkans. However, given the entrenched modern mindset, this 'return' to Islam was basically a sort of intellectual somersault whereby, "perfectly rational, modern individuals, quite suddenly (have gone) to the other extreme and become insufferably religious, hairsplittingly 'correct' Muslims. The game carries on."[13]

Post-9/11, given the intellectual somnolescence of the majority of otherwise well-educated and modern Muslims, the response is, by and large, typical to what follows a rude awakening: Namely, an emotionally driven paranoia, which while intuitively suspicious of modernity, is largely unable to consciously examine its negative currents in their own lives and by implication, what they themselves have 'done' to Islam. Thus, the response largely remains focused on the West, and a 'defense' of Islam, rather than seeing the connections within and between themselves and the West.

The few, isolated individuals who dare suggest an exercise that would be simultaneously (self)critical about prevailing modern attitudes to religion *and* the distortions it has created in their view of Islam, tend to be mostly dismissed by colleagues many of who are (ironically) simply, increasingly anti-Western or turning to different shades of fundamentalist Islam. In short, individuals who dare to criticize 'modern' Islam have little support or protection from the state or society. Given the fundamentalist impulse, s/he must either risk her life or seek refuge outside of the Muslim world.

Thus, it was also noted a decade ago, how, many Muslim women were increasingly "besieged from within and without."[14] Between being demonized without and facing repression within, increasingly, there are fewer places to go. Post-9/11, this condition of besiegement is encompassing numerous Muslim men and women, amounting to a sort of global psychological exile, of a crucified consciousness but also the possibility of another type of Islam(s).

For the time being, the truth is that, proportionately, more Muslims in the West are (still) free to practice and understand the role and place of Islam in the modern world than in many 'Islamic' countries. In Pakistan, sectarian politics has become so violent that numerous mosques of different communities have heavily armed guards at the gates. Ironically then, one major possibility for the reclaiming of the Islamic message of Peace may lie in the modern West, where there are many non-Muslims who also feel psychologically exiled and crucified. Fully conscious of the role of the West in various types of social and environmental destruction, many are aware that they can no longer enjoy the state of bliss which comes from ignorance and insist that the West carries its own cross of (self)knowledge. Within such contexts/communities, as a 'body', the numerous Islam(s) which constitute the Muslim Diaspora, along with the many other religions that have taken root in the West, potentially offer some Muslims a way out of the impasse/abyss that is the secular 'postmodern mind'.[15]

Concluding Part II: Mirrored Conditions

The key psychological issue has not been about one religion or another, not even about being modern or not, but about a now globally dominant, extreme heroic masculinism. It's not about Christianity or Islam, but about psycho-theologically hyper-masculine approaches to text, interpretation, meaning(s) and expression, which negate and devalue the Divine Feminine. It's about *logocentricism* at the expense and denial of the 'Other(s)': woman, body, nature, the world of *eros*, *mythos* and the symbolic imagination.

163

Similarly, it is not about male or female but about a particular consciousness, a mindset or *weltanschauung* which can be present in anyone, including women such as Condoleezza Rice or Hillary Clinton, or those who choose to render themselves invisible through the hijab. To say this, is not to suggest a wholesale rejection/indictment of modernity/masculinity/males, or rationality, but about the imbalance between various complementary psychological and/or theological factors, *all* of which are required for life. When the balance goes awry, as it has with the natural environment, it indicates a sickness which is rooted in the psychology of fundamentalism, secular or religious.

Outside of the vicious cycles of manic-obsessive-compulsive vengeance, what is required is knowledge, principally of oneself and to see how our inner conditions are mirrored in each other and in the degradation of the external environment whether natural, or in mega man-made cities. Not just in the events of 9/11, but also in the corruption, chaos, violence and decay of the Muslim states, not to mention the implications of Nagasaki, the holocaust, Rwanda, Bhopal, the steadily increasing sales of Prozac, and what has been done to the environment as a whole. Terrorism can simply no longer be denied in bland generalities, confined to the periphery, attributed to just outsiders. It is all around us and demands to be known. When we are able to do that, and recognize our own faces staring back from the darkness, then perhaps we will be able to hope for a time of healing.

INTERLUDE:
ISLAM'S FEMININE DIMENSION

We head the experience, but missed the meaning.
(T.S. Eliot[1])

Toward a Different Epistemology

If I have been critical of the West and modernity, it has not been for the sake of West bashing, nor to sentimentally suggest a return to some utopian past of 'tradition'. As a closer look at modernity reveals, the world really does not become better but simply different. A cursory survey of the state of primary/higher education in many Muslim majority states, including Pakistan, is a personal reminder of how deeply indebted I am to the missionary educational institutions where I, and many of my generation, received not only a good school and college education. It gave us access to several aspects of 'the best of the West'. Among others, this included many wise voices in the Western intellectual tradition generally and particularly feminism (which by now, has unfortunately been heavily co-opted by mainstream academia).

The missionaries also gave the gift of becoming familiar with the Bible which, years later, enhanced my understanding of not only the monotheisms, but as mediated by Jung and Muslim thinkers, also a deeper understanding of Christianity.* I am

---

* In this respect it's also notable that Mary is mentioned more times in the Quran, than she is in the New Testament and always with great reverence. It shows that the possibility for rapprochement is certainly not purely hypothetical.

convinced therefore, that part of the problem with modern Muslims has to do with their ignorance of the Bible. However, given the abysmal levels of literacy in the Muslim world, there is some justification for this ignorance and it cannot be compared to the ignorance about the Quran among the widespread 'high literate' societies of the West.

At the same time, some of the best work on Islam is coming from universities and scholars in the West, Muslim and non-Muslim. It includes, for example, translations of Islamic texts, classic and modern, from different parts of the Muslim world into global languages (English, French etc.), thereby enabling a more nuanced, deeper and expanded self-understanding for Muslims everywhere. In a way, the West is doing for the Muslims what the Muslims did for it in terms of preserving, partaking of, transforming and passing on the legacy of the Greeks.

Similarly, much of what I have said is based on Western sources, acknowledged and wise voices, which, have existed on the margins of Western culture and consciousness, and I have utilized them for a more balanced view of the present situation. This free exchange and sharing of knowledge is also a positive gift of modernity. Whereas an insatiable appetite for learning is one of the West's greatest and most distinguished aspects, it has unfortunately literalized the profound idea that 'knowledge is power'. That is, power for the sake of power, an end in itself, exercised frequently through brute, material force.

The motto of the Pakistani University I attended is taken from Kant: 'Courage to Know' (*Sapere aude!*). It sums up the spirit of the Enlightenment and still holds true, implying that it takes courage to think independently about religion, politics, or anything else. If 'ignorance is bliss', then knowledge is also a burden requiring moral responsibility. Today, I believe, the bliss factor is no longer an option for numerous individuals East or

West, Muslim or non-Muslim and all those who refuse to submit to what is actually an illusion of alternatives: "you are either with us or against us". In such a context, it's best to remember that Christ carried his *own* cross. Whether personal and/or political, we all carry different burdens. Knowledge of oneself can perhaps bring us closer and give each other courage to face what confronts us, wherever we are.

As many parts of the Muslim world become increasingly driven by the demographically ascendant, raging energy of testosterone driven young males, other demographic projections indicate that in about 10 years a quarter of Europe's population will be over sixty. According to *The Economist* "given declining birth rates and female longevity, Europe becomes a continent of the old ... especially old women. ... The majority of the very old will be women living alone."[2]

Contemplating the symbolic significance of this twin image, of a young male and elderly woman, one can keep in mind that beyond *logos*, the domain of the Feminine is above all *mythos*. Even in the West, the Muses, those that inspire the arts (and science) including philosophy, are all feminine in form. The rational intellect as *logos* has a higher dimension, Wisdom. Represented often as Sophia, it is the basis of the word 'philosophy' (the lover-of-Wisdom/Sophia).

Having critiqued the modern masculine Cartesian-Christianist approach and the manner in which it obliterates the Feminine in both Christianity and High Islam, Part III will explore how the Masculinity of 'low' Islamism also suffocates the Feminine. Yet before we can move into Part III, a different epistemology will be needed to properly understand the Feminine dimension of Islam.

Islam and the Feminine

In the West, beyond the hijab, Islam isn't usually associated with psychological Femininity. On the contrary, it is mostly seen as a purely patriarchal, misogynist and masculine religion. More specifically, to the extent that Islam is seen as part of the family of monotheisms there is, today, an implicit tendency to view it from two broad perspectives. In the first instance, it is frequently assumed that in so far as it came after Judaism and Christianity, Islam is a received mishmash of the two and has nothing new and coherent to offer. Conversely, where differences are perceived, they are filtered through an array of cultural lenses that provide largely negative stereotypes of Islam and sexuality. These assumptions must first be worked through since they preclude a nuanced and realistic understanding of the Feminine Islam, including their impact on the psychology of contemporary 'low' Islamisms.

Eve, Evil and Sexuality

The prevalent discourse on women's sexuality is of course inextricably linked with modern Cartesian-Christianist consciousness and its underpinnings in certain interpretations of the Judaeo-Christian tradition. Western models of male and female sexuality have been heavily influenced by Puritan Christianity which in turn has become the dominant lens when it comes to viewing questions of women and sexuality in other religions. For example, the archetype of Eve as seductress responsible for the Fall, does not exist in Hindu mythology, which has a very different attitude towards women and the female body. Similarly, while both Hinduism and Islam have an ascetic dimension, it has never existed in a *widespread institutionalized form* as characterized, for example, in medieval Catholicism.

Many Muslims themselves assume that the Quran endorses the

Biblical story of Adam and Eve, not only in the sense of the latter being created from Adam's rib but also that it was she who was responsible for the Fall. This is incorrect. Firstly, the name of Eve simply does *not* appear in the Quran. There are references to Adam's spouse/mate but her name is not mentioned. In fact, the only woman named in the Quran is Maryam (Mary), who has a *sura* named after her. This is not to say that Eve does not have an Arabic name, but this has come more from folklore and the traditions, in which she is referred to as 'Hawwa', related to the root of the word 'Life'.

In Genesis II, the story of Adam and Eve attributes various levels of inferiority to the female. This inferiority is anchored in the details of her creation; not only from Adam's rib but in comparison to his coming into being fully conscious, directly divine, Eve is extracted during his (dark) sleep and unconsciousness. Her inferiority and negativity is further highlighted in the role of seductress through her interaction with Satan and the ensuing Fall of Adam and herself. The contrast between the pristine innocence of Adam and the dark guilt attributed to Eve forms a cornerstone in the foundations of Western culture. As Hillman puts it, "the psychological history of the male-female relationship in our (i.e. Western) civilization may be seen as a series of footnotes to the tale of Adam and Eve."[3]

While the Quran does share many of the Judaeo-Christian narratives, there are crucial differences in details which can be considered significant, one way or the other. The story of human creation and Eve's role in the Fall, are two examples.

> Man We did create from a quintessence of clay. Then We placed him as a drop of sperm in a place of rest, firmly fixed. Then We made the sperm into a clot of congealed blood then of that clot We made a (foetus) lump, then We made out of the lump bones and clothed the bones with flesh and then *We developed out of it another creature,* so blessed be Allah the Best to create.[4]

Yet the phrase, "We developed out of it another creature" has also been translated as "then We developed it into a new creation".[5] Elsewhere, the Quran states: "He created you all from a single Person. Then created of like nature his mate."[6] However, another grammatically more accurate translation reads "He created you from a *single being*, then of the same kind He made *its* mate."[7]

Thus, references to human creation, as a whole, remain ambiguous regarding gender, the female is not created from the rib, and there are no negative connotations regarding inferiority of either. More importantly, in the Quranic version of the Fall, references are either to the couple, or when the events are described in detail, it is *Adam* who is seduced by Satan.[8] Eve clearly isn't the culprit. However both are expelled from the Garden. Thus, whether in terms of creation or the Fall, Eve's role in the Quranic narrative is radically different from the Biblical one.

Related to this, Islam completely rejects the notion of 'original sin', Adam's sin being, rather, 'forgetfulness'. Once reminded, he is forgiven. Hence, according to Islam, humans are *not* fundamentally tainted, in fact, to the extent of being created through God's 'breath' and in God's 'image', they are deiform: "Man [is] envisaged not as a fallen being needing a miracle to save him, but as man, a theomorphic being endowed with an intelligence capable of conceiving the Absolute and with a will capable of choosing what leads to the Absolute."[9] However, being prone to forget their origins and bonds with the Creator, there has been a steady and universal stream of 'reminders' through the Prophets and scriptures, including the Quran which refers to itself as 'the Reminder'. The rejection of original sin, the story of human creation and Adam's role in the Fall, are key factors which combine to form a major theological, psychological and civilizational point of departure (within the monotheisms) vis-à-vis wo(man) and Islam.

Harems, Seraglios, Odalisques

Along with ignoring such key differences, popular Western conceptions of Islam particularly, tend to see it not only as a violent and misogynist religion, but also as one which is suffused with a certain licentiousness. For example, when one considers the Orientalist view of Islam in art and literature, there is a negative stereotype of a rather rampant sexuality expressed primarily through images of women: multiple wives, the harem, concubines and odalisques. Many of these ideas are telescoped, stereotypically, in the figure of the Prophet. Hinduism, in a way, has a similar 'image' problem when it comes to sexuality, the naked female form evidence of a wanton-ness in such matters. The main point at this stage is the *assumptions* that filter our understanding of not only Islam and sexuality, but other religions as well.

These assumptions manifest themselves in the images that are selected or imagined, and possibly reveal more about the Western observer than the observed. Kabbani's study of how Europe viewed the Orient provides a range of visual illustrations regarding, what are basically fantasy images of Islam and Muslim women.[10] European painters such as a J.F. Lewis, Ingres and Delacroix, portrayed sensational *tableaux,* a collage of harems, odalisques and slave markets permeated with "opulence, languor and eroticism". These "imperial fictions" were reinforced and further stereotypes generated by travel writers, scholars and intellectuals such as Richard Burton, T.E. Lawrence, Edward Lane, Baudelaire and Flaubert. Commenting on the numerous images of the female body in this Orientalist genre, Kabbani suggests how "such portraits, in wishing to convey the East, described more accurately, Europe... the repressiveness of its social codes, and the heavy hand of its bourgeois morality."[11] Analyzing a range of historical, literary and cultural data, she shows how negative ideas about Islam and women remain entrenched into the present: "the whole Western debate about Muslim women is a dishonest one… The study of the Muslim world by the West has never been a neutral and scholarly exercise."[12]

A Christianist Distortion

From an archetypal perspective, each founder of a religion can be seen as a paradigmatic 'image', an archetype, highlighting a certain cluster of qualities regarding life, morality, knowledge, divinity etc. As such, many of our modern ideas about religion and sexuality are related to the archetype of Christ. It is an image of high asceticism, asexuality and a single-minded other-worldliness. In that sense, it would not be an exaggeration to say that many assumptions about male and female sexuality in Islam come from a Western-Christian gaze and its notions of a prophetic religion.

What is lost sight of is that Christ was unique. Whether in birth, or the Passion there has been no prophet like him, before or after—at least in the monotheisms. Prior to Christ, a long line of Hebrew prophets was very different, and the Prophet of Islam was very much of this prophetic Semitic 'lineage'. In varying degrees, the Old Testament prophets were men of this world; kings, rulers, warriors, statesmen, husbands, fathers etc. Yet, at the same time, they were deeply spiritual individuals. This paradigm, exemplified by figures like Abraham, Joseph or Moses, is overshadowed by the Christian one, which dominates modern ideals of piety and religiosity. Sexuality particularly, is seen as something which contaminates spirituality. In the context of Islam, these ideals create major hurdles, because while Christ is the miracle in Christianity which is built around Christology, in Islam the Prophet is *not* the miracle nor is the faith principally centered on his person. Instead, it is the Quran that is the miracle and the mainstay. However, from the perspective of the Western-Christian gaze and its assumptions regarding the separation of the spiritual from the sexual, Islam and its Prophet are regarded as suspect.

In her biography of the Prophet, Karen Armstrong has discussed how over the centuries, a negative picture of Muhammad was painted in order to discredit him and the religion.[13] Particularly during the Crusades, the most fantastic stories were fabricated and between the violent image of the sword and sexuality, Islam was stigmatized in a manner that has had a continuing impact on the Western Christian psyche into the present.[14] As she points out, these fantasies about Islam came at a time when they "reflect Christian anxieties about their own emergent identity ... at a time when the church was imposing celibacy on a reluctant clergy, the astonishing accounts of Mohammad's sexual life reveal far more about the repressions of Christians than about the facts of the Prophet's own life."[15]

The Prophet and Women

If we set aside the stereotypes about sexuality, women and Islam which as anchored in Orientalist and Christianist biases about the Prophet and his relationship with women, a very different picture emerges. For example, the Prophet's first marriage was to a *widow* who was more than ten years older than him, Khadija. It was *she* who proposed and he married her at the age of twenty-five. She was his only wife until her death fifteen years later. Among his children who lived to be adults, all were from Khadija. She was the first to accept the truth of his calling and was a source of strength and comfort in the early days of his mission. It was only after her death and the growing complexity of his task as warrior, statesman *and* prophet (like David and Solomon), by which time he was in his fifties, that multiple marriages were contracted. This is not to say that he was a sexual ascetic, but rather to put in perspective his life and the varied bases of his relationship with women.

As Armstrong's insightful biography of the Prophet shows,

polygamy tends to be the norm in tribal societies. The sexual exploits of King David and the enormous harem of King Solomon make Muhammad's "look quite pathetic."[16] The fact that he remained married to only one (and an older woman) for many years until her death, should be indicative of the essential man-woman relationship in Islam. The multiple marriages were contracted mostly for social/political reasons and bedevilled throughout this period by the contingencies of war, politics, not to mention the intense, drawn-out spiritual/physical experience of revelation and its demands. Similarly, as Armstrong notes, given the demands on the Prophet in his fifties, not only did many of the marriages have political dimensions, they also cemented ties of kinship. Simultaneously, they were also the beginning "of an alternative kind of clan…not based on kinship but on ideology."[17]

Nevertheless, the same man also stated: "Three things are loved by me, Women, Perfume and Prayer" (or "were made worthy of love to me"). As Schuon points out, those who have no idea of Oriental symbolism in general, or of the Islamic perspective in particular, find this ternary—women, perfume and prayer—as arbitrary and shockingly worldly.[18] However, one can see this ternary as a summative of the social, the sensual and the sacred.[19] These three dimensions are inextricably linked in the Islamic view on sexuality, gender and the Feminine—at the literal as well as symbolic level.

'Masculine' and 'Feminine' in Islam

The Social Balance

When it comes to the social aspect, there are no Islamic restrictions on women's sexuality in the sense that there are no remarkable differences between Islam and other theological systems regarding women, and generally speaking, the same injunctions operate similarly for men and women: to be modest and not be sexually provocative or obscene, the forbidding of homosexuality, adultery or extra-marital sex, are some common examples.*

These restrictions generally focus on maintaining a social balance and are not a set of limitations for the personal and individual. The various prescriptions and strictures regarding marital behaviour in the Quran, for example, are, at one level, clearly focussed on maintaining social order. At another level, they are contextualized vis-à-vis the realities of human nature. Thus, for example, adultery is considered a major sin, which must be severely punished since it strikes at the heart of the family and established social order. At the same time, the punishment can be carried out only if four 'well respected' *eyewitnesses* testify to having personally witnessed the act of intercourse. Clearly, this would be exceedingly rare and implies a recognition of human nature and its foibles and an emphasis on discretion and the social order. Similarly, the concept of marriage itself is, at one level, a sacrament and all Muslims are encouraged toward it, yet, at the same time, it is a *contract* based on implicit and explicit terms. Divorce, even though it is frowned upon, is fully permissible in case of breach of contract on either side. One basic condition of the contract has to do with sex, in the sense that, if there has been no sexual encounter for three months, it may become, if either party desires, the first step

---

* Within this sociological frame, one will not be considering issues such as the veiling. It has been given enough academic and popular, albeit, stereotyped attention. Suffice it is to say that there is no definitive agreement about it. From the Jungian perspective in any case, the presence of the veil in Islam and the current obsession with it by both insiders and outsiders, suggests a literalizing process to a symbolic and archetypal reality. That is, one can argue that the Feminine in Islam remains veiled, and as such, a tantalizing mystery to masculinized consciousness.

towards dissolution of the marriage. So sex becomes a crucial part of the marriage bond and, as in Judaism, it is an established right of both parties.

This does not imply, however, that sexuality in Islam is simply about common rules and regulations or social mores. In fact the enjoyment of sensuality and sexuality are given ample space in the Islamic view.

The Sensual Balance

Muslim poets and philosophers such as Rumi and Ibn 'Arabi often used sexual imagery to speak of the Divine. Ibn 'Arabi's exegesis of what the Prophet meant when he said he most loved women, perfume and prayer draws on a sophisticated analysis of Arabic psycho-linguistics, suggesting that "the contemplation of God in women is the most intense and the most perfect; and the union which is the most intense (in the sensible order which provides support for this contemplation) is the conjugal act."[20]

As complimentary manifestations of Divine Unity, and given that Islam considers the quest for God as the ultimate aim of existence, male and female sexual union (in this traditional, conjugal and ideal sense) in Islam, is already a sacred act. This *a priori,* inherent metaphysical significance, is what enables the Islamic perspective to highlight the positive dimension of this all too powerful human impulse, even as it functions (ideally) within the parameters of the Law.

Discussing the connections between erotic desire and the pursuit of truth, Katherine Ewing shows how certain motifs in Islamic mystical writings have an analogous relationship to pleasure. One of the most prominent Islamic philosophers, al-Ghazali, explains how the desire of the mystic who yearns for God is essentially indescribable and impossible to realize. Within the vast canvas of mystical Islam, therefore, the themes of desire and truth have been addressed by philosophers, scholars, mystics and poets alike in a bewildering spectrum of desire ranging from the uplifting and sublime to the scatological and scandalous.[21]

This interlinking of the flesh and the spirit are part of the cultural underpinning in vast parts of the Islamic world and have permeated its civilizations. They include a substantial body of erotic literature of which *The Perfumed Garden* is best known in the West and can be considered another *Kama Sutra*. While these texts have been criticized by Muslim and Hindu feminists as exploitive of women's sexuality, they are not sex manuals in the modern sense but rather, have to do with the esoteric dimension of what is best termed as sacred sexuality, the 'meanings' of which were never meant to be easily accessible to a paperback, mass market, readership.[*]

Thus, as Bouhdiba has detailed, there are numerous texts in Arabic and Persian which delineated an 'Islamic art of sexual ecstasy' and which incorporate much more than sex.[22] Through language and speech, they evoke an entire sensory universe: tactile, olfactory and visual, and are replete with not only references to personal hygiene, but to a wide and exotic array of incense, oils and perfumes. Like many dimensions of the Hindu Tantras, they are to be understood primarily symbolically but have literal under-pinnings in, of course, the body and other, physical substances. Similarly, the institution of the *hammam* or public bath in many Islamic countries reflect a sensuous culture in which individuals learn to become comfortable with their bodies. The *hammam* culture provides a social and sensory education, and has profound ramifications—albeit differently— for males and females.

*

---

[*] But which is happening now as is evident from the growing sales on Tantra as well as such books as the lavishly illustrated *Sacred Sexuality* by Mann A. and Lyle J.; Element Books. Shaftesbury. 1995.

All of this eventually portrays how Islam strives for a balance between the corporeal and the spiritual, between the sensual and the metaphysical, between the feminine and the masculine. As a religion claiming to be rooted in a nature ruled by natural laws (God's, that is) there is an explicit and implicit understanding and acceptance of human nature in Islam, its drives and requisite constraints. There is, so to speak, an economy of pleasure in Islam, not in starkly sexual terms, but in terms of human nature and the human sensorium.

We are as much creatures of the flesh as we are of the psyche, which includes the human imagination. Death can only be imagined. As beings capable of desire, we are simultaneously capable of imagining the nature of pleasure. As Bouhdiba suggests, desire consists of both volition and imagination, and in this sense, paradise is the reign of the imagination.[23] Or as Schuon puts it, "we know metaphysical Reality not only by what we understand or conceive, but also by what we desire, and therefore by what we are."[24]

From an Islamic point of view then, life as such is woven around the warp and weft of what, in Western philosophical terms, is called 'paradox' or 'contradiction'. In a Cartesian-Christianist approach, the word 'contradiction' has connotations of negative problematics requiring 'resolution'. Yet stepping out of a judgemental frame which demands 'resolution', contradiction(s) can simply be seen as givens, multiple impulses which underpin human and earthly existence. The human psyche itself is capable of turning every proposition on its head with an equally valid, opposite proposition. The only domain where this does not hold, is death—or in certain religious perspectives which seek to transcend this crucifixion of consciousness in perceived warring opposites. Thus, in Islam, "The apparent contradiction in the moral comportment of

Muslims is not in their philosophy, *it is in things themselves.*"*

Given that two opposing forces always coexist, the Islamic (earthly) ideal is not so much a heroic negation of one over the other but of balance. 'We have made you (the Muslims)', says the Quran, 'a people of the middle way' (2:143). Thus, even though this book mostly discusses the positive role of sexuality, this emphasis on order and balance needs to be kept in mind. Which is also why, even the most radical Islamic mystics insist on clinging to exoteric Law (*Shariah*). Inner, psychological and spiritual freedom, is meant to be balanced by outer constraints.

The sacred balance

Perhaps more than most religions, the division between the exoteric and esoteric is vividly present in Islam. That is, there is the level of the codified, textually based Law (*Shariah*) and the informal, also textual, but overwhelmingly orally transmitted idiom of the 'Path' or 'Way' of mysticism (*Tariqah*). Within an Islamic vocabulary, these differences pertain to the visible (*Zahir*) attributes of God as compared to the hidden (*Batin*) respectively. "Woman ... in a certain manner incarnates esotericism ... 'esoteric' truth, the *haqiqah*, is felt as a 'feminine' reality."[25]

This nature of gender relationships in sapiential Islamic cosmology, theology and spirituality, have been explored in depth by Murata in her path breaking *The Tao of Islam* which identifies profound similarities between certain Islamic epistemological frameworks and the Chinese-Taoist concepts of *Yang* (masculine) and *Yin* (feminine) as two fundamental principles of existence, namely, the Active and Receptive respectively. As a whole, these two broad approaches in Muslim

---

* "... if Islam on the one hand recognizes the positive quality of sexuality, on the other hand it is aware of the danger involved in pleasure as such, the two points of view coexisting and interweaving in practice as well as theory." (Schuon Frithjof; *From the Divine to the Human*; World Wisdom Books. Indiana. 1980. p. 140.)

and Chinese spirituality can themselves be seen from within the *Yin/Yang* frame, reflecting the Active/Receptive principles: the Islamic legalistic and Confucian view emphasizes the *Yang* (masculine) aspect whereas the sapiential and Taoist stresses the *Yin* (feminine). As conceptualized in the circular symbol divided by a sigmoid line with each half containing the other, *Yin* & *Yang*, constitute 'the Great Ultimate'.[26]

Based on a system of correspondences and the relationship between these two principles, Islamic and Taoist philosophy can be seen as deeply similar in their approach to the three inter-related levels of the metacosm, macrocosm and microcosm—or God, the cosmos, and the human being.[27] It is impossible to attempt to summarize the complex dimensions of these gendered ideals as conceived and articulated over many centuries and Murata's work remains a milestone on the subject of gender relationships in traditional Islamic thought.

We need to keep in mind, therefore, that simplifications are inevitable when talking of, what is in reality, a highly sophisticated, vast body of metaphysical thought developed over more than a millennium across different languages and cultures. Similar to many other traditions, the male and female dyad in sapiential Islam is part of a larger intellectual and philosophical framework based on a system of polarities, and is in turn based on a recognition of the centrality of polar relationships that are not so much oppositional, but rather, complementary. The ultimate aim of this type of polar thinking is to establish the idea of Unity (*Tawhid*) which in fact manifests itself principally through the dialectics of polarity.[28] Thus, to reiterate, male and female, masculine or feminine, are not so much literally man and woman as they are qualities within a human being.[*]

---

[*] One can note the similarities between this and Jungian concepts, which is not surprising, given the extensive references in his writings to Gnostic Christianity,

Of course, in Islamic theology, God is ultimately beyond gender. The use of the masculine 'He' is more a linguistic constraint of Arabic and not a gendered entity. Thus, for example, there is no gender specific notion/term 'God the Father' (or 'Mother') in Islam. However, to the extent that humans 'reflect' different attributes of God who created male and female, "at another level there is an implied androgyny to the Divine Nature."[29] Within this system of polarities, the proverbial 'Ninety-Nine' names of Allah, God's Attributes, can be broadly classified as Names of Grandeur and Majesty (*Jalal*) and those of Beauty and Graciousness/Compassion (*Jamal*). In this sense, the former can be considered 'masculine' and the latter 'feminine'.

> The differences between the sexes cannot be reduced to anatomy and biological function. There are also differences of psychology and temperament, of spiritual type and even principles within the Divine Nature which are sources *in divinis* of the duality represented on the microcosmic level as male and female. God is both Absolute and Infinite. Absoluteness and Majesty, which is inseparable from it, is manifested directly in the masculine state and Infinity and Beauty in the feminine.[30]

---

alchemy and Chinese philosophy (but very little on Islam). (See: Ahmed; *Islam and the West*. op cit.)

Beyond the broad categories of masculine/*Jalal* and feminine/*Jamal* attributes, many commentators have pointed out the significance of the names *ar-Rahim* and *ar-Rahman*. Referring to different aspects of Mercy, Graciousness and Compassion, they are derived form the same root (*rhm*) as the Arabic word for 'womb'.[31] *Ar-Rahim* (The Merciful, He who saves by His Mercy) and *ar-Rahman* (The Compassionate, whose Mercy embraces everything) are perhaps the most well-known names of Allah, given that, with one exception, every chapter of the Quran begins with them. Apart from statistically being the most often repeated Name of God in the Quran, *ar-Rahman* is the *only* Name made synonymous with Allah in the Quran.[32] In short, the 'feminine' attributes emerging from *ar-Rahman* and *ar-Rahim* as (Maternal) source of Mercy, Grace/Graciousness, Compassion, dominate all others, forming a significant and dominant dimension to the Islamic idea of God.

Islam and the Masculine

Balanced Masculinity

It must be reiterated that what is being presented here are generalizations regarding a fraction of an entire system of cosmology, theology and spiritual psychology vis-à-vis gender. One should also keep in view that while the focus has been on the feminine as an essential counterpoint to the masculine, it is not to imply that the latter is all negative and the former purely positive. In keeping with the principle of polarity, both feminine and masculine have their own positive and negative dimensions. And in keeping with the Islamic focus on balance, taken to exclusive extremes, both can turn into negativities.

In psycho-spiritual terms, while the feminine may be a symbol of life, birth, nurturance, grace, beauty, compassion, it can also represent, as women's bodies also do, decay, dissolution, inertia and death. The negative aspects of the feminine would also include an extreme surrender to impulse and sensation, which becomes in the absence of rationality, a cognitive darkness, that is, ignorance-as-unconsciousness. This ignorance can be about oneself, the material world and God. Similarly, positive aspects of masculinity, such as determination, discernment, detachment, chivalry and reason, when taken to subjective extremes (as in the heroic ideals of self and God), can turn into violence, literalism, and to deny, if necessary by force, anything that differs from itself. All these can be present in both men and women. As Rumi puts it:

> To abandon anger, sensuality, and greed is all manliness and a trait of the prophets. ... Manliness is this manliness, not beard and penis: Otherwise the ass's implement would be the king of men.[33]

The current abysmal state of education in the Muslim world belies the enormous emphasis on knowledge in Islam as evident in the well-known saying of the prophet to seek knowledge, even if one has to 'go to China'. Being the fountainhead of spiritual/religious knowledge (for Muslims) it is unlikely that he was referring to knowledge about Islam, but rather about other types of 'secular' knowledge. Additionally, and equally important, beyond urging Muslims towards different types of 'worldly' knowledge even if one has to 'go to China', implies the possibility of gaining crucial knowledge about one's *self* through travel, leaving the familiar and encountering the foreign/other.

The physical human sensorium functions on the principle of contrast, that is, our senses process information only in the presence of contrast. For example, consider our olfactory sense. When you enter a room which has a bad smell, you will register it as a contrast to the outside. However, if you stay in that room, after a while, in the absence of contrast, the smell will no longer be prominent. Stepping outside once again will provide a new set of sensory information. As Bateson said: "Information is a difference that makes a difference."[34] Similarly we can only understand our self when it is confronted with a different 'other' self. This is why, apart from the Prophet, sages/teachers from all traditions urged/instructed the student/seeker to travel.

The Prophet's statement 'man's knowledge of himself comes before knowledge of his Lord' indicates the primacy of self-understanding, warts and all, and the profound links of individual subjectivity and its relationship with the Divine. It is in this sense of spiritual/intellectual self-awareness that 'masculinity' may have a higher status than the 'feminine' in *certain* contexts. But such a masculinity needs to be grounded in its archetypal dimensions of a receptive approach to knowledge and spirituality, which is in any case inseparable from the Divine Feminine. At another level, and important for our purpose, the overall significance of the Feminine is indisputable:

> the Feminine is not opposed to the Masculine... but encompasses and combines the two aspects, receptive and active, whereas the Masculine possesses only one of the two... This intuition is clearly expressed by Rumi: Woman is beam of the Divine Light/ She is not the being whom sensual desire takes as its object/she is Creator, it should be said/she is not creature.[35]

This intuitively perceived, and largely unconscious, reverence for the Creative-Maternal aspect of Divinity, is possibly one of the few vestiges of the positive dimensions of Islamic masculinity today, manifest in the combination of respect and love that many Muslims—men and women—show toward their mother(s).

Negative Masculinity

Despite the tendency towards balance and the undeniable presence of the Feminine in the broader Islamic tradition, the current Muslim world, as a whole, is dominated by a negative masculinism, especially in the high Islamist mindset, linked as it is to the heroic psychology of modernity. As such, many of the problematics around Islam and women today have to do with customary practice rather than religious injunctions. This dimension has been addressed by many scholars but was not the focus in the present analysis since issues such as female circumcision have nothing to do with the Islamic view of female sexuality. They have everything to do with cultural practice and an ambitious masculinist political policy. To the extent that Islam is often used to justify these acts, the real battle has to do with the politics of interpretation and the reclaiming, by women, of all dimensions of their humanity as sanctioned by Islam since both religion and women's sexuality have come to be dominated by modern masculinism.

At this stage then, the main point was to highlight what is eventually, either way, the all-encompassing significance of the (Divine) Feminine and the possible impact of an absence of its positive side in Muslim psychological and theological consciousness. Emphasizing the positive Feminine in this framework is not to deny gender complexities which are widely available for those interested in Islamic philosophy and theology. But in the present context of this book, the idea is to highlight the extreme valorization of what is essentially a negative masculinity at all levels of existence.

This 'interlude' and the broad range of issues it has touched upon, has attempted to highlight certain aspects of Islam which provide a different framework for a psychological understanding of gender, Islam and its Feminine dimension. As one proceeds to discuss this dimension in the chapters to follow, this epistemological framework/context needs to be kept in mind.

PART III:
PSYCHOLOGICAL EXPLORATIONS OF 'LOW' ISLAMISM

Chapter 6:
Academic Religion and Mystical Islam

There cannot be a universal definition of religion, not only because its constituent elements are historically specific but that definition is itself the historical product of discursive processes.
(Talal Asad[1])

Religion and Academia Today

The postmodern ferment in academia has led to a recognition that as an intellectual/academic discipline the study of religion is fraught with methodological inconsistencies, contradictions and disorder. Reflecting on this academic crisis in the post-9/11 context, Bruce Lincoln discusses the 'serious disarray' in the discipline during the last decade. Singling out anthropologist Talal Asad as a major contributor to the reformulation(s) the discipline is undergoing today, Lincoln acknowledges that earlier, dominant paradigms were in fact implicitly based on Protestantism, and were as such not universally applicable.[2]

In a similar vein, other scholars have also suggested that the concept of 'religion' itself is 'highly dubious' and like any other social construct, laden with biases of politics, gender, race and

191

ethnocentricity.³ Thus, the role of the modern academic gaze and its construction of "religion as conceptual category which is then applied universally, needs serious reconsideration."⁴ In short, and most importantly, it is widely acknowledged today that almost all scholarship is simultaneously a discursive exercise having constitutive implications.⁵ Additionally, it is increasingly evident that there is an academic bias towards "textual and elite manifestations of traditions as opposed to their oral, visual, and popular counterpoints ... reflecting the androcentric assumptions of the male and female scholars."⁶ The collective implications of these critiques and emerging conceptual changes, particularly for the study and understanding of Islam, are significant. The inordinate focus by Muslim and non-Muslim scholars on geopolitics as an important factor in the rise of Islamism has obscured other crucial issues pertaining to the production of knowledge about religion, including Islam. It is important not to ignore this dimension since it implicates not only Muslim scholars but also those in the highest echelons of Western academia.

Scholarly Islamism

Within (and outside) the post-9/11 Muslim world, it has almost become *de rigueur* in moderate and liberal Muslim intellectual circles to point to the Wahhabi/Saudi inspired role in the rise of Islamic extremism in different Muslim countries. In Pakistan, these analyses tend to highlight the politics of the cold war and Afghanistan during the seventies and eighties including a military dictatorship, the influx of foreign Muslims, Saudi money and American policies and weapons, all of which indeed did contribute to growing Islamism. More recently, the subsequent 'Talibanization' of the society at large and the role of education in creating a mindset of violent, religious extremism, has come under discussion, especially regarding the system of education and the place of Islam in it, including the *madrassahs*.

However, what is not discussed/debated are the monetary-theological dynamics in the production of such knowledge in which the *madrassah* is simply the tail-end financial/theological recipient of a simplistic version of an Islam. One that has been 'officialized' not only by the state and various governments but more importantly, claimed as 'authentic' by the *ulema* and scholars of Islam at the level of institutionalized 'higher' learning about Islam.

The epicenter of Sunni Islamic thinking, Al-Azhar in Cairo, is a case in point. Despite steady decay during and after the colonial period, it was nevertheless open to intellectual diversity. The founding of the Muslim World League by Saudi Arabia in 1962, initiated the steady flow of vast amounts of money into Al-Azhar through endowments for scholarly chairs and handsome grants and prizes to individual scholars. Within four decades, the Saudis had 'steadily purchased the ideological direction of Al-Azhar'.*

Western academia has also not been immune to Saudi attempts at gaining prominence and scholarly legitimacy for Wahhabism through monetary incentives. In 1997, Oxford University was given more than $30 million for its Islamic Studies Center, a $20 million grant was given to University of Arkansas to begin the King Fahd Program for Middle East

---

* Egyptian professor of Islamic jurisprudence at UCLA and author of books critical of Wahabism, Khaled Abou El Fadl, recounts how "one of his most beloved teachers, Mohammad Jalal Kishk, had mocked the ignorance of Wahabi Islam when El Fadl was a student at Azhar. But, in 1981, after Kishk received the $200,000 King Faisal Award and the $850,000 King Fahd Award from the Saudi Government, he published a pro-Wahabi tome called 'The Saudis and the Islamic solution'." Foer; *'Moral Hazard': Interview with Khaled Abou El Fadl.* 11-18-2002.

Studies in 1994. The Program in Arab Studies at U.C. Berkeley was given $5 million. Whether the motives behind such largesse were altruistic or not, scholars who have refused Saudi support claim that they declined because of the proviso that the 'final editorial control' of their work would rest with the Saudis.*

According to the critic of Wahhabism and scholar of Islamic jurisprudence Khaled Abou El Fadl, the monetary subversion of scholarship in Western academia has exacerbated the shift in Middle Eastern studies away from critical, secular analyses of modernization toward celebrations of Islamist "civil society". Apart from *not* adopting a critical stance on Wahhabism and Saudi Arabia, such scholarship also indirectly reinforces and projects Wahhabism's claim to be the *only* legitimate Islam. For example, Frank Vogel's book *Islamic Law and Legal Systems: Studies of Saudi Arabia* has been termed "an embarrassment' by colleagues and scholars such as El Fadl. Vogel himself claimed that taking money from the Saudis for such scholarship is in "… the greater good of the Muslim world and particularly Saudi Arabia."[7] In 2007 Vogel retired as the Director of Harvard's Islamic Legal Studies Program which was subsidized by at least $5 million from the Saudis.[8] He occupied an endowed Chair in the program. Its title encapsulates the Saudi attempt to Vaticanize Islam by evoking the idea that the Kaaba 'belongs' to the Royal Family (and Wahhabism): 'The Custodian of the Two Holy Mosques Chair for Islamic Legal Studies.'[9] The Custodian, of course, being the King. What is forgotten is that such titles come and go and has not eternally belonged to the House of Saud. Thus, whether in the West or the Muslim world, recent and contemporary scholarship on Islam has been overtly and subtly skewed towards Wahhabism and the Saudi regime. As an

---

* Khaled Abou El Fadl turned down a $100,000 offer by the Muslim World League to write a book on Islam. See: Foer; 'Moral Hazard', in *New Republic*. 11-18-2002.

analyst puts it "The last places to look for anything critical are Berkeley and Harvard. There is nothing out there on opposition trends in Saudi Arabia. Because even if you aren't getting money, you are trying to get into the game."[10]

Almost all Muslim countries have participated in this game of Islamic money-theism. Pakistan is no exception and in fact can be considered an enthusiastic player. Caught up in larger geopolitics of the 'Great Game' and Afghanistan since the late seventies, governments, scholars and institutions have increasingly been recipients of Saudi largesse and explicitly or implicitly projected and privileged Wahhabism/Salafism at the expense of numerous other types of Islam(s). This 'academic' support spans the *madrassah* to the huge International Islamic University established primarily with Saudi funding. Numerous books remain to be written detailing the social, political, cultural, religious and educational impact of Saudi money and its empowering of Wahhabi inspired versions of Islam in the Muslim world.

The main point here is that, as poststructuralist and especially feminists have argued for decades, all scholarship and the production of knowledge is situated in a field of multiple overt and covert factors which influence authors and subjects. Dismissing everything Western as suspect, this dimension of scholarship remains ignored in Pakistan especially when it comes to writing on/about Islam. By its very nature a detailed analysis of Saudi monetary-theological impact on Pakistani scholarship generally and on Pakistani Islam in particular, is a hazardous undertaking. It is also extremely difficult since it has by now become endemic and institutionalized over four decades. Stories such as those recounted by Khaled Abou El Fadl, and which I have mentioned earlier, are common across the Muslim world where scholars have been handsomely (re)awarded/ supported for affirming the Wahhabist perspective. Those who refuse to submit to theological conformity frequently find themselves without a job, intellectually homeless or in exile. In all instances, at home or abroad, criticism of Saudi Arabia or Wahhabism, more often than not, invites hostility from Muslims and threats of apostasization and death.

The example of privileging Wahhabism/Salafism in scholarship on Islam demonstrates the constitutive implications of such scholarship for Islam and Muslims in general, and one has not even touched upon the question of women and the implications for them, particularly those who are neither Arab nor Wahhabi. Given the intervening decades and the combination of massive wealth and co-optation of elite minds/institutions worldwide, one can only speculate on the long term implications of what is, by now, a huge body of biased, propagandized and discursively loaded 'knowledge' directly or indirectly privileging Wahhabism. It is increasingly present and getting steadily entrenched in universities and libraries across the world. A few decades hence, researchers may well come to the conclusion that the only academically 'kosher', 'true' or 'dominant' Islam is Wahhabism. This scenario seems very possible in places such as Pakistan—the libraries in Harvard and Berkeley will perhaps confirm such 'knowledge'.

Apart from the Saudi-Wahhabist money driven impetus, generally today it is Islam's macho public image that is given prominence in media and scholarship. Such an exclusive focus on the political/ideological and codified aspects of Islamism has its pitfalls, treading as it does a razor's edge. Even when critical, it (in)directly legitimizes, strengthens and ultimately encourages the proponents of extremism at the expense of the less strident, often silent majority. As a whole, between the money-theists and the relentless focus on extremist visions, Islam continues to be publicly and academically constructed along unbalanced lines. This situation has serious intellectual, political and spiritual implications for Muslim men and particularly women. It is no coincidence that Wahhabism and other extremist Islams share a misogynist attitude and an abhorrence of mysticism. Even though it was/is women and the vast majority of the 'masses' who have traditionally been comfortable, 'at home', within mysticism(s).[11]

Mysticism and the Feminine

Mysticism in Islam

According to Amaury de Riencour:

> The massive theological superstructure that Muslim's elaborated during the first three or four centuries following Muhammad's death was a replica of the Christian one, but it never satisfied the Muslim soul: sternly ethical and dryly philosophical, it made no appeal to sentiment, emotion or intuition. So, it was that mysticism soon appeared ... in the guise of Sufism, to enlist the enthusiastic support of the masses, not expressed directly in the increasingly repressed Muslim women, but in the feminine emotionalism of Islamic mysticism ... In the end, Sufism defeated and routed the ulemas.[12]

As the feminine expression of the religious impulse, and as Murata's work—which was discussed in the interlude on Islam's Feminine Dimension—shows, the sapiential and mystical tradition has been long and powerfully present in Islam. Popularly known as Sufism, and its inevitable decay notwithstanding, as Nasr points out, it is still a vast and living tradition.[13] Its strength has frequently been brutally contested, and mystics such as Mansur al-Hallaj and Shahab al-Din Suhrawardi are legendary because of the terrible violence directed at them. To this extent, the Wahhabis/Salafists are not unique. But whatever their claims may be, it is important to note Winter's observation that Sufism is an integral part of Islam, not an esoteric sect.[14]

As scholars like Karen Armstrong[15] and others have pointed out, what we broadly term Sufism today, was the *normative* form of Islam until the end of the Nineteenth Century. As such, people did not see themselves as 'mystics' or 'Sufis' but simply Muslims living in what was/is a vast, multilayered canvas of what I term as a variety of *indigenous* Islam(s). I myself have been raised within this complex and multifaceted religious perspective(s), and am old enough to bear witness to its widespread normative presence and existence in South Asia and elsewhere.

To this extent Abdulwahab Bouhdiba was entirely correct in saying that "[it] cannot be repeated enough. There is no one Muslim society, but a multiplicity of social (and cultural) structures all claiming allegiance to Islam."[16] Or, as Edward Said put it, there are actually "innumerable Islams".[17] And since Sufism reflects the diverse nature of Islam itself, at one level, it is impossible to define this multifaceted phenomenon, for what applies to one Sufi order may not apply to others. Yet, within a vast and nebulous arena having a wide range of styles and expressions, one significant dimension emphasizes the cultural/imaginative such as music, dance, and poetry. Thus, the creative imagination played a major role in ecstatic Sufism all over the Muslim world and was an important part of many regional and local cultures.

From Africa and the Middle East across Central Asia and China to South Asia and Indonesia, there are innumerable places where this expression of ecstatic abandonment has a central place in the Islamic subjectivities of its adherents. This expression is, yet again, just one end of a spectrum, the other being different schools of extremely sophisticated metaphysics such as of the Andalusian Ibn al 'Arabi and the Persian poet and philosopher Jalaluddin Rumi. Both are well-known proponents of the creative imagination and who, till today, inspire and influence the spiritual lives of millions, not only in the Muslim world but also far beyond, including the West. Even though, during their lifetime and over the centuries, Rumi, Ibn Arabi and numerous other mystics, philosophers, poets and theologians were/are periodically branded as heretics by orthodoxy.

Within Islam, the different forms of mysticism incorporate and span their own types of 'high' and 'low' religio-spiritual and epistemological frameworks. Reflecting the inherent diversity of religions, including Islam, Islamic mysticisms also offer(ed) a spiritual-religious *smorgasbord* catering to the spectrum of human capacities, predispositions, and cognitive abilities. Given that, even till today, literacy is still not widespread in the subcontinent, historically it was the multiplicity of mysticisms which provided spiritual sustenance, and hence, the capacities to cope with situations of extreme deprivation that were the lot of the majority. By definition, then, along with the usual theological hairsplitting, religious expression also had a strong component of one aspect or another of popular culture.

Islam's Secret Backbone

By and large, religious mysticism and any ideas/framework associated with it tend to be viewed as academically, analytically, and even religiously suspect. It is also too 'anecdotal', 'subjective', 'not scientific', etc. Hillman's observations on the lack of the initiatic experience in Western culture,[18] implies a paucity of living and widespread Judeo-Christian mystical traditions in the West, which maybe a reason for mysticism's pariah and secondary status. But what is lost sight of is that the mysticisms are exceedingly widespread elsewhere, witness the Hindu, Buddhist and Muslim spiritual universe(s), not to mention the 'religions' of many indigenous peoples and shamanisms. Of course, all these traditions also face inner decay and marginalization by dominant macho perspectives from within each of them. But that is a different order of debate/conflict. In the context of academia and its norms, especially in the light of the rapid deconstruction of the notion of 'religion', there is no reason why the significance and utility, of the discourse(s) labeled as 'mysticism' should remain intellectually ghettoized.

As utilized in this exploration of 'low' or mass Islamism, an idiom/framework derived from Islamic mysticism is, in turn, closely related not only to Jungian ideas but also to some currently important discourses in feminism around issues related to woman, body and knowledge.[19] As a contrapuntal response to the problematics of the Cartesian mind-body split, there are by now, numerous perspectives converging on the body as a central category of analysis. The inherent differences of the male and female body can be seen as related to differing subjectivities and these concepts have been applied to a range of scholarship from literature and social theory to religion and gender. Collectively, they are part of a widening and extending of questions relating to the study of religious phenomena. More importantly, they have rendered:

> ...impossible the disassociation of questions of value and power from questions of knowing. The body as central category has reinforced critiques of assumptions taken as normative since the Enlightenment, especially assumptions regarding universal claims about the nature of reality and the human condition, and claims regarding certainty and objectivity in respect to knowledge.[20]

However, in being a central category of analysis, the body also becomes inseparable from questions of sexuality. As was mentioned earlier, the language of mysticism is deeply similar to aspects of sexuality. Based on contrasting sexual metaphors of the male and female sexual organs, mysticism can thus be considered the 'inner', 'private' and 'hidden' dimension of religion. As the 'feminine' counterpoint to more public, outer, 'masculine', moralistic, codified expressions, the doctrines and practices of mysticism tend to focus more on the *inner* experiential dimension of the Divine, rather than, cerebral *outer* explanation and scriptural dogma. Perhaps this is why much of the modern academic view of mysticism reflects the Cartesian mind-body split, seeing the latter as 'subjective' or 'soft' data as opposed to the 'hard' (phallic) facts of patriarchal historically legitimized texts and codified commentaries. As Jung said: "Rationalistic materialism, an attitude that does not seem at all suspect, is really a psychological countermove to mysticism— that is the secret antagonist to be combated ... they are a psychological pair of opposites, just like atheism and theism."[21]

The external aspects of monotheism can be similarly seen as 'masculine' in the emphasis on an active, self-assertive will, seeing God more in a linear sense of collective history and an uncompromising view of textual revelation. In contrast, as de Reincourt says:

> The feminine nature of mysticism is obvious; the surrender to nature or God, the passive attitude waiting for the spiritual blessing and uplift to ecstasy, essentially quietist, contemplative and resigned ... an expression of femininity as expressed through the feminine side of all human beings.[22]

In its theories and especially initiatic practices, mysticism aims to psychologically 'de-masculinize' consciousness, feminizing it to the extent that heroic-ego attitudes such as mastery, control, action, and a narrow material notion of rationality, must take a back seat to a more receptive-contemplative attitude. "In relation to God, we are all—men and women alike—basically feminine. Macho insights reveal nothing of God."[23] Such religious 'feminization' of the psyche exists across cultures, from the shamanistic religions, to Hinduism, Judaism, Buddhism, Christianity.[24] When it comes to Islam, the name of the religion itself has profound connotations of 'submission', 'surrender.'

Finally, to say that mysticism is the experiential, softer aspect of religion is not to suggest that it is devoid of political and social consciousness. Ample historical evidence suggests, in fact, an undercurrent of a different type of revolutionary religiosity which challenges the political status quo. For example, Joan of Arc or the Muslim martyr Mansur al-Hallaj. Ewing's[25] and particularly Soelle's[26] studies on mysticism and resistance make a strong case for the intertwining of mysticism and political actions, and delineate how mysticism finds its natural expression in striving against all forms of injustice, ecological trauma and global chaos. Like many other women scholars/theologians, Soelle sees the rejection of the experiential as rooted in the trivialization of children and women's experiences. She makes a compelling argument for the relevance of mysticism to common life and its capacity to challenge and upset 'the powers and orders that be'.

Within the Muslim world, tens of millions of individuals remain actively linked to the mystical dimension, prompting Jung to call it Islam's 'secret backbone'.[27] Certainly when it comes to sheer numbers, especially in contexts of overwhelming illiteracy, it is women and the widespread popular spectrum of Sufi Islam that still form the 'body'/backbone of the religion rather than the official, dogmatic, scriptural/textual facades, and commentaries devoted to theological hairsplitting. Even contexts of high literacy have solid intellectual traditions within Islamic mysticism(s). But given the general level of poverty and illiteracy in the Islamic world, it is unlikely that these texts form the basis of large scale praxis or comprehension. Nevertheless, for those familiar with both the elite and popular forms of mysticism in Islam, its breadth and scale is undeniable. With reference to women, Schimmel's observations not only highlight the changes of the last century but remain valid until today:

It is remarkable that in modern times Sufi teaching is, to a large extent, carried on by women again. Not only does the interest in the mystical path—modernized as it may be—apparently appeal to women, but some of the most genuine representatives of mystical tradition, 'directors of the soul', in Istanbul and Delhi (and probably in other places as well) are women.[28]

CHAPTER 7:
THE DESTRUCTION
OF ISLAM'S FEMININE DIMENSION

So go before the teachers of conventional knowledge, busy
yourself with jurisprudence and become a master of the science
of "This is permitted and that is forbidden" … By the time
intellect has found a camel for the hajj, love has circled the
Kaaba.
(Jelaluddin Rumi[1])

Non/Literacy, Drugs and Mania

Most analyses of the literalist and violent tendencies in 'low' or mass Islamism inevitably relate them to poverty and lack of modern education. However, one should not forget that as a general state of affairs, these factors have been widely prevalent for centuries. Yet, there has rarely been such a culture of widespread violence and bigotry in the past, as is evident today, for example, across almost all strata of Pakistani society. The modern explanation for linking religious extremism to poverty is, of course, because religion is seen as an 'opiate' of the poor. Setting aside the Marxist denigration of religion-as-drug, and taking as we are, the indelible reality and necessity of religion for providing meaning beyond material life; in this context poverty and illiteracy per se, are not the issue. Which is not the same as saying that the socio-economic status quo is fine in Pakistan. Particularly in view of the psycho-theology of educated 'high' Islamist violence, the idea here is to discuss how the socio-economic-educational diagnosis is inadequate in terms of both explanation and prescriptive policy.

Underlying the use of the term 'opiate' is the idea of a blanking out of all consciousness. Today, however, the clinical view of drug taking (licit and illicit) refers more to the idea of the desire for an 'altered state(s) of consciousness'. The burgeoning, global psycho-pharmaceutical industry self-evidently points to this human desire and simultaneously highlights the psychological toll of modernity through prevalent norms for 'normal' consciousness. Strictly speaking, the opiates offer one end of a spectrum, in this context, basically the pole of *unconsciousness*.

The attribution of such a vacuous state to religion as it has existed in the lives of the vast majority of humanity is untenable simply on the basis of cultural and civilizational evidence such as architecture, art and poetry inspired by religion. The relationship between socio-economics, religion and (non)violence, then, is deeply related to culture as a manifestation of the condition of its sacred and creative imagination, as is most evident in its various mystical expressions. The modern undermining, weakening and obliterated absence of these positive cultural dimensions, existing as they had for centuries, are a key factor in the widespread appearance of 'low' Islamism.

This is not to suggest that, prior to partition, Islam in the subcontinent was just a conglomeration of peaceful Sufi communities. All religions contain within them schisms, 'heresies' and sects, reflecting ultimately, the psychological diversity of their adherents *and* a Providence equally responsive to Its creative aspect of infinite possibilities. Given the inevitable reality of earthly decay and (possible) renewal, internal differences within religion not only enable spiritual pluralism but also a certain continuity of a religion as a whole. To this extent, there have always been severe, extremist and violent perspectives in Islam and even within Sufism. But, as was discussed in Part I and II, the problem arises when one vision attempts/manages to overwhelm all others and create a 'monotheism of consciousness'.

Along with a range of more diffused, culturally hybrid expressions of Islam, the creative imagination existed in numerous theologically 'softer' Sufi *silsilahs*. There is no doubt that many of these orders have themselves decayed internally and continue to do so. Nevertheless, as a whole, they ensured that, in spite of low levels of literacy/education, the popular and intellectual imagination was, even at a minimal level, free and active in terms of dance, poetry and other spiritual-cultural expressions. Their present marginalization/decay has led to a condition whereby the gentle haze of a moderate 'opiate'-induced altered state, has been replaced, so to speak, by an amphetamine induced macho-mania that is inevitably part of modern life. This is further fueled by a prematurely administered dose of a testosterone driven, hyper-macho Islam. The bulk of 'low' Islamists, let us not forget, are young males. Untethered from its earlier 'opiates', the sheer physical energy of that age propels it towards a sort of adrenaline-amphetamine induced 'high', in which externally eyes are wide open, but internally/psychologically, shut.

To some, this 'mania' of the 'low' Islamists might look like a form of 'hysteria', but in a sociological, theological and psychological sense it has little to do with the 'hysteria' which their (grand)mothers or (grand)fathers sometimes experienced (as trance, etc.) in certain places of worship, during pilgrimages or at religious festivals. The energetic and macho 'mania' of the 'low' Islamists is a form of unfettered masculinity, while forms of spiritual 'hysteria' are closely linked with the feminine and mystical side of Islam.

Religious Hysteria

As was mentioned in Chapter 2, hysteria has a special place in the annals of Western psychology and the emergence of psycho-analysis as a method for treatment. It was the first dis-ease to be 'discovered' and as such became the gateway to the concept of the unconscious. Literally, it means 'the wandering uterus/womb' and the behavioural extremes, from screaming and 'being out of control', to trance like states, have come to be universally associated with women. More often than not, the diagnosis of these behavioural extremes are seen as the 'conversion' of the sexual impulse and the patient seen as dishonest, manipulative, infantile and basically sexually 'frustrated'.

Within the symbolic narrative of the 'ascent of the Hero', the epidemic of hysteria that surfaced in Europe during the late 19th and early 20th Century was a psycho-cultural response to the long and often violent repression of the inherent diversity of the psyche, including its feminine dimensions of, by then, 'modern' Western consciousness. Thus, following hysteria (the feminine), the next 'disease' to be 'discovered' was schizophrenia or 'multiple personality' (diversity).

Pathologizing the feminine aspect of the psyche with the label of 'hysteria' in the West should not be confused with seeing a particular constellation of behaviours which have existed around women in different cultures from ancient times to the present. In the West, 'hysteria' can be traced to the mists of the ancient past in descriptions of women's mysteries around the cult of Dionysus, the god who represents the counterpart to Apollo. While even Hippocrates and Plato viewed hysteria with negative connotations of female inferiority, its close associations with Dionysus and therefore, spirituality and religion, remained. As such it was not considered a mental illness in the ancient world.

Tracing the psycho-religious history of hysteria in the West, Hillman has documented how in medieval times hysteria was seen as fundamentally religious, having to do with a crisis of faith. As he says, "'hysteric and witch' never lost their close association"[2]. From viewing women as religiously inferior—the witch had to be saved by God—the diagnosis of hysteria underwent many transformations but was always linked to female inferiority. By the 19th Century it was regarded as a weakness of women's reproductive organs, such as the ovaries and uterus. By the time Freud came along "the witch is now a poor patient—not evil but sick"[3], now no longer in the ovaries/uterus but in her head. Freud's mentor Kraeplin, whose textbook on psychiatry was seminal to the discipline till well into the 20th Century, continued "the great misogynist tradition" in which the description of hysteria "still echoes the description of the witch."[4]

The ancient connections between women's mysteries and the cult of Dionysus, and their subsequent negativization as 'pathology' suggests how one is dealing with two very different cognitive and spiritual styles. The Apollonic and Dionysian, as worldviews and analytic categories, are commonly used concepts but rarely in terms of their sexual and spiritual connotations. As compared to Apollo's beautiful masculine form, Dionysus has, among his many images, some very unattractive ones, both in physique or predispositions: wine, women, the *bacchanal* etc. (The root image perhaps for the phrase 'wine, women and song'.) While the orgies and other excesses associated with this rather decadent god may be coming from the Apollonian gaze, they nevertheless suggest a certain sensual abandon and general disregard for the 'establishment' (religious and political).[5] More importantly, he is bisexual, not as the feminine element added on to a male, rather, he is born androgynous. As a bisexual archetype, Dionysus is the force behind both masochism and hysteria, representing an androgynous consciousness and an 'image' that is a primordial unity of feminine and masculine. Interestingly, many millennia later, Freud could not help but observe that "an hysterical symptom is the expression of both masculine and feminine unconscious sexual fantasy."[6]

Given the recurring theme of the hermaphrodite and Divine 'Androgyny' in so many religions, including Islam, hysteria in women can be seen, either as a psychological attempt to transcend what are culturally imposed divisions of this intuitively perceived androgyny, or then, more often, manifesting a particular state of 'intoxication' when this trance-ascendant Unity is experienced. In short, the Freudian 'cathexes seeking discharge' can be primarily spiritual and manifesting a sexual counterpoint. It can also simply be a deep rage at life-as-woman in certain hyper-patriarchal cultures.

That these 'symptoms' have more to do with religion is evident in the sheer frequency with which they occur at religious locations. The images of women (and men) in what would be labelled as a state of 'hysteria' at shrines, is a common one in the Islamic world—certainly in India and Pakistan. Frequently accompanied by powerful rhythmic music, these trance like states are a regular phenomenon epitomized in the 'mad' man (or woman) known as the '*qalandar*' in Sufi Islam; and who in folklore and the real world, is frequently both rebellious and saintly.[7] Even if purely 'secular' frustration and rage is being expressed, such locations seem safer in which one can 'let go'. Not surprisingly then, one of Dionysus' many names was 'the Loosener' (of bondage).

All of this is not to suggest that women in Islam literally worship Dionysus in this state. Rather, it is to point to the psychological similarities of these themes across cultures and centuries. In the ancient Islamic world, hysteria was not regarded as a mental sickness. As pointed out by Dols, "hysteria is not found among the maladies of the head in Arabic compendia of medicine."[8] Following Galen, Ibn Sina (Avicenna) saw hysteria as *ikhtināq ar-raham*, the constriction or suffocation of the womb.[9]

It should be kept in mind that 'hysteria' is actually a vast behavioural spectrum in reality difficult to diagnose or treat and one is speaking here in terms of broad generalizations. But such mythic-poetic connections are important for not only manifesting the spiritual urge towards experiencing a trance-ascendent Unity, but also as a mode of resistance to established social norms about women, sexuality and religion. Some other names of Dionysus thus include 'The Dancer and Ecstatic Lover', 'The Liberator' and 'The Deliverer'.

These connections between women, sexuality and religion, certainly in the Islamic context, can only be fathomed within a framework of its psycho-spiritual poetics, and outside of pernicious epistemologies which dominate our understanding about these matters. As was explained in the previous chapter, the differing views on the sexual and spiritual, the concept (and reality) of functions such as desire, the specific Islamic history, the different theological discourses etc. render this an extremely complex area. It is made even more complex by modern masculinist attitudes, which, having firstly obfuscated the issues, then wants simple answers. The latter becomes evident every day in a country like Pakistan. Though the more fluid, hybrid and 'Dionysan' dimension of Islam was strongly present for centuries (and in many places still is), Cartesian-Christianist-Islamism has thoroughly penetrated all matters of religion, identity, politics etc. collectively besieging the Feminine.

The Hyper-masculinity of an Islamic State

As a literal embodiment of a 'monotheism of consciousness', almost from its inception the Pakistani state has had to confront questions of religious identity-politics.[10] And whereas questions of gender per se may not have been prominent in the construction of national identity, the emergent profile—and the status of its women—indicate its largely negative and hyper-masculine nature. Masculinity in Pakistan today has less to do with the visions and teachings of Islam (or of the secular founder, Jinnah) but more with literalism and the pursuit of heroic-patriarchal power agendas in the name of Islam.[11]

With the advent of the modern state which chose to promote orthodoxy for its own gains, Islam was given an 'official' composite face: one part consisting of a professionalized *ulema*/priesthood; the other, a by now thoroughly 'Islamized' military. Additionally, both created/promoted a false religio-cultural narrative of an Arabized Islam at the expense of an all embracing Indo-Persian Islam which had existed for centuries prior to the creation of Pakistan. This cross-pollination of Persian/Indian/Hindu culture had led to a unique indigenous Islam which many consider to be the 'jewel in the crown' of numerous Islams. By now, this composite of militarist machismo and *ulemasculinized* theology of a culturally barren Arabized Islam has been fully assimilated into the collective psyche of numerous extremist groups and also large segments of 'civil society'.

The steady, state sponsored empowerment and ideological convergence of various hyper-masculine perspectives (Wahhabi-Salafi-Deobandi), have a singular vision of the Divine: a terrifying, monolithic (rather than monotheistic) God, sans all Attributes except those that service goals of brute power. In tandem with the marginalizing as well as internal decay of the mysticisms, the ascendance of this singular vision ensured a steady repression of different and diverse expressions of Islam. The role of Saudi money-theism in further accelerating cultural erosion has been noted earlier. As a whole, a self-reflexive, self-perpetuating movement gained momentum, and continues aiming at making a monolith of a tradition that has historically and theo-culturally, been exceedingly diverse.

The narrowing of Pakistani/South Asian/Indo Persian Islam's cultural spectrum and a corresponding increase in religious bigotry, has come about due to the steady ascendance of a masculinist vision and dominance of a particular 'malestream' Islam which will not tolerate anything different from itself. Thus, for example, whereas the impulse to hereticize difference is one thing, to institutionalize it through the Constitution of the nation-state, is another. Violence against the perceived 'heretic' becomes sanctioned by the nation-state itself.

As pointed out in Chapter 3, this is what happened in the case of the Ahmadi *silsilah* and it being constitutionally declared 'non-Muslim' in Pakistan. In view of the problematics around even defining Islam as a religion,[12] and what Edward Said has referred to as its (Islam's) "basic resistance to reductive formulas,"[13] after 1500 hundred years the modern nation-state finally managed to 'define' a Muslim. Thus, in Pakistan, Islam as a faith is no longer the affirmation of God and the Prophet as his messenger but in the *denial and denigration* of a particular community/individual.* This theocratic move by the state enshrined in the constitution more than forty years ago, evoked scant intellectual resistance from the Muslims inside and outside of Pakistan. The legislation was inspired by both religious and secular 'high' fundamentalists such as the Berkley/Oxford educated prime-minister Z.A. Bhutto, who was himself a secular socialist.

The heriticization of the Ahmadi sect also illustrates the heroic, modern-rationalist tendency discussed in Chapter 3 of seeing life as a series of 'problems' in need of 'solutions'. Frequently, the 'problem' is about difference(s) as perceived from the position of the dominant ego/group. Instead of seeing diversity/difference as actually a routine difficulty, which has to be tolerated and coped with, once the problem/solution formula is applied, it can only generate more serious problems. This is what happened after the Ahmadi's were hereticized in 1974. By now, large scale violence and accusations of heresy/'being not-Muslim' regarding many other minorities have become part of daily life. A study of one such sect indicates, that the prominence given to the Feminine, through either text, ritual, doctrine, interpretation, along with a generally positive status of women in these communities, is what evokes violence towards them through the accusation of 'heresy'.[14]

---

* For example, as was already explained in Chapter 3, a Pakistani Muslim cannot obtain a passport or identity card unless s/he signs a declaration stating that the founder of the Ahmadiyya sect was an 'imposter' and that his followers are non-Muslim. All individuals claiming to be Muslim must first sign this statement before being eligible for a passport. For the legal human rights implications, see p. 126 and following.

Hereticization of Feminine Islam

As pointed earlier, terms such as canon, dogma, creed, heresy etc. are derived from Pauline Christianity. There are no precise equivalents in other religions, partly because no other religion has had the strong, centralized institutions which began emerging in Christianity around 300 AD. This is not to say that other religions did not have internal dissent or sects which were considered 'deviant' and worthy of persecution by others. The difference is of scale/ratio, particularly large, centralized, institutionalized authority, which can 'officially' decide to define and execute by force, its own interpretation. Thus, for example, although patriarchy has long prevailed in all religions, there is no parallel regarding the sheer scale and violence of the inquisition, especially the 'witch hunts'.

Regarding heresy—which basically means 'to choose for oneself'—instead of getting entangled into an infinite regress of competing interpretations, ultimately the question is: *whose* hermeneutics and *whose* interpretation? It is therefore more fruitful to ask not what heresy *is*, but what it *does* in a particular context in terms of being situated within a religion, as well as its relationship to other traditions. It has been suggested that the 'heretic' tends to have a larger, more inclusive vision of his/her religion, crossing so to speak, malestream boundaries set out by the professional theologian.[15] Frequently, in the face of persecution, the heretical crossing of boundaries is also cultural and geographic. Affirming as it does the inner and outer diversities of religious consciousness, the hybrid nature of heresy makes it a cross-cultural pollinator of civilizations.[16]

Jung's metaphor of Islam's 'secret mystical backbone' encapsulates the idea of distinct yet interconnected elements, *all* of which are necessary for upholding the 'body' of Islam. Hereticizing, ignoring, stifling and marginalizing its more mystical-radical expressions is not only to repress (and oppress) the Feminine dimension, but to also steadily erase the magnificent rainbow of the Creative Imagination that is its mystical tradition(s). The result is what has been described as the "monochromatic bigotry of modern Islam."[17]

As was explained in the introduction, according to Jung, the main tragedy of Christianity was the loss of its mysticisms. By now, there is ample evidence that this was indeed the case. For example, the work of Elaine Pagels clearly shows how in the earliest stages of Christianity, the 'woman friendly' Gnostic Gospels emphasizing the subjective/experiential were de-legitimized, excised and eventually forgotten.[18] The subsequent steady decline of mysticism with its emphasis on individual subjectivity, was accompanied by the consolidation of patriarchal, centralized, hierarchical institutions. By the 16th Century whatever traces remained of mysticism were obliterated.

Today, a similar momentum is prevailing within Islam. Between Cartesian-Christianist modernity and the monolithic Saudi-Salafi theo-cultural bulldozer, the psycho-cultural-spiritual diversity of Islam is being steadily obliterated. This is a disaster for any natural phenomenon, and religion is no exception. All religions are languages of the soul, and like all languages, have numerous dialects and accents. Today, this idea has its literal counterpart in the notion that all Muslims must 'speak' with just *one accent*, in *one dialect*, namely Salafi Islam— even though 85% of more than a billion Muslims are not Arabs. If this momentum continues, it will eventually result in the extinction of 85% of the Islamic spiritual/cultural kaleidoscope.*

---

* This is most evident in the outer, performative aspect of hijab, historically a cross-cultural, colourful, multi-styled expression of female sartorial 'modesty'. The black/white canvas of Saudi female/male attire is symbolic of the monochromatic mind.

Given the vast and shifting spectrum of Islam, what is required are frameworks that can accommodate all its colours and shades, not hypermasculine macho exclusionary ones.

In short, between the 'high' Islamism of the nation-state and its theo-cultural nihilism, along with an abdication of intellectual responsibility/interest that could have stemmed and rejuvenated the decaying *silsilahs*, Islam's spiritual 'backbone' has been severely damaged—not only in Pakistan but thanks to the power of Saudi money-theism, across the entire Muslim world. As a whole, the Feminine has receded, virtually vanished/banished from Muslim religious consciousness.

CHAPTER 8:
THE TERROR WITHIN

No one who does not know himself can know others and in each
of us is another whom we don't know.
(C.G. Jung[1])

'Low' Islamism and the Absence of Education

The previous chapters have attempted to set out a range of broad issues which will now allow a more detailed analysis of 'low' Islamism. As should be clear by now, modern secular consciousness, particularly science, traps women and their sexuality through masculinist ideals and the machismo underlying modernity is a mirror image of the misogyny underlying religious fundamentalism. Both modernity and fundamentalism can be said to reflect a fear of the Feminine which has been relegated into the unconscious. Rather than integrating the Feminine into individual and collective theological and spiritual consciousness, it has become wholly the 'Other'. Thus, by re-visioning the Feminine within Islam and describing its destruction, I have tried to sketch an analytic frame from within Islam and Jungian psychology that will now allow us to approach the (psychological) realities of 'low' Islamism.

In view of the critique of modernity and trying to understand the psychology of those deprived of modern schooling, the question becomes, like so much else in life, of having to choose between the lesser of two evils. History in any case cannot reversed. Thus, in the absence/erosion of compensatory cultural factors, the childhood rite of passage to a 'modern' school is the only way left for the young psyche and its need for developmental pathways, not to mention acquisition of skills for livelihood. Keep in mind that the main purpose of the rite is the development of reason/rationality through exposure to experiences relevant to the emergence and cultivation of abstract concepts. At the very least, well-developed literacy provides the *possibility* of a modicum of *logos* to come into consciousness, and may be an exposure to ideas other than extreme Islamism. To this extent, modernizers are correct about the necessity for education that assists in developing rational thought, including science. One's opposition, in any case, is not to rationality and science per se, but to the denial/denigration of the symbolic and creative imagination in (Muslim) modernity. *All* of these are absent in the *madrassah*.

Absence of Eros and Logos

Vast numbers of poverty stricken parents send their young boys to *madrassahs*, lured not just by simplistic ideas of 'education', but more importantly, to be relieved of having one less mouth to feed. Trapped between globalizing modernity and an obliterated/vanishing local culture, male rites of passage that are utterly vital for psychological (self)development become distorted. What is psychologically even more serious is that this vestigial shadow of the rite is merged/conflated with other stages of development which would normally occur much later in life, especially those related with religion. Thus comes the premature psychological encounter at an exceedingly young age with an abstract, enormous and complex concept like 'God'. Literally and brutally *enforced*, it is inevitably mediated by someone who is, by now, himself a product of this super-speeded-up psychological and cognitive 'development'.

The 'education' starts with the foundations of *logos* in language and its building blocks, the alphabet. As research (and personal observation) on literacy primers used in the *madrassah's* show, the phonetics of each letter are accompanied by corresponding images of weapons and their names that begin with the same letter, such as tanks, guns, swords, daggers, bomber aircraft. The United States Agency for International Development distributed $13 million worth of textbooks in Pakistani *madrassahs* where students learned basic arithmetic by counting dead Russian soldiers and AK-47 rifles.[2]

Coupled with a banning of art and music,[3] the combined impact of this 'education' leads to a psyche that can know nothing else but violence and hatred, setting the stage for what is clinically called the persecutory paranoia of adulthood.

As contextualized in the critique of science and modernity, 'high' Islamism has an overly developed *logos*, leading to literalist reductionism and denial of all that is different not only externally but more crucially, inwardly. What is repressed primarily are the feminine dimensions resulting in the psychological absence of *eros*. As a function of relatedness, *eros* has to do with a sensitivity to the interconnectedness of life which requires emotionally nurturing capacities developed over time. In contrast to the logocentric high ideologue, the 'low' Islamist faces a psychological double jeopardy: youth and poverty ensure that *logos* remains undeveloped. A culturally eroded spiritual environment along with extreme economic conditions, ensures that the feminine remains inaccessible. Hence *both logos and eros* remain absent/undeveloped.

The absence of the Feminine in 'low' *and* 'high' Islamist religiosity means the absence of Divine ('Feminine') Attributes such as Beauty, Mercy, Compassion, Graciousness, Love, Indulgence, Peace, to name a few. But as a collective 'image', it is the Taliban who become a living symbol of what happens in the absence of the Feminine in psycho-cultural-theological consciousness.

For something to be symbolically true, somewhere it must be literally so. This is in the nature of that which is Immutable, whether or not we 'hear'/'see' or sense what the symbolic is communicating. In short, the literal remains, literally. The absent Feminine in Taliban consciousness, one can note, is self-reflexively related to a *literal* absence of the *experience* of females in the individual lives of many Taliban. As a result of the first Afghan War, starting in the eighties and which in many ways is still ongoing, large numbers of Afghan children were abandoned and/or orphaned in an unimaginably harsh, war torn and poverty stricken environment. Raised in all-male seminaries, the vast majority of Taliban did not have even the most *basic* exposure to women,[4] something which most human beings universally have at a young age. Even in the most segregated environments, young males encounter a degree of intimacy with females such as mother, sister, aunt, grandmother etc. None of these were part of the Taliban's orphanage-*madrassah* environment. In short, for thousands of young males, Woman/the Feminine became wholly 'Other'.

Whereas the rational function of *logos* can be considered a socio-cultural acquisition, the experience of emotional connectedness is simply part of natural life, like the ground

222

beneath our feet. However minimal or rocky, as in situations of poverty, it is still there and we simply take it for granted. One does not need to cite research evidence to know with certainty that children need care and love. This sense of caring and connectedness is *eros*, which in its most fundamental sense, is Life itself. Whereas Freud narrowed his view of it to focus only on the sexual, the deeper and wider meaning becomes evident in light of the principle of *Thanatos*, death, which is the Freudian postulate for the opposite of *eros*. In the absence of *eros*, physical life mutates into something else.

In situations of mass and prolonged violence and the absence of both *eros* and *logos*, once this type of psycho-cultural mutation occurs on a disproportionate and large scale, as it did over more than two decades in Afghanistan, it self-reflexively perpetuates itself through large-scale violence.

'Low' Islamism's Persecutory Paranoia

'Low' Islamism's double jeopardy, and factors of poverty, age, absence of parents and the experience of violence at a young age, starkly distinguish it from the high Islamist's background. Whereas the eventual outcome in terms of their violence and misogyny are broadly similar, there are nevertheless, differences of style. Putting it clinically, there may be a differential diagnosis of paranoia.

Adequate psychosexual development requires, above all, a situation of what Erikson called 'basic trust'.[5] Whereas paranoia as related to homosexuality may be developed (according to Freud) because of confusions linked to the Oedipal/parental context, the significance of other, trust related factors remain the crucial matrix for healthy psychological development. They have to do with what much of humanity takes for granted in the context of childhood/childrearing and an age when a child's physical survival depends on consistently reliable adult behavior. Young children need to believe that people in general are well disposed towards them, or at the very least do not actively want to harm them. Similarly, routine activities, such as having food and sleeping, need to occur regularly, at a minimal level, without a child feeling it necessary to take the most elementary precautions against being injured or destroyed.[6]

To this extent, mass Islamism has less to do with intellectual and cognitive capacities and more with the socio-cultural-economic environment. As studies on paranoia show, either as infants and/or young children, such individuals were not given the 'usual opportunities as infants to develop basic trust'; they lived through a childhood in which significant persons proved undependable, outright rejecting or simply disappeared or died. Consequently, "adults who develop the common persecutory form (of paranoia), almost uniformly consider themselves incapable of loving and being loved."[7] It has also been noted, that "adults who develop paranoid reactions under stress have not been able to form or have not been given the necessary intimate close relationship with a loving mother or mother substitute."[8]

The formative years of the Taliban in Afghanistan during more than two decades of a relentless and brutal state of war, and in many ways similar socio-economics of *madrassah* inmates across Pakistan, can be strongly related to an ultimately psychological experience of a 'basic trust deficiency'. Persecutory paranoia is especially related to such psychological situations, marked as it is by a deep mistrust of others and a strong tendency to deny one's own hostility which is characteristically projected onto others. There is thus, a seamless and self-perpetuating connection between the initial internalizing of a genuinely hostile environment and an externalizing of this hostility onto the world.

Given the feminine void in the socializing of these young males, by the time they reach early puberty, violent and misogynist attitudes have become part of the emergent persecutory paranoia. For example, in a poem from a *madrassah* textbook about a 'Brave Child', a ten-year-old boy kills hundreds of Russians in Afghanistan. As part of a seventh grade text, a 'letter' from a boy to his mother and sister says "If I am killed in battle, celebrate... make sure you conceal your body and never wear perfume."[9] Such statements are chillingly close to 'high' Islamists such as Mohamed Atta. As discussed in Chapter 6, he too was a consequence of speeded up rites of passage. In spite of differing psychodynamics, the emergent psyche is of a terrorist.

The enormous void of basic trust then, is the heart of the matter in persecutory paranoia, which, in such a context, has nothing to do with initial delusion. In the face of an exclusive and relentlessly inflicted violence by the adult world, the only route to survival is to perpetually remain alert to its danger. As adults, eventually, "these relatively infantile defenses take over and become predominant."[10] Finally, recent studies reinforce and confirm the link between child neglect/abuse and political consequences. Early and prolonged exposure to an environment saturated with uncertainty, fear and pain can lead to breakdown, which can only be avoided by repressing these experiences. As adults, they are then unconsciously driven to reproduce these repressed scenes over and over again in the (false) hope of liberating themselves from these memories. Thus, victims create situations in which they can assume the active role in order to master the feelings of helplessness and its attendant anxieties.[11]

Cultural Vandalism (Part 2)

Inspired and financially supported by the high ideologue, 'low' or mass Islamism flourishes in a fragmented culturescape. Both types share behaviors, particularly in terms of the body as it becomes the locus of a wholly externalized view of God. There is an enormous emphasis on physical, outer aspects, such as beards, veils, clothing and headdress. During the sixties and seventies, there was scant visual evidence to link appearance with religious practice. Which is not to say that there were fewer devout Muslims across the socio-economic spectrum. Social networks of any individual would confirm knowing persons who, even after a life time of concerted prayer, rarely carried the 'mark' of prostration(s) on the forehead, even in old age. That is, in spite of doing tens of thousands (and more) of prostrations required in carrying out the daily prayers, the darkening/hardening of the skin at the point of contact between the forehead and the ground started becoming visible, if at all, during old age. Today this literal 'mark' of devotion is common, not only on sundry televangelists, but also among many born again Muslims, sometimes within weeks/months of his 'rebirth'. Experience and common sense indicates that this mark usually appears after a lifetime of prayer unless the devotee is actively seeking out ways to accelerate the process. Often this is achieved by exerting inordinate pressure on the forehead against hard straw mats.

There is an extraordinary preoccupation with the body and bodily taboos which function more as obsession-compulsions. Psychologically this syndrome is related to the anal personality whose hallmarks are pedantry, parsimony and petulance and an overwhelming desire to control others. Hence, a compulsive preoccupation with the body and similar paranoid obsessions around women's bodies and what a woman can/cannot do as sanctioned on the grounds that 'it is our culture/religion'.

In recent years, easing of restrictions on private media have led to a boom of television channels catering to a broad spectrum of spiritual seekers. Most of these channels promote a hardline Islam. While due lip service is paid to women's rights it is invariably in a restrictive manner, justified through the need to 'respect' and 'protect' women. The only woman to have had a show to herself appears in full Saudi style hijab. Apart from the voice, there is really no way of ascertaining the gender. In contrast, the spectrum of male apparel is more diverse. Apart from Western trousers and/or jackets and the Pakistani/South Asian *shalwar-kamiz*, there are peculiar hybrids which combine the Arab robe with a variety of caps, turbans never seen before in Pakistan or India. Certainly, in comparison to the somber black of the veiled women, the male presenters are far more colourful suggesting, perhaps, an atavistic dimension of the male species and its 'performative' contingencies in the evolutionary mating battle.

The content of these myriad programs is quite similar to the fire and brimstone of Western televangelists. Most are in Urdu but one of the most popular channels is in English, Peace TV. Ostensibly devoted to rationality and logic, and its name notwithstanding, the primary aim of its widely popular founder (the previously mentioned televangelist Zakir Naik) is to demonstrate how every other religion is inferior to Islam. As a whole, Islamic televangelism has contributed in creating a mindset that is more intent on the particularities of *halal/haram* (permissible/forbidden) and on generating guilt, rather than a spirituality that is contextually lived. Thanks to the globalization of the media such televangelism is no longer restricted to Muslim countries such as Pakistan but is increasingly available to the Muslim Diaspora. Interestingly, the more shrewd and sophisticated of these Muslim televangelist follow their

American counterparts in entrepreneurial skills offering products such as tapes, CD's, etc.

Between the television and the mosque amplifiers, the senses are assaulted by an audio-visual aesthetic terrorism. Home is no longer safe. Just when some are seeking an 'altered state' of consciousness through quiet contemplation, or others attempt to escape into chemically assisted oblivion; the ear is assaulted by a terror that is relentless in its regularity: the sound of mega-amplified, screeching, pre-pubescent voices of young males, and/or the blood curdling howls of those masquerading as *muezzins*. Once considered an art form that took years to cultivate, today one simply recoils at the call to prayer as made from the ubiquitous mosque.

Outside the homes, it's no better—witness the polluted, decaying, filth-filled cities. This literal garbage is then literally presented in different ways as 'art' by those who think it is somehow post-modern and profound to confront a viewer with what may not be so visible in the West, but is self-evident and literally present on a large scale in Pakistan. But one is digressing here into the psycho-cultural domain of 'high' artistic/liberal fundamentalism which requires a full-fledged analysis on its own, particularly regarding its masochistic tendencies vis-à-vis the creative imagination.

The Hero's Shadow

For the Jungian psychologist, the psyche is both personal and collective including the archetypes of 'ego' and 'shadow'. If the former stands for reason and willpower, the latter provides a balance consisting of our dark side, of inferior, uncivilized, almost animal-like traits. At the collective level, as in the individual personality, ego and shadow are inseparable.

The ego is closely linked to the archetype of the Hero. To repeat what was explained in Part I: it is a universal mytheme about a young male in search of an elusive treasure, and the trials and battles he endures in the quest for victory after which he is acknowledged as the Ruler and Law Giver. However, either because of *hubris* (arrogance) or the fact of mortality, he ultimately suffers a 'fall' and dies. The Heroic Quest represents the emergence of the psychological faculties of willpower and reason and the transition from adolescence to responsible adulthood. But, according to Jung, the Western manifestation of this motif indicates a fixation with power and violence and a refusal to move towards a more mature and complex sense of identity. Instead of seeing the Quest as a rite of passage and a symbol of a process eventually leading to wisdom, of becoming homo-sapiens ('man of wisdom'); the adolescent hero's quest becomes an end in itself culminating in brute assertion of power as sanctioned by a virulent and narrow idea of reason (techno-science).

In contrast to the ego, the shadow frequently remains unconscious since it is socially unacceptable. The more unconscious it is, the greater the tendency for the heroic ego to become inflated, making the individual or group believe that he/they are god-like, all good and powerful. The (unconscious) shadow is then projected onto others, identifying them as inferior and evil. At an international level, the current impasse between the West and Islamism can be seen as a mutual projection of their collective shadow(s). Since the West has a long history of internal critique, Jung being just one example, it is best to take a look at one's own (Islamic) shadow. Not only as it mirrors the West's trigger-happy, macho ethos, but also what it is saying about the state of masculinity in Pakistan as exemplified by an increasing number of young males enthralled by religion.

This is not about male bashing. As an illustration of archetype and counter-archetype, take the example of the barely clothed or naked female. It is an image that is endlessly encountered by the Western/global gaze particularly via the media. But its countervail (so to speak)—the hijab—is also increasingly visible. Here, I am not discussing the individual as stereotype, but the Jungian idea that the psyche's collective dimensions can be inferred from the widespread prevalence of certain images and ideas which, unlike stereotypes, carry a certain emotional 'charge'. Topics such as religion and the 'place' of women elicit intense views and feelings for or against and today this is so in both Islam and the West with reference to women and the hijab. This is an indication of the problematics of *both* protagonists as they mirror their differing styles of what nevertheless is a shared misogyny. In short, as 'imaged' in modernity, the Feminine archetypes of Love, Compassion, Beauty, to name a few, recede in psycho-theological consciousness. What prevails in such a lopsided psycho-cultural individual and collective universe is a grim, undiluted hypermasculinity as exemplified in the archetype of the conquering Hero.

In Pakistan, the archetype of the Hero's Shadow is evident not only in the relative invisibility of women but more so in the demographics of a steadily increasing population of young males, brought about principally by the widespread presence of technologies that either increase the chances of bearing sons or facilitate early aborting of the female fetus.* Even in the best of circumstances, young males are more responsive to the physical and external, inherently passionate and volatile, raging hormones and all. Between widespread poverty and inadequate systems to channelize this volatility (school/university, sports, etc.), huge numbers of testosterone driven males are finding refuge in an idea of religion in which weapons become an erotic

---

* Since 1980, male-female ratios have been 1.08 and the gap is increasing.

substitute for a need which, it seems, can only be fulfilled in the hereafter, preferably with a *houri*. As was mentioned, the fusion of unacknowledged sexual energy and violence leads to a condition which Western feminists call phallogocentrism. In the self-destructive context of Pakistan we could call it *ewrecktionism*.

In an atmosphere of cultural nihilism and the suppression of anything close to the idea of pleasure, fun and laughter, ewrecktionist terrorism prevails, not only in the periodic blood baths of sectarian politics but at all levels of life. For example, decreeing as 'un-Islamic' events such as kite flying festivals (*basant*) which are ancient rites of spring, a symbol of renewed (Feminine) fecundity. Celebrated with joy, color and abandon for centuries in South-Asia, including Pakistan, until the nineties, the festival is now banned and finished. Similarly, there are continuing and violent attempts at suppression of more modern ritual events like the New Year celebrations. Either way, the state of the Pakistani psyche—secular or Islamist—seems to be in deep distress if not outright depression with very little by way of comic relief. No wonder, a worldwide survey of happiness refers to "troubled Pakistan" being "near the bottom at 4.3" on a happiness scale of one to ten.[12]

A Collective Crisis of Masculinity, Religion, Sexuality and Love

The prevalence of pedophilia among those men who have adopted religion as a profession in Pakistan is not unlike its occurrence in the Catholic Church in Europe and the U.S. In a way, both point to a similar psychological malaise of an exclusivist hypermasculinism. However, differing injunctions about religious celibacy, but especially his inherent paranoia, impel the mass Islamist to demonstrate his 'masculinity' vis-à-vis women in the most macho ways, verging on the grotesque. Beyond the obvious socially negative attitudes towards women, extreme individual pathology becomes symptomatic of a collective, misogynist, paranoid, religiously rooted, psychosexual syndrome. In 1994, an *imam* of a mosque brutalized his young wife by first placing iron rods in her womb and anus and then subjecting her to electric shocks, leaving her severely burnt and mutilated.[13] Outside of the religious world, one of the most grotesque episodes in the nation's history had to do with the alleged murder of more than a hundred adolescent boys by a pederast.[14] Secular or religious, the brutalizing and obliteration of the Feminine is all pervasive.

A collective crisis of masculinity, religion, sexuality and love is evident in the nature of advertising directed at the masses. A psycho-cultural reading of these texts indicates that they are primarily addressed to males. Basically brief, widely prevalent slogans/messages in Urdu and other regional languages, they are painted/written on rocks, walls and different publicly visible structures. The scale and frequency is impossible to ignore from roads and thoroughfares. In the last two decades, these advertisements are increasingly around three themes reflecting the mix of concerns dominating mass (male) Pakistani-Muslim consciousness.

At least till 9/11, and even now in the North-West-Frontier Province, the most frequent ad is the call to *jihad*, inviting/urging 'men' to join one of the numerous fundamentalist organizations that have proliferated in the country. As was explained earlier, *jihad* is primarily an inner, and therefore psychological/symbolic concept, the pre-requisite being a subjectivity that is aware of its inner diversity, positive and negative, feminine and masculine. The inward, subjective primacy of *jihad* is self-evident in the Prophet's referring to this as the 'greater *jihad*' (*jihad-i-akbar*). In contrast, the external, literal form is seen as 'lesser' (*jihad-i-asghar*). But given factors ranging from cultural erosion to state sponsored religiosity, *jihad* has been totally externalized in the service of a persecutory paranoia that is focused on single mindedly routing out all perceived 'enemies of Islam' everywhere.

The second type of advertisement, and of equal scale and frequency as the call to *jihad* concerns all manner of quick and sure cures for what is euphemistically termed 'male weakness', that is, impotence. The invisible, global underbelly of masculinist machismo as evident in the current militaristic mood of the West *and* militant Islamism, can be glimpsed in the sales of Viagra which in 1998 became the fastest selling drug in history. In 2003, revenues for the market of erectile dysfunction (ED) drugs was over $4 billion in 2012 and expected to remain around $3.5 billion in 2019.[15] While precise figures for the Pakistan market are not available, interviews with CEO's of pharmaceutical companies suggest that there is, so to speak, stiff competition from the informal sector and which is borne out by the nationwide presence of the popular marketing of sundry *kushtas* or aphrodisiacs for 'male weakness'.

Between the popularity of these cures and the modern Viagra, lies the phallic symbol of a (inter)nationally flaccid phallogocentricism. Islam and the West, ego and shadow come together in the billboard(s): 'Make a Zero into a Hero: Tremendous Masculine Strength'. Since the Feminine is denied/absent, full-fillment remains elusive. Yet the need remains; but only as experienced/expressed literally, as in adolescence, mainly through the genitals. The archetype of love and relatedness, *eros*, remains unmoved, dormant. Artificially propped up, so to speak, it is expressed in a sexual rage against women's bodies or the despair of a particular sort of depersonalized homosexuality, both experienced and conducted as compulsions. Beneath the self-glorifying, self-gratification of 'handling' all types of guns and weapons, these advertisements for old (and new) Viagra provide a fearful, yet poignant sub-text, to the strident calls for *jihad*.

The state of both spirituality and sexuality are encapsulated by a series of three advertisements on a wall. The middle one offers the 'spiritual' service of *istikhara*, a special prayer for guidance when difficult decisions are required. This is framed on one side by a promotion for 'Dynamic Gold' promising to make a (male) zero into a hero. On the other side, a text promotes the 'Royal Clinic' and its specialists dealing with 'hidden' ailments, that is, impotence and hemorrhoids. The sheer scale of advertisements for cures of these two conditions encapsulate the spectrum of the masculine malaise in Pakistan.

Interestingly, despite of the hatred for all things Western (except techno-weapons), when it comes to naming these centers of treatment it is 'French Laboratories', 'German Health/Clinics' and 'Cheen (China) Health Clinic'. Somehow, these are the most credible nations when it comes to alleviating 'hidden' ailments. Eat your heart out U.S.A.[16]

A third type of advertisement relates to the services of practitioners of healing through magic and other 'spiritual arts,' promising especially, instant fulfillment in love and seduction. The appeal to absolute power and control is vividly summed up by the guaranteed goal of bringing the victim, the 'beloved, at your feet within twenty four hours'. To the extent that the market for this promise of 'love' includes women, *eros* is present, albeit minimally, and in an infantile 'magical' conception, typical to a situation of helplessness and disempowerment.

When occasionally, *eros*/woman does surface in the masculine-dominated culture, it is in extremely crude, literal and brutal ways such as the episode of the *imam*, or collectively, in the regional cinema and portrayals of women either in fully armed fury and/or, eventually, as extremely vulgar and obscene sex objects. Mostly, it tends to express itself not only in direct physical violence to women but also in terms of a peculiar and crude (homo)sexuality, which is perhaps inevitable in exclusivist male environments.

Given the emergent demographics of a growing and ever younger male population in Pakistan, the collective manifestation of the Hero's Shadow and its implications for Islam and women, does not bode well for the future. But we can all take comfort in the fact that modern, internationally bestselling drugs, particularly for anxiety and depression (Prozac, Zoloft, Xanax, etc.) are available over the counter to enable us to endure this relentlessly grim 'Land of the Pure'.

Incidentally, the only advertisements aimed specifically at women, pertain to different brands of pressure cookers. Therein lies another symbol of the present and future.

Concluding part III: Masculine Delusions

Within a backdrop of inspiration and support of 'high' Islamism and its sources in modernity, the preceding analysis of 'low' or mass Islamism has drawn from a number of perspectives. These include parallel conceptions of gender in both Islam and Jungian psychology as organizing principles. To this extent, the terms 'masculine' and 'feminine' have been applied to dimensions of the human psyche, the idea of the Divine, as well as to different categories of religion. As the 'feminine' side to Islam, the Sufi *silsilahs* can be considered the religion's 'secret backbone', many of which had strong bonds with the creative imagination including local/regional popular culture. 'Low' Islamism's influence as exercised through the state, inflicted severe damage to this backbone, psycho-spiritually cutting adrift an already brutalized, overwhelmingly poverty stricken population, especially young males.

The different types of cultural terror unleashed by and through mass Islamism indicate a major psychological crisis in self-conceptions of masculine identity, sexuality and religion. The violence of the 'low' Islamist has its roots in a specific type of 'education' and circumstance, namely war and poverty and an absence/erosion of restraining cultural factors. Psycho-dynamically, they form the foundations of what eventually surfaces as persecutory paranoia that is both violent and misogynist.

The differences between 'high' and 'low' fundamentalism are ultimately a matter of style. To the extent that the high ideologue, like so many modern persons, prides 'the mind', his paranoia is related to delusions of grandeur which is much more of a 'mental' condition than delusions of persecution. As clinical evidence suggests, and the socio-historic situation of mass Islamists confirms, persecutory paranoia has very real reasons underlying its 'delusions'. In this case, child abuse is an understatement for describing the impact on young children of war, extreme poverty and parental absence.

Given the well-educated 'mind' of the high ideologue, its violence is accordingly, sophisticated, insidious, covert, systematically thought out in scientific detail. Deeply influenced by the psychology of modernity, different types of high fundamentalisms, globally display not only a masculinist love of violence, weapons, and technology, but also generate, as does science, its own predispositions towards literalism. There are similar modern biases towards woman/body/knowledge. The ethos of modernity is also literal, cut off from the feminine in body and consciousness. While emerging from a different psycho-cultural history, it too harbors a Talib(an) within, exhibiting a psyche that is violent and macho.

As a whole, high fundamentalism inspires, and morally,

intellectually, financially and politically, supports low fundamentalism. Given the ensuing cultural destruction, low fundamentalism tends to surface and be strengthened. But in the absence of scientific, rational education (*logos*) as well as absence of *eros* and the Feminine in most aspects of life, mass fundamentalism's violence is even more literal, hence more overt, direct and crude. Together, both types exhibit a crisis of masculinity in religion, sexuality and love.

PART IV:
PSYCHOLOGICAL EXPLORATIONS OF GLOBAL PARANOIA

We are all sufferers from history,
but the paranoid is a double sufferer,
since he is afflicted not only
by the real world, with the rest of us,
but by his fantasies as well.
(Richard Hofstadter[1])

CHAPTER 9:
INTELLECTUALS, (HOMO)SEXUALITY, RELIGION AND PARANOIA

No wonder the Western world feels uneasy, for it does not know
what it has lost through the destruction of its numinosities
[symbols]. It has lost its moral and spiritual values to a very
dangerous degree. Its moral and spiritual tradition has
collapsed, and has left a worldwide disorientation … The great
religions of the world suffer from increasing anaemia.
(C.G. Jung[1])

The Rise of Paranoia in the West

In discussing modernity and fundamentalism one has frequently used the term paranoia and juxtaposed connections with male homosexuality. Both warrant further scrutiny particularly since the latter is today located in the no-(wo)man's-land of political (in)correctness.

A closer look at how paranoia has been historically and clinically constructed may tell us more about, what is surely, *the* all-pervasive mood (if not dis-ease) of the times. Actually, in the US this mood has been around at least since the 19th Century, indicating yet again certain psychological tendencies inherent to modernity. In this respect, Richard Hofstadter's classic essay *The Paranoid Style in American Politics* remains a landmark of political psychology indicating the longstanding presence of paranoia in American political discourse.

Among the many examples Hofstadter provides, is the inventor of the telegraph, S.B. Morse, who in 1835 described a new danger to the American way of life in his book Foreign Conspiracies against the Liberties of the United States. Based on anti-Catholic sentiment Morse argued that Jesuit missionaries were plotting to install a member of the Austrian House of Hapsburg as Emperor of the United States.[2] Similarly, the witch-hunts of communists in the 20th Century during the McCarthy era are well known. As a historian, Hofstadter makes no claims of clinical/therapeutic competence but rather, by "borrowing the clinical term" his aim is to show "the use of paranoid modes of expression by more or less normal people that the makes the phenomenon significant ... The paranoid style is an old and recurrent phenomenon in our public life which has been frequently linked with movements of suspicious discontent".[3]

Given the problematic of clinical paranoia I have referred to earlier, Hofstadter would have been none the wiser even if he had been a clinician, hence perhaps his recourse to the term 'paranoid style'. As discussed in the theoretical framework of this book (see Chapter 1), Archetypal Psychology adumbrates the idea of un/consciousness as being constituted around different archetypes, what Hillman terms "structures of consciousness". Each is a different perspective, expressed as a psychological attitude and a distinct style. As a kind of web of inner (unconscious) meaning, archetypes are the foundations of our basic assumptions about life and it is from these inner dispositions and the feelings and images clustered about them, that we form a sense of who we are collectively and individually.[4]

As discussed in Chapter 1 and 2, through this archetypal perspective, the main myth/image underlying modernity, is of the youthful Hero who by his 'nature' (psychology) has some strong and positive aspects but is also violent and paranoid at many levels. In short, Hofstadter is intuitively and psychologically correct in saying that "style has more to do with the way in which ideas are believed and advocated than with the truth or falsity of content".[5] As he says:

> The paranoid spokesman sees the fate of conspiracy in apocalyptic terms, he traffics in the birth and death of whole worlds, whole political orders, whole systems of human values. He is always manning the barricades of civilization. He constantly lives at a turning point. Like religious millennialists he expresses the anxiety of those who are living through the last days.[6]

Similarly, as discussed in Chapter 2 and 3, the heroic style of dealing with political conflict tends towards extreme violence with no room for options such as negotiation or reconciliation. The fact that Hofstadter wrote his essay in the 1960's and its uncanny relevance for the present indicates the existence of a genuine archetype rather than 'just' a literary trope. If anything, given the global presence of paranoia, the essay is not only incisive but unwittingly prophetic regarding the grip of the Hero archetype on contemporary politics East or West. Similar to the Hero mentality, increasingly politicians everywhere, do:

> ... not see social conflict as something to be mediated and compromised in the manner of the working politician. Since what is at stake is always a conflict between absolute good and absolute evil, what is necessary is not compromise but the will to fight things out to a finish. Since the enemy is thought of as being totally evil and totally unappeasable, he must be totally eliminated—if not from the world, at least from the theatre of operations to which the paranoid directs his attention. This demand for total triumph leads to the formulation of hopelessly unrealistic goals, and since these goals are not even remotely attainable, failure constantly heightens the

paranoid's sense of frustration. Even partial success leaves him with the same feeling of powerlessness with which he began, and this in turn only strengthens his awareness of the vast and terrifying quality of the enemy he opposes.[7]

It is no wonder then, that the current global presence of paranoia was evident well before 9/11. Ironically, around the same time as the birth of the European Community and heralding of the New World Order in the early 90's, there was simultaneously a steady rise in racism, xenophobia and a growing appetite for conspiracy theories in the West. Titles of editorials in prominent mass publications encapsulate the emerging syndrome in the US: *Xenophobia's High Cost*,[8] *From There to Intolerance*,[9] *Sam, Sam, the Paranoid Man*.[10] As early as 1991, *Time* magazine noted that "America is becoming a nation of crybabies and whiners ... twin malformations are cropping up in the American character: a nasty intolerance and a desire to blame everyone else for everything."[11] The next year, *Newsweek* noted that "xenophobia and paranoic nationalism" was gaining momentum in Europe and "in spite of 45 years of unprecedented economic and democratic growth ... demons of racism and authoritarianism (had) popped out of the European psyche."[12] In short, the present situation of internal and global tensions and mutual paranoia between Islam and the West is not simply because of terrorism post-9/11.[13] It indicates the presence of a deeper psychological syndrome.

Definitions and Descriptions of Paranoia

The Oxford dictionary defines paranoia as a "mental disorder characterized by systematized delusions, as of grandeur and persecution." Both psychiatry and the dictionary define 'delusion' as a "false belief". Given human subjectivity, this is really not very helpful, especially since ideas of grandeur in one individual/group tend to usually evoke a logical counterpart of a sense of persecution in the other. They can also co-exist within the same individual. This sort of cognitive impasse is typical to paranoia and may become understandable as one proceeds.

Apart from its popular and widespread manifestation, the etymology of the word 'paranoia' suggests it also concerns those who place a premium on a 'life of the mind'. 'Para' means along with, parallel to; 'noia' is from 'nous' or mind, intelligence, perception. Noeisis means existing or originating in the intellect. To be noetic is to be 'an intellectual person'. Thus, paranoia can be seen as a paradigm for mental illness and concerns both, reader and writer, Muslim and non-Muslim.

In ancient Greece, paranoia was a non-specific term that referred simply to a distracted mind 'thinking beside oneself'. The first modern classification by Heinroth in 1818 states it is "essentially a disorder of the intellect".[14] Beyond Freud's attempts at linking it with male homosexuality, modern psychology today refers to it in terms no better than the Greeks, as a "thinking/personality disorder".[15] Following are some salient features from standard sources on psychiatry on how paranoia is understood: (all emphases are mine):

> A psychoses without known brain pathology ... intelligence is well preserved ... a complex, slowly developing system often *logically* elaborated after a *false interpretation* of an *actual occurrence* ... no hallucinations ... personality is intact... *preservation of clear and orderly thinking* ... a century ago called

> *intellectual mono mania* ... a disorder of the intellect ... highly
> systematized incurable delusions but without general
> personality deterioration[16]... Delusional disorder ... is a type of
> serious mental illness ... the main feature is the presence of ...
> unmistakable beliefs in something untrue... These delusions
> usually involve the misinterpretation of perceptions or
> experiences. People with delusional disorder can often
> continue to socialize and function normally, and generally do
> not behave in an obviously odd and bizarre manner...
> Delusional disorder usually occurs in middle to late life...[17]

Basically, modern psychiatry until now has not really managed any significant improvement in understanding the more than 2000 year old, triumphant presence of something purely 'mental', a 'belief', whose central concern is *meaning*. As Jasper's puts it, for the paranoid: "The environment offers a world of new meanings. All thinking is a thinking about meaning. There is an immediate, intrusive knowledge of the meaning and it is this which is itself the delusional experience."[18]

To sum up and add a few more facts: In a century that has seen almost every behavioral condition reduced to brain pathology, paranoia remains outside of bio-chemical and genetic considerations. Furthermore, the paranoid is frequently of above-average intelligence and personality remains firmly intact through a 'preservation of clear, orderly thinking'. Thus, it is primarily a disorder of the intellect having its roots in a 'false *interpretation* of an *actual* occurrence'. It is an extremely intransigent condition, almost impossible to cure.

While there are many different types of paranoia and we have already considered the specific persecutory form in 'low' Islamism in part III. The focus here will be on the most frequent and most important variety, namely the Grandiose/Persecutory as basically one condition, two sides of the same coin. In short, paranoia is a disease that afflicts intelligent, mature individuals, without impairing their personality and general functioning. Its central concern is epistemological and related to it, the construction of meaning. This brief profile in terms of age and intelligence, make the 'high' ideologue (religious and non-religious) the indirect but primary focus of this section. That is, while we will be discussing issues such as the Western construction of homosexuality and paranoia, they should be understood in the context of the (post)Jungian critique of modernity and the impact of modernity on not only high Islamists but also their high liberal/secular counterparts, Muslims and non-Muslims.

Paranoia and Homosexuality

The most controversial and well known theory of paranoia was put forward by Freud who placed the root cause of paranoia in repressed male homosexual desire. Reducing all types of paranoia to a single etiology, Freud stated that "the familiar principal forms of paranoia can all be represented as contradictions of a single proposition: 'I (a man) *love him* (a man)...'"[19] Before going further, given my own paranoia about political correctness, it needs to be clearly stated that I am not suggesting that homosexuality is a disease that must be cured, or that all male homosexuals are paranoid. In the context of the present discourse, which is located somewhere between post Jungian Archetypal Psychology and frameworks about gender derived from religion, two points need to be kept in mind. The first has to do with Freud and the entire edifice of psychoanalytic theory regarding paranoia which is based on specific conceptual underpinnings pertaining to repressed male homosexuality. The second point has to do again with Western constructions of sexuality.

Concerning the first point, an entire book could be devoted to

Western academic psychosexual and cultural politics, whereby on the one hand, Freud's ideas continue to be attacked/discredited, but nevertheless, they remain powerfully alive in the public imagination and continue playing a major role in medical training/practice across the world. By the eighties, homosexuality was declassified as a psychological disease, and this revisioning is to be applauded. Meanwhile Western intellectual-cultural politics continue insofar as Freud was nevertheless proclaimed among the '100 great individuals', who shaped the mind of the 20th Century.[20] In spite of feminism and myriad schools in psychology challenging Freud, his hold on the public imagination is nothing short of remarkable. W.H. Auden's comments after Freud's death that "if often he was wrong and at times absurd, to us he is no more a person now but a whole climate of opinion", is echoed in Time Magazine stating that "today we all speak Freud," or in Newsweek saying that his ideas are today part of "universal common sense."[21]

This brings us back to the second point about Western constructions of sexuality which are still deeply influenced by Freud and Cartesian-Christianism. Beyond the academic, they are evident in the continuing and self-evident obsession with sex in the West and now also the Muslim world of a still rather black and white approach to questions of (homo)sexuality and gender. The fact is that when the West was firmly anti-homosexual and had morally reduced it to a disease or crime, there were/are many other cultures where it has basically been a non-issue. This was primarily because, like the Greeks, these cultures distinguished between the homosexual act and homosexuality as a 'state of mind'. As such, both had always had a place, albeit, different from the current aggressive-defensive 'out-of-the-closet-and-in-your-face' Western style, which is now also spreading to non-Western societies. The main point is, religious injunctions everywhere notwithstanding, homosexuality has basically been, till recently, more of a 'problem' in the Western world. In any case:

> Freud's theory, accepted even today by many analytic workers, is that paranoid delusions result from repressed homosexual impulses striving for expression ... handled primarily by the defense mechanism of ... attributing to others feelings that are unacceptable to one's own ego. Freud considered the common paranoid delusions of persecution and grandiosity to derive from distortions ... of this basic homosexual urge.[22]

It should therefore be clearly understood that this discussion does not reflect any personal bias. To each their own. Nor is it interested in the recent debates about genetic predispositions in these matters. The issue is not the literal act or the following of a 'lifestyle'. Rather, it is a tracing of certain *themes* that go back to the Greeks and its modern intellectual and collective manifestation in various political, religious and academic discourses. Given the absence/marginalizing of feminine or feminist perspectives the bulk of contemporary discourses remain within what feminists call an exclusivist 'male imaginary'.[23] One can note in passing that icons such as Sappho notwithstanding, since the Greeks, the theme of homosexuality remains historically and primarily linked to males. The main point in any case is not the literal fact but the idea, the (myth)theme, in this case the phallocratic Rooster factor and its implicit denial of the feminine. Thus, before moving to our main focus on the links between paranoia, homosexuality and modern religious *and* non-religious fundamentalism, a feminist review of religion and psycho-sexuality needs to be considered.

Modern Masculinization of Sexuality

Jungian psychology sees the implications of the Biblical story of Eve as a recurring theme, its biases evident even in the seemingly objective world of science. Bringing together a vast body of research ranging from anatomy to chemical embryology, Hillman shows how the idea of Eve, as the Christian 'abysmal side of bodily man', *evil*, dark and unconscious, has remained a leitmotif in medical science.[24] In psychology, this presumed inferiority surfaced in the Freudian concept of a controlling, masculinist 'ego' and *its* ideas of women experiencing 'penis envy' and 'immature' versus 'mature' female orgasm, the latter essentially being in the context of male dominance. (It can be noted in passing that Freud never analyzed even one little girl in proposing the concept of 'penis envy'.) In spite of the feminist de-bunking of Freud, from the Jungian viewpoint as well as contemporary feminism, the motif of female inferiority, including the sexual, in actual fact remains entrenched.[25]

Consider, for example, the Masters and Johnson's studies on human sexuality which are part of modern medical training across the world.[26] In contrast to the earlier Freudian notion of a scientifically proven widespread female 'frigidity' in the Kinsey reports,[27] these studies disproved Kinsey, highlighting instead, the female capacity for 'multiple orgasm'. Overtly 'superior' to males in quantitative terms, the possibility of multiple orgasms for women continues to convey an impression of functioning *below* a desirable threshold. Whether frigid or otherwise, once again vast numbers of women are left feeling 'inadequate' (envious).

The modern 'freedom' of women is modeled on a male idea of consciousness, which sees all issues in terms of power and quantity and a moral reductionism related to them. By making a technology of the orgasm, along with the steady refining of other technologies such as contraception and abortion, women can more closely approximate male sexual patterns in the prototype of a 'free' and 'healthy' male sexuality.[28] Thus, though Freud has been 'debunked', penis envy lives on.

The Masters and Johnson studies provide a perfect symbol for the present state of many modern women (and men) as they remain trapped in masculinist sexual and bodily norms/consciousness. As documented by Hillman, scientific theories of the female body are preponderantly based on the observations and fantasies of men. They are "statements of masculine consciousness confronted with its sexual opposite".[29] Insofar as one investigator of the Masters and Johnson team was female, it clarifies the question of consciousness as not necessarily being only that of man or woman, but of a certain *type/style*, in this case the heroic, and whether or not it gives adequate recognition to the feminine not just physically, but also metaphysically/ psychologically.

Religion and Sexuality

One of the Freud's major contributions was to bring to the surface Western civilization's neuroses about sexuality. Rooted in Puritan Christianity they can be summarized, first, as seeing sexual pleasure being indelibly linked to guilt and sin. Related to this, secondly, that spirituality/religion are incompatible with sexuality. The two are (or should be) separate. Thus, the more religious a person the less interest in sex and 'vice' versa. This is not to say that Freud's prescriptions for the neuroses were salutary. Dismissing religion as an 'illusion' without a future, his solutions, in a way, simply compounded the problems, witness the growing obsession with sex in the Western media over the last century. Nevertheless, he can be credited with acknowledging and articulating the presence of deep-rooted unconscious issues. To this extent his ideas remain relevant in the context of the psychology of young males. The problem therefore isn't that Freud is completely wrong. The problem lies in imposing that particular adolescent template onto women and subsequent stages of life for males and females.

Similarly, between the feminist critique of Cartesianism (including of Freud) and the views of Foucault,[30] there is a consensus that Western culture's understanding of sexuality remains anchored in its *religious* unconscious. This anchoring in Cartesian-Christianism remains covertly present in numerous negative biases towards women and their bodies as they appear in different types of scientific-philosophical-cultural discourses. As was explained in Chapter 6, their roots go far deeper than Puritanism, into the archetypal story of creation and the Biblical role of Eve in the fall from Paradise. To repeat the words of Hillman: "The psychological history of the male-female relationship in our (Western) civilization may be seen as a series of footnotes to the fall of Adam and Eve,"[31] and for which Eve is held responsible. In this context, while remaining anchored in many ways within the monotheistic narrative of the Adam and Eve myth, Islam presents a significant psychocultural, civilizational point of departure from its Judeo-Christian counterpart since Eve is not considered to be the culprit of 'the fall'. Of course, this is not to suggest that the Islamic ideologue is somehow less misogynist. If anything, as consistently stated, his type of modernity propels him in to possibly more rigid Cartesianist-Christianist attitudes, ironically, in the name of Islam.

My highlighting the psycho-theological roots of Western or modern constructions of sexuality, aims to avoid a psycho-analytic framework in which there is, in reality only *one* sex: the male. Such uni-sexual frameworks make women's identities (and the feminine) invisible, nonexistent. In the exclusive world of a unisexual male imaginary, much of Western philosophy and particularly psychology, leave women without a subjective sense of identity and a symbolic self-image.[32]

Islamic or Christian, ultimately the dominant constructions of (hu)man sexuality of course resonate with patriarchal views on women as sanctioned by particular readings of religion, both in terms of an invisibility as well as inferiority. But equally important may be the fact that such masculinist exclusivism leads to an 'inbreeding' which can create psychological and philosophical problems for males, and also for our understanding of psycho-pathology and religion. As I will shortly discuss, perhaps it is this exclusivist, monochromatic male worldview that creates the problem in (mis)understanding homosexuality and paranoia. But this can only be seriously considered once a framework of difference has been established.

Fortunately, the emerging realization of the significance of difference between men and women, creates a space from where religion and sexuality can be viewed more comprehensively. The 'essentialist' versus 'diversity' debate notwithstanding, as Irigaray says: "Sexual difference is one of the questions, if not *the* question to be thought in our age. According to Heidegger, each age has its issue. One alone. Sexual difference is probably that issue in our own age, which could be our salvation on an intellectual level."[33]

Psychological Interiority

To talk of difference in the present context is to talk of women's bodies, which in contradistinction to existing phallocratic norms of identity, provide a different vocabulary of concepts. As Ong puts it:

> The internality of the female, sexual organs, is crucial ... biologically and psychologically. Woman's body is a mystery, for what is most distinctly feminine about it, its reproductive equipment is largely invisible. ... In a profound sense, by contrast to man, woman is interiority, self-possession. She relates to herself interiorly, and others relate to her interiorly, her lovers, her children.[34]

Many qualities of consciousness can be related to this physical (literal) aspect of interiority. In fact, as experienced by us, consciousness itself is an inner phenomenon (reflecting perhaps the original feminine meaning of 'psyche' as a woman). Our sense of 'I'/'me' is *within*. Interior/feminine qualities include receptivity, reflection, synthesis, contemplation, silence, darkness, mystery. When contrasted with those as symbolized in the male body, different qualities (as modes of cognition) are involved. Thus, action, mastery, analysis, and serial/linear cognition, are as important as the ability to assimilate, receive, reflect, synthesize and provide meaning. Prose and poetry, speech and silence, explanation and understanding, *logos* and *eros*, both dimensions and many others are united in the imagery of sexual union between male and female.

These dimensions to knowledge and consciousness and the connection between religion and sexuality can be meaningfully understood only if one acknowledges the idea of interiority as it suggests itself in the female body. It is in this sense that Cooey considers the growing research emphasis on woman's body as extremely significant since it serves as a metaphor for alternative knowledge, that is, "knowledge that escapes cultural determination."[35]

Psychology, Theology, Paranoia and Meaning

Trying to psychologically deconstruct the links between religion, (homo)sexuality and paranoia entails a recognition of one's own paranoia. Thus, a few observations on psychology/psychiatry are in order. For a start, as people like Jung, Hillman and others have pointed out before, this discourse itself can be considered as being paranoid about a masculinized modernity and its connections with all types of religious and secular fundamentalism. However, the correlation of method with topic is actually in keeping with both Archetypal Psychology and numerous non-Western, including traditional Islamic methods, of medicine, that is, 'the thing that harms is the thing that heals'. In short, if one is to understand paranoia one must enter the condition oneself.

As a quintessentially modern discipline, psychology itself incarnates paranoia within its epistemology. To begin with, like philosophy, psychology's roots were/are in religion. As much as it has tried to 'secularize', it has not managed to do away with the performative dimension of religion like private confessions behind closed doors, etc. Depth- psychology particularly, relies on thoroughly training the practitioner in the art of suspicion: to constantly decipher behaviors, identify hidden connections, and eventually construct elaborate explanations about them. Frequently, this deciphering of (to the psychologist) hidden forces, has to do with the invisible, but nevertheless sinister, ever present, 'unconscious'. Strictly speaking, in the absence of brain pathology, the entire exercise is based on theorizing, that is, various concepts are imagined, and hidden connections 'discerned' according to a logically well-developed system (theory). Eventually, it too, is about interpretation and meaning.

*

From the outset, the parameters of the present discourse have been situated at the juncture of psychology and religion. Following Hillman, it is a juncture at which one can perceive religion as relation with divinity *and* as relation with community, in other words, where psychology is drawn to consider theology and politics.[36]

More than a century ago, the psychologist William James suggested that at the most general level religion consists of the belief that there is an 'unseen order' and the larger good lies in "harmoniously adjusting ourselves there to it."[37] Similarly, the entry on 'Revelation' in a major theological dictionary states:

> All religion is concerned in some way with the manifestation of deity. This consists in removing concealment... Even primitive man knows this. On the other hand, there could be no dealing, let alone fellowship with a God who remained permanently hidden. In the broadest sense then, all religion depends on revelation... it belongs to the nature of deity to manifest itself. What really counts is the correct method....[38]

The theologian's reference to 'primitive man' is perhaps an allusion to the 'primitive's' sense of the symbolic. Whereby, for example, he 'sees through' a thunderbolt towards an even greater force/presence. The sense of being connected with the transpersonal, thus, has to do with relating to phenomena meta-physically. That is, for the 'primitive', thunder is not reduced to 'nothing but' this or that physical cause. Instead, its subjective sphere of meaning is enlarged symbolically to include divine manifestation/presence. Put another way the 'primitive' view makes thunder more 'full' of meaning whereas the scientific-materialist vision is relatively 'empty' and hence 'meaning-less'. In light of the critique of modernity and erosion of *mythos* and the symbolic, paranoia can be considered a symptomatic, unconscious response to this condition. By clinging to the literal (the sacred text, money, etc.), some-thing becomes better than no-thing. In this sense, all 'isms' become the final refuge against meaninglessness. This is of course, a common explanation for religious fundamentalism in modern times. But it is a simplistic response and the question remains unanswered: how and who is to decide what is the (in)correct meaning in both revelation and paranoia? The answers may lie in a post Freudian review of some seminal case study material on paranoia.

Case Studies of Paranoia

Three Men in a Tub

Freud's own bias against religion ('infantile neurosis'), and also possibly his own latent homosexual fears[39] made him dismissive of the strong, religiously based delusions that were also part of the data he relied on for developing his theory of paranoia. That is, while the data were complex, Freud focused primarily on the sexual/physical material as presented in the autobiographical account of the German judge Daniel Paul Schreber, *Memoirs of my Nervous Illness*.[40] This book provided the bedrock for Freud's theory of paranoia and homosexuality. As explored by Hillman, and in order to enlarge the present scope of understanding the gender dynamics of paranoia, let us first look at two other case studies before discussing Schreber (and Freud).

Anton Boisen

Anton Boisen, author of *Out of Depth: An Autobiographical Study of Mental Disorder and Religious Experience*,[41] was an American Presbytarian minister and author of many works in psychopathology as well as the relationship between psychology and religion. He wrote his book in 1960, forty years after a breakdown during which he was institutionalized for more than a year. As stated in his 'Foreword': "I offer this as a case of valid religious experience which was at the same time madness of the most profound and unmistakable variety." Boisen was forty four when he had his paranoid breakdown, 'coincidentally' during a period when he was trying to formulate a Statement of Belief, related to his advancement within the official structure of the Church. At some point while writing the third paragraph he noticed a 'transition into an abnormal state' in which certain ideas came 'surging into his mind with tremendous power'. Shortly thereafter, Boisen was hospitalized and remained under psychiatric attention for more than a year. The ideas had to do with impending world change,[42] classificatory schemes of power[43] death and rebirth and of course, God;[44] "... it seemed the world was coming to an end ... Only a few tiny atoms we call 'men' were to be spared. I was to be one of these ... [to] be of help to others ... the motive that has sustained me throughout this whole affair is the conviction that I was really acting in obedience to a divine command."[45]

During periods of intense delusion, Boisen was obsessed with the sun and especially the moon. He "succeeded in climbing into the sun"[46] and discovered that the moon was a highly sexual place. Upon arrival there one's "sex was likely to change and doctors tried to determine whether you were a man or woman."[47] While he was seen as neither, he felt he was a woman named Magdelen. Sacrifice meant "becoming a woman" and he believed that "he must descend to the lowest possible level". This urge to abase himself - abjection - was done by taking on various provocative postures on the floor to which attendants would respond by beating him.[48]

Finally, Boisen was continuously thinking of plans to thwart enemies, "constant watchfulness". "Christian civilization seems doomed"[49] and the impending "titanic struggle" depended entirely on him.[50] Randomly opened Biblical passages "bear with amazing directness upon the questions uppermost in my mind ... something more than coincidence was involved here."[51] Given the cosmic nature of events, no one could be trusted, including doctors/staff. "Everything had some deeper meaning ... patients, attendant and the doctors ... different kinds of food, all stood for something else."[52] One can clearly see here the overarching theme of religion, the sexual inclinations towards femaleness and the search for (hidden) meaning.

John Perceval

Born in 1803, the son of the British Prime Minister, John Perceval's autobiography meticulously documents his descent into paranoia. Edited by Bateson, *Perceval's Narrative: A Patients Account of his Psychosis*[53] is based on two volumes published by Perceval after his recovery.[54] Similar to Boisen, Perceval was haunted by religious questions and just prior to his breakdown had been praying and fasting as participant in a sect.

Perceval recalls the precise time related to his institutionalization. He had been invited to a dinner and believed he had to convince the host family of his religious beliefs. This would entail that "I was to speak in an unknown tongue ... other marvelous feats ... it came into my head ... to put my hand in the fire."[55] Subsequently, he woke up at night hearing voices, a violent state of conflict "between Jesus and Satan" and was ordered to take "a position on the floor."[56] He felt his body was half white and half scarlet.[57]

Perceval's detailed narrative indicates patterns similar to

Boisen: "the end of time was at hand,"[58] constant references to God, lewd and lascivious compulsions,[59] the urge to debase himself "...gave myself up to every low, groveling, base, often savage feeling and thought that came upon me."[60] They included strong homosexual fantasies with himself as the abject (female) partner. Like Boisen, he felt love for another man, there were voices, violence, singing and suicide attempts and above all lengthy ratiocinations, reflections on the meaning of everything, not only the hypocrisy of doctors but also the meaning/ intentions of the commands and suggestions coming to him.

Daniel Paul Schreber

The most famous patient of paranoia 'probably the most famous in all of psychiatric history' and who became the prototype for paranoia, was a man whose job was to know the truth, and *interpret meaning*, that is he was a lawyer and later a judge:

> ... probably the most famous case in all of psychiatric history was that of the gifted jurist Daniel Paul Schreber. This remarkable man wrote an autobiography 'Memories of my Nervous Illness' in which he described his imaginary transformation from man to woman ... he made no attempt to repress his homosexual aspirations. Rather, he made them into a kind of religion, albeit a glorified and personal religion. ... Freud's masterful analysis of its contents (the autobiography) ... was that paranoid reaction and homosexuality were inseparable ... Freud's brilliant interpretations of the paranoid components has since held the major attention of psychiatrists.[61]

Daniel Paul Schreber was born in Leipzig in 1842, trained as a lawyer and was active in politics. As a jurist, by 1893 he was appointed *Senatspräsident*, or presiding judge of the Supreme Court of Appeals. Around this time he started having a series of psychotic episodes which continued for almost nine years and entailed long periods of incarceration. He died at age 68, a few years after publishing his *Memoirs* which became the inspiration for Freud's theory of paranoia.

Like Boisen and Perceval, Schreber's overarching delusion was religious. "I had to solve one of the most intricate problems ever set for man … to fight a sacred battle for the greatest good of mankind,"[62] "my person has become the center of divine miracles"[63] and "if I succeed in putting forward the truth of my so called delusion … mankind (may) gain a truer insight into the nature of God."[64] Schreber's battle had to do with the realm of God and the "Order of the World". According to Schreber, God "saw living human beings only from *without* … His omnipresence and omniscience did not extend *within* living man."[65] God was neither psychologically, existentially, phenomenologically evident and this was a major problem in the 'Order of the World'. Schreber had to solve this problem *within* God even as he experienced great torment and the 'testing' of his soul by the same God.

Like Boisen and Perceval, erotic sexuality permeated Schreber's delusions.[66] He described this frequently experienced feeling as 'voluptuousness', in German *entmannung*, unmanning, that is being 'feminized'. *Entmannung*/unmanning does not mean literal emasculation or castration but removal from the category of men. In the earliest stages of his illness he wrote:

> One morning while still in bed … I had a feeling which … struck me as highly peculiar. It was the idea that it really must be rather pleasant to be a woman succumbing to intercourse. This idea was so foreign to my whole nature that … I would have rejected it with indignation, if fully awake.[67]

Later, he concluded that *entmannung* or (feminine) voluptuousness "is the soul's form of existence within the Order of the

World."[68] "This state of Blessedness is mainly a state of voluptuous enjoyment which ... needs the fantasy of either being or wishing to be a female being."[69] "I could see without doubt that the Order of the World imperiously demanded my unmanning, whether I personally liked it or not ... nothing was left to me but reconcile myself to the thought of being transformed into a woman."[70]

Apart from the sexual and religious delusions, Schreber's more than five hundred page *Memoirs* resonate deeply with the experiences of Perceval and Boison: suicide attempts, violence, hatred and distrust of his doctors, solar and lunar fascinations, bathtubs, world catastrophe, preoccupation with the body and an intense concentration on meanings, especially of words as well as the statements/actions of people, but above all, the meanings of God's communications, what Hillman calls his "agony of theologizing."[71]

Paranoia and the Feminine Soul

Paranoia and Anima

The three cases of clinically diagnosed paranoia clearly show the strong links of the syndrome with religion and the feminine. A major underlying theme of this book has been the loss of the feminine dimension in modern psycho-theological consciousness and it would be useful to briefly recap its main features: what we consider the 'ego' ('I') is an unbalanced sense of self, one-sided in its emphasis on willpower and a narrow scientistic notion of rationality and reason. Accordingly, modern consciousness has become 'heroic', essentially Aryan, Apollonic, Protestant Christian, positivistic, scientific, Cartesian, rational and overwhelmingly masculine. It opposes as immoral and abnormal that which is ambiguous, intermediate, dark, symbolic, metaphorical and feminine.[72]

To repeat oneself yet again, the 'feminine' here does not refer literally to a woman but to a particular style(s) of consciousness which spans contemplation, receptivity to the symbolic, the capacity for interiority, depth etc. In Jungian terms it is the *anima*, which means air, breath, life, soul, and refers to the feminine principle within masculine consciousness. The *anima* or soul is used here not in terms of a pseudo religious substance but rather a *viewpoint* towards things rather than a thing itself.[73] Apart from its usage in Archetypal Psychology, 'soul'/or *anima* is not seen as scientific by psychology even though there are many words which 'speak' to us but find no place in modern science.

To fully grasp what is at stake here, we need to digress a little further on the essential concepts of soul and image. Once these become more clear—by looking at them through the lens Archetypal Psychology—we can return to our case studies of paranoia.

Soul, Psyche, Nafs and Archetypal Psychology

A central idea behind the psycho-therapeutic enterprise is that human behavior is understandable because it has *inner* meaning and this meaning is suffered, experienced. The meaning of 'soul' is best amplified by the wide range of contexts it is embedded in and associated with: ... mind, spirit, heart, life, warmth, humanness, personality, essence, innermost, purpose, courage, virtue, morality, wisdom, death ... one can search one's soul or one's soul can be on trial. There is the journey of the soul, selling it to the devil, yearning for a soul mate etc. It is a 'deliberately ambiguous concept, in the same manner as all ultimate symbols which provide the root metaphors for the system of human thought. 'Matter', 'nature', 'energy' have ultimately the same ambiguity, so too, have 'life' and 'death'.[74]

The *psyche*, as defined by the dictionary is 'the principle of mental and emotional life', encompassing soul, spirit, mind.

Hence psychology originally refers to a *logos* of the soul. In late Greek mythology the soul was personified by a young woman with butterfly wings named Psyche.

In the Quran the word for soul is the feminine *nafs* which comes from the same root (nous/*anima*) in Arabic as in Latin.[75] For example, it is the initial creative substance. "We created you from a single soul" or 'single being' (39:7). Elsewhere there is "the soul and its perfect proportioning, He revealed to it the right and wrong of everything" (91:7-11). It has distinct archetypal dimensions, "the self-accusing/reproaching soul" (75:3) "the soul that incites to evil" (12:53), "the soul at peace" (89:28)... (Asad translates "soul at peace" as "the human who has attained peace").[76] The Quran also talks of the soul's evolution, development, innocence, not being burdened beyond its capacity, its responsibility, its capacity for knowledge and its inevitable encounter with death. Other connotations include vital principle, blood, spirit, person, individual, the 'self' as an essence of a human being or thing, intentions, desire, pride, essence, precious, much sort after ring leader, clearer, relative, punishment.[77] It is evident that the word *nafs*/soul has a complex spectrum of meaning centered around the idea of *being human*.

Chittick has dicussed how in Islamic philosophy and theology, the notion of '*nafs*'-as-soul is extensive: it can have to do with appetites, animal qualities, a child of spirit, body, human, earthy, heavenly, inspired, angry, capricious, opposing religion, at peace, rational, receptive, fiery, dark, capable of ascending. The spectrum of qualities and corresponding commentaries, has raised considerable confusion when it comes to translating *nafs* into English. Generally, its negative dimensions are equated with 'ego' and the positive with 'spirit' but which is closer to 'soul'.[78] In short, it has a multifaceted phenomenological nature, as is human nature. Murata thus, translates the *hadith* (which was discussed earlier) "whosoever knows his soul knows his God" as "whosoever knows his *self* knows his God".[79]

All this is not to suggest that the Jungian and Islamic view of soul is identical. Of course there are differences between spiritual theology and speculative/imaginative psychology. At the same time, given that Hillman himself categorically points to Corbin as the second immediate father of Archetypal Psychology (after Jung), there are overlapping areas and the notion of soul in the present context may form the middle ground between the two (psychology and religion).* In either case, Islamic or (post)Jungian, the idea of 'soul' is not just restricted to religion but is also the inner subjective mosaic that constitutes every individual. As summed up by Hillman, it implies both psyche and religion: "That unknown human factor which makes meaning possible, which turns events into experiences, which is communicated in love and which has a religious concern."[80] Such a psychological perspective, aims to 'humanize' religion, or at least its more virulent and pathological forms. In sum, the feminine dimension of the psyche which is its 'soul', and the depth and complexity of its twists and turns, its joy and despair, are what makes us human.

Images, Imagination and Archetypal Psychology

As mentioned in Chapter 2, 'Imagination' is not just flights of fancy or day dreams but a complex epistemological framework exemplified in the work of, among others, Gilbert Durand, Carl Jung, Mircea Eliade, Paul Ricoeur, George Dumenzil, Henry Corbin, James Hillman and Harold Bloom. As used by them, the terms 'imaginal', 'creative imagination' are echoes of their source in Islamic metaphysics. Catherine Wilson points out that within

---

* The Islamic connection with the idea of the *anima* is evident simply in the title of one of Annemarie Schimmel's book: *My Soul is a Woman: The Feminine in Islam*, which does not rely on any Jungian ideas.

the vast canvas that is Islamic philosophy, a particular strength has been its theory of imagination, the impact of which goes back to, among other, Locke, Berkeley, Montaigne, St. Thomas and Paracelsus.[81] In Islam, this highly developed philosophical tradition includes Al-Farabi, Suhrawardi and Ibn 'Arabi and also forms the philosophical bedrock of the poetry of Rumi. In our times, Henry Corbin's work on Ibn 'Arabi, Avicenna and Suharwardi has highlighted the significance of concepts such as the 'imaginal' and 'creative imagination' in the context of Sufi metaphysics, as has the work of William Chittick.[82]

Since this is not a book on Islamic philosophy, and given the depth and span of sources, one can only resort to simplification in the present context. The Imaginal or Creative Imagination is that domain between sense perception and intuition on the one hand and what we call intellect or thinking on the other. According to Chittick, Ibn 'Arabi employs 'imagination' to refer to everything that pertains to an intermediate state and the standard example of an imaginal reality is a mirror image, which is neither the mirror nor the thing that is imaged, but a combination of both. This intermediacy, in-betweenness is also the domain of the 'soul' and one has already noted the multiplicity of meanings and associations linked to it (soul/*nafs*). Meaning and sense perception, or the spiritual and the physical interact with the soul (psyche) through language and imagery. These are as ontologically real as the idea of a mirror image.[83] In short this language and imagery is both literal and symbolic.

Similarly, within Rumi's poetry there are numerous references to the 'world of the Imagination', or *alam-ul-khayāl*, which Rumi credits as being the source of his inspiration. Observing how relatively impoverished the English word 'imagination' is to explain *alam-ul-khayāl*, Chittick adumbrates it as a mental faculty which not only conjures up images and ideas in the mind but also pertains to these images and ideas collectively and individually, including the entire realm, or 'world' from where they emanate. In short, ideas and images are not derived from within the mind, not something that 'we have', rather *they* come to us from a separate world of Imagination. Thus, *khayāl* can be understood as the mental faculty of the world of 'imagination'; or as "image"/form/idea/concept contained within the imagination.[84]

Having devoted a lifetime researching this subject, Corbin himself was aware of the problematics that could arise when these terms are decontextualized from Sufi Islam and transposed into aesthetics, literature, psychology, etc. He warned against the degradation and loss of meaning that could occur when these terms are used indiscriminately by moderns inhabiting the contemporary 'civilization of the image':

> We have come to see for ourself, with pleasure though not unmixed with some anxiety, that the word "imaginal" as used specifically in our researches has been spreading and even gaining ground. We wish to make the following statement. If this term is used to apply to anything other than the *mundus imaginalis* and the imaginal Forms as they are located in the schema of the worlds which necessitate them and legitimize them, there is a great danger that the term will be degraded and its meaning be lost. By the same token we would remind the reader that the schema in which the imaginal worlds is by its essence the intermediate world, and the articulation between the intellectual and the sensible, in which the Active Imagination as *imaginatio vera* is an organ of understanding mediating between intellect and sense and as legitimate as these latter and that world itself. If one transfers its usage outside this precisely defined schema one sets out on a false trail and strays far from the intention which our Iranian philosophers have induced us to restore in our use of this world. It is superfluous to add—the reader will already have understood this—that the *mundus imaginalis* has nothing to do

with the fashion of our time calls 'the civilizations of the image'. [85]

This in fact has happened. Jungian and Archetypal Psychology, for example, use the term 'active imagination' as a central therapeutic technique in a rather ambiguous manner. And frankly, at times I find Archetypal Psychology to be a pale reflection of Ibn 'Arabi and Rumi's ideas. The literary critic Harold Bloom, however, is of the view that Corbin's note of caution on this matter does not consider "how electric in their spirituality his (Corbin's) Sufis are, and he himself was"[86] and that these ideas in fact should be available outside their original Islamic frameworks. Whereas Corbin wished to reclaim the Creative Imagination as cognitive power in spiritual life, its necessity for Bloom is prompted by contemporary realities in which both art *and* spirituality need to be rescued from cultural materialism:

> ... for our culture, at this time, it may be more pragmatic for seekers to discern the reality of the Active Imagination in Shakespeare, rather than Ibn 'Arabi, though under Corbin's guidance Ibn 'Arabi and other Sufi sages will help us define the imaginal realm ... while Shakespeare needs no rescue, *we* badly need to be rescued from the cultural materialists who are alienating students by reducing Shakespeare to the supposed 'social energies' of what they call 'Early Modern England'.[87]

The contemporary use of the concept/terminology of the 'imaginal' or 'creative/active imagination' confirms Bloom's notion that the Sufi's "imaginal realm is a concept generous enough to embrace both the spiritual and aesthetic".[88] Fundamentally rooted in Islamic/Sufi metaphysics, they nevertheless resonate with currents in contemporary discourse which may or may not be directly theological but whose concerns encompass the virulent and shriveling dimensions of modernity. For the Muslim psychologist and student of culture who is still idiomatically/ culturally/spiritually located closer to Corbin's original sources, the space created by Bloom et al. offers a vast potential for research in (cross) cultural studies and the Islamic humanities.

Art, Image and the Feminine Imagination

For Jung, "image *is* psyche".[89] Within the context of the earlier discussion on soul, Hillman takes this further and sees the source of images in 'the self-generative activity of the soul itself'. As such, they don't 'stand' for anything and are not mental constructs. Soul is primarily an imaginative activity the paradigm for which is the dream. In a dream, the dreamer herself can be one image among many, that is, the dreamer is *in* the image rather than the image in the dreamer.[90] In a similar vein, Casey claims that an image is not what one sees but the *way* in which one sees and this is the act of imagining.[91]

The arts and humanities are also the domain of the creative imagination whose span of course extends beyond the usual way we think of 'creativity-as-art'. From within Islamic philosophy, the images of art are perhaps the most literal expression of the human imagination which in any case, are not meant to be taken literally. Art is literal evidence of the inherent and powerfully tendency of the psyche's image-making capacities, especially regarding religion. As such, art and what is referred to as creativity is perhaps the palest reflection of these ultimately, spiritual potentialities and ideals and thus, a possible bridge towards them. That is, when linked with lived experience, art and imagination can offer a way of thinking about alternative realities. That is why art and cultural expression are vital antidotes to fundamentalism. At its best, art is ambiguous, metaphoric, having the power to 'move', transform and open us to reflection. In Western civilization, the arts/humanities were traditionally linked with the feminine as the Muses, the nine goddesses who among other disciplines also 'inspire' poetry, music, dance, history, comedy, etc. However, today, unfortunately, the emphasis is on the consumption of images rather than their appearance within.

*

Returning to the experiences of our cases of paranoia: in all three, the strong experience of the feminine was not just an obvious, literal affair in terms of physical desire. All three cases talk of visions of beautiful women. At times formidable, but more often the women were loving, tender, gentle. More important, all the men experienced a powerful urge towards unmanning/feminizing which, to repeat, is not necessarily emasculation but rather, a removal from the category of men. Into a more passive-receptive state of female-ness and more fecund, imaginal state of mind. Similarly, all the cases report the varied and voluptuous nature of *entmannung*/feminizing: physically *experienced* retraction of the genitalia, swelling of breasts, quickening of embryo, desirous of childbirth. Perceval and Schreber cultivated femaleness, by wearing ribbons and jewelry, sewing, dusting—and contemplating pictures of naked women.[92] These descriptions illustrate the multiple layers and nuances of the word 'feminine' as it is being used here, including the connections to art and the symbolic/imagination:

> There are periods every day, when I float in voluptuousness ... an indescribable feeling of well-being corresponding to feminine feelings... It is by no means always necessary to let my imagination play on sexual matters; on other occasions too, like reading a particularly moving part of a poem, playing a piece of music on the piano ... or enjoying nature ... soul-voluptuousness creates ... a kind of foretaste of Blessedness.[93]

As if anticipating the masculine heroic mode, a few pages earlier he had noted "manly contempt of death, as expected of men ... such as soldiers and especially officers in war-time, is not in the soul's nature".[94]

CHAPTER 10:
PARANOIA RE-VIEWED

Just because you're paranoid
doesn't mean they're not out to get you.
(Anonymous)

Inwardness, Mysticism and Spiritual Feminizing

The main points to consider in these three autobiographical accounts of paranoid breakdown are, first, the men were well educated, intelligent individuals (one can surely call them intellectuals). Second, all of them were troubled by religious questions and all believed they were having a religious experience. Third, the homosexual desire was part of the experience, not isolated from it in terms of guilt vis-à-vis religious injunctions.

The Freudian verdict of repressed homosexual desire becomes understandable—at a stretch—only if religion itself is seen as an 'infantile' illusion and hence, psychoanalysis looked to the literally infantile experiences of childhood in order to trace the origins of homosexual inclinations in parental dynamics. But if one were to read these cases from within the metaphysics of the psycho-sexual dynamics of religious mysticism, a very different picture emerges. This would not be inappropriate particularly since Freud and psychiatry notwithstanding, the men themselves, without exception, placed the *meaning* of their breakdown in a religious context.

*

To reiterate, sexuality and spiritual experience have traditionally been linked in the literature of mysticism, the great spiritual current running beneath all religions. Terms such as 'rapture', 'passion', 'union', 'ecstasy', 'ravish', occur frequently in mystical texts. Many so called 'esoteric' (to the Westerner) psychologies in the East, including the perspectives of certain types of yoga, tantra and sufism, would say that sexuality is really unexpressed and unfulfilled religious experience. This becomes understandable if one sees the word 'esoteric', not in its modern derogatory sense, but as the *inner* aspect of a spiritual/religious tradition, that is, mysticism.

In discussing the psychodynamics of 'low' fundamentalism, I had utilized a framework of gender based in an Islamic idiom in which mysticism can be viewed as the 'feminine' expression to religion. Similarly, many other mysticisms employ imagery pertaining to different types of knowledge based on bodily difference and a third unifying element that emerges when there is a union of difference. This union is frequently symbolized in the form of the hermaphrodite or androgyne, a common theme in many mystical/mythological systems. One can note here that all the three men experienced some form of androgyny and Freud's colleague, Bleuler, had noted that uncertain sexual identity, gender ambiguity, is present in nearly all cases of paranoid schizophrenia.[1]

In the context of mysticism, the figure of the hermaphrodite or androgyne and the disclosure of its meaning lies in initiatic systems, not only as it did for men and women of antiquity, but in many traditions today, as for example, in certain schools of Tantra, Tibetan Buddhism and Sufism. To quote Hillman, "initiation as a transformation of consciousness about life involves necessarily a transformation of consciousness about sexuality." He goes on to observe that, "the absence of initiation and of mysteries in Western culture is one main reason for its (west's) preoccupation with sexuality."[2]

The earlier example of the Master's and Johnson studies highlights this paradoxical modern preoccupation with sex and the underlying themes of what happens when sexuality is cut off from its spiritual counterpart. Like much else, sexuality keeps changing through life's phases, and has numerous expressions even in the phallic world: Pan, Priapus, Hermes, Dionysus, Zeus, Eros, are just some male images in this context. According to Hillman, the figure of Jesus as a rare exception both textually and iconographically wholly omits this phallic dimension. Individuals in Western culture are given no God-image as an example for the initiation and recognition of sexual being as spiritual being and vice versa.[3]

One could of course further discuss the intellectual and moral dimensions of the interplay of sexual images and initiation ceremonies. But there is no need to digress for the main point is that apart from the Gnostics in early Christianity and certain mystics in the Middle Ages, till today these ideas remain a significant part of almost all major religions via their mystical dimensions, except in contemporary Christianity.

The central role of initiation and its deep links with formalized rites of passage within an overall context of a 'mystery', has played a major role in the discrediting and/or marginalizing of mysticism in academic and theological discourse. The accusations range from a 'subjective' approach to knowledge and religion, to seeing initiatic communities as elitist. There is no doubt that these (self)revelatory dimensions to sexuality are not meant for everyone. However, in the context of the project of psychotherapy, this elitism is not any different from many types of depth psychologies and their analytic modes/vocabularies which also rely on an implicit elitism of intellectual ability and cultural sophistication, not to mention other high scientific/cultural/political/economic (post)modern knowledge contexts. To this extent, the secular world of various knowledges also remains an elitist enterprise.

What is more important, is to be aware of the consciousness behind the demand to know about such matters in mysticism 'clearly', and the resultant double bind regarding knowledge. As it is said, 'those who speak do not know and those who know do not speak'. Put another way, rationality in its power aspect, is unable to deal with silence and mysteries, and hence this type of knowledge is considered illegitimate, 'subjective', 'soft', useless. If this is so, it is because once again, the feminine side of the body is absent in consciousness. Secrets have to do with what is hidden, inward—and silent. Thus, whether in terms of the Cartesianist mind-body split, or in the view of 'those who believe can't think', there is the tendency to pathologize the religious impulse and which then indeed 'returns' as genuine pathology.

Beyond questions of initiation, the issue here is of analytic perspective. Namely, given the actually mutual concerns of psychology and religion in terms of self-knowledge, modern tendencies inherent in the former have largely excluded what the latter may have to offer, particularly in understanding the religious dimension of the psyche. A brief re-view of mystical religious symbols shows that this theme of feminizing/ *entmannung* is in fact widespread.

Starting with the 'primitive', as Eliade has written about the Shaman,[4] in some cultures initiatic rituals into priesthood involve a symbolic change of sex, including transvestism and homosexuality, living as a wife to another man. He is called a 'soft man' or a 'man similar to women'. That epitome of manhood, Hercules, after completing his labours did not go onto endless conquests but became a servant to a woman, Queen Omphale. Similarly Ulysses and Circe. Contemplation and worship of the feminine is an integral part of the statuary and practice of Hinduism. The Buddha's feminine characteristics are obvious: 'full-bellied, soft-breasted receptivity', large ears indicating a 'taking in' and the lotos posture representing compassion. The Sabbath in Jewish tradition is feminine. It is welcomed as a Queen, Shekinah, bringing peace and joy.[5] Finally, and interestingly, what is overlooked by Hillman in his writings, is that the most often repeated Attribute/Name of God in the Quran is Al-Rahman, the Gracious and Compassionate One. As was explained before, the etymological roots of 'Rahman' are directly related to those of 'womb'. The word 'Islam' then means to surrender to God's intentions for example as Mary did in her acceptance of her role in bearing Christ. As one moves towards a reconsideration of paranoia from within this alternative psycho-spiritual-sexual framework, one can arrive at a very different view of paranoid 'homosexuality'.

Eruption of Eros

The Freudian view of paranoia assumes that the material cause/drive of paranoia is homoerotic desire. This desire is then converted using standard modern logical frames such as the principle of contradiction etc. to arrive at a given meaning. Thus, the proposition 'I (a man) love him (a man)' can be contradicted by delusions of persecution, stating 'I do not love him, I hate him'. Since this is unacceptable to paranoid consciousness, it is projected into 'I do not love him, I hate him, because he persecutes me' or 'I do not love anyone'. In short whereas the material cause is homoerotic, the formal cause is noetic, that is, intellectual.[6]

Freudian theory postulates two basic instincts, *Eros* and *Thanatos* but the latter actually receives scant attention in Freud's writings. His focus was on the energy of *eros*, libido, which is a life integrative force and as such more than sexuality. To this extent, homoeroticism is one dimension of *eros* which contributes to "friendship and comradeship, to *esprit de corps* and to the love of mankind."[7] While recognizing the wide scope of *eros* as an instinct/function of relatedness, Freud's writings as a whole nevertheless clearly reduce it to sexual energy. As mentioned earlier, it was this attitude of literal reductionism which led to Jung saying, only half in jest, that the penis is 'nothing but' a phallic symbol. In short, the problem lies in how desire is *interpreted*, given meaning and place, or in psychoanalytic terms how libido is expressed. To quote Freud: "...Libido must go somewhere."[8]

(Post)Jungian psychology conceives of libido as *eros* itself and sexuality as one literal expression of it. A cat or dog rubbing itself languorously against the leg of its owner is manifesting *eros*-as-connectedness as much as the sexual act. Today even the most functionally oriented 'schools' of clinical psychology recognize that the problem with paranoia centers around relatedness, what depth-psychology calls *eros*. "No other problem can compare with paranoia in its power to negate trust and capacity to empathy that are required for intimate relatedness."[9] In our three cases of paranoia, the libido flows nowhere except in circles of words and language. All three detail at great length their almost constant preoccupation with words, literally. This atomizing obsession with words (*logos*) can be seen as prefiguring Derrida and the postmodern 'condition' today, which many see as an abyss of meaning-less-ness.

Deconstructed Logos

In the pre-modern world, words had a sacred/archetypal function, considered as repositories of sacred (mantric) power. They were seen as divine 'messengers', evoking presence(s) and hence to be used carefully. Many religions which retain a sacred liturgical language, including Islam, place great significance on the sacred nature of words. 'In the beginning was the Word' may also refer to the deep link between language and consciousness and one has noted the connections between *Logos* and Christ. (See Chapter 1.)

However, with the rise of science and modernity, words increasingly became a vehicle for accumulating facts rather than conveying meaning. Far too little attention has been paid to the fact that, for all our irreligiousness, the distinguishing mark of the Christian epoch, its highest achievement, has become the congenital vice of our age: *the supremacy of the word*. It prompted Jung to state that the 'congenital vice of our age' is that "the word has literally become our god and so it has remained, even if we know of Christianity only from hearsay."[10]

Once again, as Jung makes clear, this 'congenital vice' refers to a particular *attitude* within modern consciousness. It has nothing to do with being a practicing or even believing Christian, but rather, it's the result of a reductionist literalizing of Christ-as-*Logos* through language. Jung is thus referring to the modern tendency of concretizing concepts into words and then relating to them as if they were extraordinarily powerful forces in themselves. Words such as 'society', 'the state', 'nationalism', 'Islam', 'freedom', 'terrorism' have become like persons and we respond to them in intense and emotional ways. Similarly, in both academia and psychoanalysis (i.e. the 'talking cure'), there is increasing overvaluation of language and theo-ry in contrast to the cultural and experiential.[11]

As discussed in Chapter 1 and 2, *logos* is itself a powerful archetype and symbol with multiple meanings. Having a strong phallic/lingam dimension, it is a creative, spiritual, commanding force having Divine and human connotations in many religions. As an aspect of the creative force of the Divine, all language is a manifestation of the unity of *Logos*. Many religions reflect this feature of the word as sacred but Christianity is unique in the incarnation of Christ-as-Logos. As such, how He (Christ) is *interpreted* becomes crucial. In the absence of seeing His symbolic significance, or simply denying Him altogether, either way, there is a tendency to literalize this undoubtedly unique and important symbol. Both instances lead to a 'worship of the word'.[12] Differently put: *The Word became word.* The modern mind believes that by stating or explaining something one can generate change, even though daily experience constantly demonstrates otherwise, since most people simply don't do what they are told. (At which point there is the tendency to become violent.)

Imagine then, Jung's response if he had lived to witness postmodern linguistic deconstruction. From the literal point of view, linguistic deconstruction can in fact be seen as the culmination of the cult of the literal, seeing no inherent meaning in words, reducing them to quasi-mathematical units whereby both fact *and* meaning are rendered suspect. However, in keeping with what Jung called the psychodynamics of *enantiodromia*, that is, when taken to the extreme, a phenomenon starts exhibiting its opposite, linguistic deconstruction can also be seen as an interesting symbol.

To the extent of attempting to literally kill the literal (word), Derridan deconstruction can be seen as an attempt to rectify the excesses of modernity by attempting to undermine and destabilize its logocentric biases. Equating logocentrism with phallocratic patriarchy as done by feminists, it could also be said that the Derridan endeavour is also an attempt at linguistic/cognitive *entmannung*/unmanning, but unfortunately conducted in the most literally literal manner: castration will not suffice, the entire body must be chopped up until it is mincemeat. Only then can the tyranny of a modernized *logos and* the relational demands of *eros* be held at bay. Interestingly, Derrida was given to cross dressing and Foucault who was gay, it seems chose suicide through AIDS.

Returning to paranoia, the struggle with meaning and language of our three cases can be placed parenthetically between two statements encapsulating Derridan deconstruction: The first concerns deconstruction's "heightened sense of suspicion about the constructedness of our discourse" locating postmodernism in the trajectory of what Huston Smith calls "the latest brand of our [i.e. the West's] century long hermeneutics of *suspicion*."[13] That is, many dimensions of postmodernity are actually allied with modernity's self-destructive nihilism and paranoia. This is not to say that neither discourse has anything positive to offer, witness feminism, the critique of science, etc. But to claim on the basis of linguistic theories—and as Smith observes, they come and go in academia—that everything including religion is meaningless, is another matter.

This brings us to the second statement between which we can locate our three cases: Deconstruction's claim that 'there is nothing outside the text'. While I am aware that this can be understood variously,* one can say that had our three males read Derrida, this statement could have been one key cause of their paranoid agony. Since it is also asserted that deconstruction

---

* The original quote is "Il n'y a pas de hors-texte", which literally translates as "there is no outside-text". The more typically used translation "There is nothing outside the text" therefore puts an extra emphasis that is not necessarily contained within the original. (See https://en.wikiquote.org/wiki/ Jacques_Derrida)

actually affirms "openness to the other",[14] Boisen, Perceval and Schreber were doubly victims. Located temporally at the heart of modernity and having intellectually absorbed its 'hermeneutics of suspicion' their deconstruction of words and language was an attempt to establish precisely that there *was nothing* outside the text. But from the perspective of the Imagination, perhaps there was, an 'other'.

The belief that God was communicating with them as the 'Other' was filtered through a hermeneutic of suspicion only to be confounded by the demand/necessity of *entmannung*. Since, God was/is conceived in logocentric/phallocratic terms this actually makes literal (grammatical) sense but goes against traditionally normative human ideals of masculinity. Rather than be suspicious about the dogmas of (Christianist) theology, the response is an obsessional preoccupation with language, of being suspicious about words themselves, looking endlessly searching for disguised, hidden, coded meaning since there is nothing outside the text. Note that 'sanity' in Latin, originally meant the *rational* use of words. However, in deconstruction they have been reduced to nominalisms and ultimately to their suicide/murder. The word 'rational' itself being made into nominalism, no longer reflecting its meaning in the idea of *ratio*, of proportion between different elements.[15]

Since libido must indeed go somewhere, instead of *eros*/relationship there is sexual arousal denied/defended against by a logocentric ego through semantic-compulsion. The constant mental activity shows the "formal cause at work, converting the libidinal, erotic relation to the world into a semantic, hermeneutic relation to the world ... instead of desire, meaning."[16] That is, instead of *eros*, a pseudologos that literalizes desire as equivalent to sex. All the while accompanied by what has in fact become the hallmark of postmodern expression: a compulsive, endless, intense preoccupation with subjectivity for its own sake, as processed through words. The notion of doing something for its own sake, be it art or curiosity, is a crucial area of the difference(s) between the mundane imaginaton and the Imagination of Sufi metaphysics. While both give a central significance to individual subjectivity, their potentialities in terms of outcome/experience/knowledge are vastly different. Whereas the latter may lead to the Imagination and the Feminine, the other ultimately leads to endless navel gazing; literally, looking at a symbol (the navel) of what was once a locus of connection to a feminine origin/Source.

Among the three cases, Boisen recovered fully and to a great extent so did Perceval. A crucial factor for recovery was ultimately being able to distinguish the particular from the universal, and the literal from the symbolic or what Perceval called the 'poetic'. As Boisen wrote, "things are working out more literally than I had anticipated" and "I went too far and attempted to universalize my own experience."[17] Similarly, Perceval: "I suspect that many of the delusions which … insane persons labor under consist in their mistaking a figurative or a poetic form of speech for a literal one … the spirit speaks poetically but the man understands it literally … the lunatic takes the literal sense."[18] Perceval's narrative indicates that his insights were inspired from within himself and not by his doctors and their methods of healing which were/are entrenched in modern scientism.

The Freudian Error

From the perspective of religious mysticism, and also Archetypal Psychology, the Freudian error lies not so much in the importance given to sexuality, but lies, firstly, in its androcentricity and then reading all manner of absurdity into female consciousness, which, in its 'plumbing' (anatomy), is of course quite different from a man's. Even more importantly, in its literalization of the symbolic, it offers the delusion that sex is only sex and the penis simply a tool for physical gratification.[19]

Literalism of course leaves no room for the symbolic, poetic, metaphorical and ambiguous, leave alone concepts such as humor, playfulness. All these are absent both in paranoia and religious fundamentalism. Similar to science, all is dry literal 'facts' or then simply unknowable. From the evidence we have, none of our three cases were particularly helped by their physicians. Rather, as in the case of Boisen, eventually it was his faith and insight which enabled him to see the mistake of universalizing what was nevertheless for him a religious experience.

To this extent, Boisen's way out of the disease was to go further *in* to it. He was aware that his carefully listed delusions such as self-sacrifice, the end of the world, global disaster, rebirth, mystical identification with the cosmos, prophetic mission, all had to do with religion. Because of "the curative forces of the religion which was largely responsible for the disturbed condition,"[20] he recognized that his cure and salvation lay in the "faithful carrying out of the delusion itself."[21] By maintaining this multiple vision of both psychology and theology he recovered. That is, accepting the authentically religious basis of his condition while not attributing universality and literalism to it. In sum: it was only by *surrendering* to his delusions that he regained his sanity.

*

In religious mysticism, desire as a function of *Eros* can be related to the Divine. The mythic roots of this are vividly illustrated in the ancient story of (the human) female Psyche and the god Eros in which he seduces Psyche without first disclosing his identity. Eventually, Psyche's curiosity gets the better of her only to discover that she has fallen in love with (the god of) love-as-desire. There follow many troubles and travails of Psyche, but eventually, they are married and have a *daughter*, Voluptas, (Pleasure). This archetypal theme of the human soul's quest for Divine love is powerfully and beautifully adumbrated in the Biblical 'songs' of Solomon and David and numerous mystic Sufi poetic traditions across the Muslim world, especially in Iran and the Indian subcontinent. The poetry of, for example, Rumi or Bulleh Shah could not possibly have survived and have widespread appeal till today, had its essential content been understood in Freudian/sexual/literal terms. (Though it is dreadfully easy to do so in modern times.)

Eros, one should keep in mind, is a male god, representing the function of desire-as-relatedness and the need for connection which can be experienced as sensuous yet not sexual. *Eros* can also span the aesthetic experience or a child's sense of wonder in discovering sand. While at one level, it has a phallic dimension, at another, the filial connection with Venus along with his love for Psyche (and vice versa) gives Eros, a 'feminine' if not androgynous dimension. In linking paranoia to literal male-homosexuality, the Freudian error—like so much of modern academic/psychological discourse—was to take metaphysical ideas literally.

Writing the preface for the Hebrew edition of *Totem and Taboo*, Freud stated that whereas he was "completely estranged from the religion of his fathers," nevertheless he was "in his essential nature a Jew."[22] Eilberg-Schwartz's study on masculinity and monotheism shows how the social and political pressures of the time Freud lived in, impelled him to distance himself from femininity especially within Judaism.[23] In concurrence, Santner also notes that *Moses and Monotheism* "does indeed construct an image of Judaism as a sort of hypermasculine, neo-Kantian religion of reason ... the conception of Jewish spirituality and intellectuality proffered by Freud suggests a posture of severe self-control grounded in an endless series of instinctual self-renunciations."[24] Yet another study of Freud/Schreber sums up these strands as follow:

> Renunciation of the fulfillment of desire, which is encoded in Freud's text as masculine, is occasioned as a submissiveness vis-à-vis a male other, whether it be the 'great man' Moses or the deity. But that very submissiveness, the mark of the religious person, is itself feminizing in terms of nineteenth century culture.[25]

Since Freud's time till now, little has changed in these matters. The gay movement and 'metro sexuality' notwithstanding, if at all things are worse when one considers the widespread nature of masculinity inspired ('secular') violence. When it comes to religious fundamentalism, cultural, philosophical machismo prevails even more intensely. In sum, Freud's entire opus can be seen as an ultramasculine, sexualized theology which is widely manifest.

Eruption of the Feminine

Metaphor, symbol, is the soul's *logos*. That is, *eros*, the relational feminine dimension, functions symbolically. When conceptions of both God and (hu)man become singular, overly masculinized and literal, the result is a double literalization, *Eros*/sex, *Logos*/semantic logic. That is, when desire is understood only literally, then 'the defeat of that desire is also literal': "In the tandem, material and formal, when either is literalized, the other follows. When fellow feeling becomes homosexuality (even if only in theory and not in concrete behavior) then the countermove becomes equally fundamentalist."[26]

Thus, 'fellow feeling' within an exclusivist male imaginary, when expressed literally, leads to conditions such as our three case studies, who even while having homosexual desires, simultaneously envisioned women and also felt and behaved like women. In short the feminine was both real and imagined. As Ong says "in relation to God we are all—men and women—females. Macho insights reveal nothing about God."[27]

When repressed, *eros* and the Feminine are held at bay through reason and will power. But since one cannot entirely obliterate that which is the Source of life itself, the movement is of a recoiling which surfaces as paranoid suspicions directed at an outer, 'other'. The sense of connectedness is there, albeit negatively as 'suspicion' in our case studies. Whether religious or not, the psyches of the men as they experienced it eventually had to be broken down. Clinically a breakdown, it can also be seen as a 'break through' of something 'other' entering into an undiluted masculinity, creating a sense of interiority-as-experience. Unable to distinguish between an interior 'effeminization' having to do with the needs of soul, interiority is understood/experienced as (passive) homosexuality which cannot distinguish between effiminization and homosexuality. Hence, the experience of the feminine that is both voluptuous and fearfully alien. As such, the issue here is not a fear of homosexuality but simply of *relationship* with (hu)man or God.

Our three cases represent rational, educated individuals who ultimately had a partial view of self and the Divine. In an exclusively male imaginary, they experienced an intrusive eruption into ego consciousness of an unacknowledged, unknown 'other' which for them, by definition, could only be theologically male. In contrast to a wholly externalized consciousness, one way or another they underwent an experience of (feminine) interiority. Initially resisted and feared, eventually the ego had to surrender to 'unmanning'. While no doubt the Freudian 'return of the repressed', it all depends on what exactly was repressed and whether it is seen as salutary or sinister, symbolically or literally.

Beyond the 'secular' world and of psychopathology, from within Islam, one could add to Ong and Hillman's observations on inner, psychological femininity many times over as expressed through the myriad Sufi poets and the theme of Love as 'realized gnosis'. As Nasr says, it is a theme that "dominates Islamic spirituality," in which "God appears as the Beloved and the female as a precious being symbolizing inwardness and inner paradise."[28] Or Schuon: "Even without knowing that femininity derives from an 'Eternal Feminine' of transcendent order, one is obliged to take note of the fact that woman, being situated like the male in the human state, is deiform, because the state is deiform."[29] 'Esoteric' truth, the *haqiqah*, is felt as a 'feminine' reality.[30] And to this we can add yet another quote of Corbin:

> ... a mystic obtains the highest theophanic vision in contemplating the Image of feminine being, because it is in the Image of feminine being that contemplation can apprehend the highest manifestation of God... The spirituality of our Islamic mystics is led esoterically to the apparition of the Eternal Womanly as an Image of the Godhead.[31]

One difference between our Islamic mystics (including those of other traditions) and the three cases of paranoia, is that whereas the former were 'led' by esoteric teachings/teachers, the latter were culturally, intellectually and religiously bereft of such an idiom/community/guides. In keeping with their cultural context, all three relied unsuccessfully on medicine, psychiatry and psychology. Regardless of what the modern mind may 'think' about religion, Nature it seems, does not give a damn. In short, whether denied, resisted or narrowly conceived in male terms resulting in paranoid pathology, or consciously surrendering (Islam?), by being 'led esoterically' through self-knowledge and spiritual practice, to be receptive to divinity, is to be feminine. "For it is as a woman, the psyche in its female form, that the soul knows *and* receives God."[32]

The Best Medicine (for Paranoia)

Perceval's road to recovery took a somewhat similar route to Boisen's insofar as eventually he too, largely on his own, eventually 'saw through' the literal into the symbolic realities of his experience. Though he continued to have brief episodes, he learned to live with them in what was basically a normal life. "The revelation of the Spirit is not so much literal command as it is through allusion, hints, symbols and poetic intention ... the spirit speaks poetically, but the man understands it literally." Additionally, in the Spirit's tendency to allude and hint Perceval observes a sort of playful humor at work. "... the Deity ... often intimates his will by thus jesting', it has 'a spirit of humor ... of irony ... of drollery."[33] This sort of humor again is not meant to be taken literally but rather to nudge one towards a state of creative confusion. Confusion of course leads to doubt which is the prime antidote to fanaticism.

Mythologically speaking, the divinity of this sort of creative confusion is the Trickster archetype which invariably carries a strong element of humor. In Pakistan and other parts of South Asia, there is the devious *ayyar* of epic tales, or the living hermaphrodite, the *khusra* as one embodiment of this archetype. As a fertility symbol, traditionally the *khusra* sings and dances at celebrations linked to marriage and childbirth. The image confounds, confronts us with paradox, gently taunting our minds as we desperately attempt to define, contain, isolate and freeze meaning into an unsubvertible fixity.[34]

There is safety in certainty. The Trickster prevents certainty, opening up possibilities of multiple meanings. For the Greeks this idea was represented best in the symbol and etymology of Hermes Mercurius. The hermaphrodite/androgyne in ancient times was a profoundly spiritual symbol. Like its elemental namesake (quicksilver/mercury) it is impossible to pin down and slips through our fingers. Hermes was the winged messenger of Zeus. Simultaneously male and female, winged and walking, dark and light, this and that, may be. His insignia is a staff with wings and two serpents twined about it, symbolizing moral duality and he was considered a peacemaker, mediator (between heaven and earth), standing for conciliation, tolerance and peace. Till today this remains the emblem of the medical profession.

The meaning and significance of the Trickster archetype has been all but lost to the modern study (and practice) of religion. Researching the religion of Native Americans, "Western anthropologists found it incongruous that joking and humorous activities occurred simultaneously with rituals and ceremonies and often parodied and mocked them." (Note the etymology of delusion: *de ludere*, to play with, to mock.) Even though these modern observers assumed the incompatibility of humor and religion, credit is due to them for at least recognizing the function of this 'incongruity', albeit within a secular frame of social critique which "permits criticism without being overly aggressive."[35]

Humor happens when our usual way of thinking and perceiving is challenged. At its best, it is neither abrasive not unkind, but a playful presenting of *possibilities*, such as, for example, the ambiguities of meaning in a pun. Thus, when confronted with spiritual incongruity in a spirit of playfulness, we are rendered (potentially) vulnerable, made 'open' (interiorized/feminized) to possibilities and meanings *other* than established ones. Without aggressively forcing one to abandon existing belief, a good joke may provide us with choice, a different meaning. In passing one can note that studies of women's spiritualities suggest that many women, including gurus and teachers, has been termed as devout 'pundamentlists'.[36]

Boisen, Perceval and Schreber dwell in detail on the constant mind-word-games they experience, puns, *double entendres*, breaking up words to arrive at alternative meanings. Perceval's experience of the Trickster god led him to reformulate the Fall as the Loss of the Spirit of humor. Recognizing and accepting this aspect of divinity/spirit does not mean that God literally cracks jokes. Rather, it is to be confronted with the narrowness of one's personal conception of deity and to be released into doubt and re-visioning It. One can note in passing that in the Quran, God is also referred to as the Greatest of Planners, Strategizer or Deceiver (3:54). The root word *makr* has connotations of plotting, planning secretly with a view to circumventing, to practice deceit. Hence Rumi saying: "God has hidden severities within Gentleness and gentlenesses within Severity. This is God's trickery, concealment, and deception, in order that the people of discernment—those who see with the light of God—... may be separated from those who see only the present and outward situation."[37]

Thus, destabilizing meaning in image and word becomes a liberating catalyst of consciousness, throwing the 'mind' into (potentially) creative confusion. The work of religion, said Rumi, is bewilderment. And like Rumi, rather than try and reduce experience to legalistic dogma, Perceval surrendered to it, all the while listening with a poetic ear. "I could not seek health by sane conduct. I could not recover sanity, but by ways which can alone be justified by insanity."[38] In short, like Boisen, Perceval basically surrendered himself to the experience. While he does not refer to this in the Schreber case, even Freud acknowledged that analysis comes to an end when the struggle against "passivity", "repudiation of femininity" is abandoned.[39] In (post)Jungian terms this means when phallic ego-consciousness surrenders without feeling defeated.

The surrender of the ego is to that which it has repressed, that is, one's inner diversity especially the feminine. In Islamic terms this means when one stops regarding one's inner life only in terms of *jihad* and includes the notion of *ijtehad* which has to do with consensus and diversity of viewpoints without prejudice, seeing one's inner diversity as aspects of one's soul. Only then, perhaps, can events be released from their literal understanding into a more symbolic appreciation which in turn opens up the questions of life onto a wider transpersonal canvas of imaginative reflection. Thus, to be psychologically 'unmanned' is to let in the feminine "... weakness, submission, learning the art of surrendering first to art, humor... doubt ... fear of one's own certainty rather than suspicion of the other."[40]

All this and more is what the mystical experience is about without attaining pathological status. Rumi's mentor, Shams, can also be seen as an archetype of the Trickster, appearing disappearing, taking an irreverent and perverse delight in carnivalizing established religious norms thereby precipitating a creative confusion in Rumi's personal/professional/religious world *all* of which had to be abandoned in his surrender to Shams. The resulting transformation in Rumi brought about by the Creative Imagination was such that the poetry he was inspired with itself became a source of spiritual transformation for countless Muslims over centuries and into the present. Of the innumerable books written on Rumi's poetry as well as on Shams, not one would claim that their spiritual styles reflect the stereotypical notion of holy piety. At one level indescribably moving and beautiful, their language and discourses also use all manner of word play and a healthy dose of hilarious, even scatological references and images.

Summing up his cure, Perceval unwittingly relies on the image of Mercurious/Trickster seeing the two serpents as male and female aspects of a dual human nature: "The weaker or more 'feminine' brings humor, mirth, and merrymaking [which] are necessary to the minds' pliability"[41] By not literalizing and universalizing, but surrendering while remaining receptive to humor and poetic allusion, Perceval learned to doubt: "I perished from a habitual error of mind, common to many believers ... that of *fearing to doubt.*"[42] Behind every fanaticism, said Jung, lurks a secret doubt. Fundamentalists refuse to give themselves the benefits of doubt.

Of the three cases, Boisen and Perceval recovered. Both of them lived into their seventies, married after being released and devoted themselves to an active concern with lunacy laws and the plight of the insane. The paranoid sense of prophetic mission was transformed into a social mission. Schreber did not recover and had to be intermittently institutionalized till his death. Nevertheless, a hundred years later Western academia remains fascinated by his case. As such, he remains a symbol of an ongoing malaise.

Chapter 11:
Modernity and Paranoia

*The European, or rather the white man in general, is scarcely in
a position to judge his own state of mind. He is to deeply
involved. From time immemorial, nature was always filled with
spirit. Now, for the first time, we are living in a lifeless nature
bereft of Gods.*
(C.G. Jung[1])

Schreber's Memoirs and the New World Order

The significance and impact of Schreber's *Memoirs* has
extended beyond psychiatry/psychology and the clinical
understanding of paranoia. Since its publication more than a
century ago, prominent thinkers have analyzed the text
including luminaries such as Elias Canetti,[2] De Leuze and
Guattari,[3] Foucault,[4] Niederland,[5] Lothane,[6] Schatzman[7] and
Chabot.[8] Jacque Lacan's medical dissertation was on paranoia
including the Schreber's case. A major theme in these studies is
the psychological link between the Schreber material and various
collective modern pathologies spanning Nazism to psychiatry
and psychology, both of which can be seen in terms of

convictions verging on a sort of religious perversity. Canetti discerned strong parallels between the totalitarian leader and the paranoid as linked with a thirst for power. Schreber's delusions "prefigured the totalitarian solution to the crisis afflicting the bourgeois-liberal order at the turn of the 20th Century."[9]

Post analytic studies of Schreber suggest that the continuing fascination with the significance of the *Memoirs* is that his "madness (paranoia) is not a particular madness, it is *general*."[10] The general madness of which Schreber is an image/idea/symbol, has to do with the nature of (post)modernity as contextualized in discourses of history, power and knowledge, including medicine and psychiatry.

Eric Santner's is a notable post-analytic, postmodern study of the *Memoirs*. It is an analysis of the dark underside of modernity which, if not recognized, contains in it the seeds of facism. Santner's *My Own Private Germany: Daniel Paul Schreber's Secret History of Modernity* is a psycho-historical deconstruction of Schreber's *Memoirs and* Freud, not only as analyst of the *Memoirs* but also as a man dealing with his own unconscious homosexual impulses, professional ambitions, and issues related to his ultramodern rejection of religion including Judaism.

Locating both patient and his various doctors in the context of wider socio-political and intellectual issues, Santner shows how Schreber's paranoia and Freud's *ideas about* Schreber's paranoia can be seen as two sides of the same phenomenon: both were part of a historical anxiety created by rapid sociological and technological change manifest in "feelings of extreme alienation, anomie and profound emptiness."[11] Schreber's *Memoirs* and Freud's analysis become symptomatic of what happens to individuals when there are quantum changes in "the fundamental matrix of the individual's relation to social and institutional authority."[12] That is, when 'official' power and authority are no longer capable of "seizing the subject in his or her self-understanding."[13] The simultaneous emergence of new and different authorities, for example, disembodied modern knowledge systems and institutions, experts/specialists legitimized by science and technology—and this is what modernity created—serve to alienate the individual further.

Santner points out that the post Cold War period has many psychological similarities with fin-de-siècle Europe and the enormous upheavals of that time. Writing in 1996, about the New World Order proclaimed by George Bush Senior, (reminiscent of Schreber's Order of the World?) Santner notes that "there has been a disturbing rise of expressions of paranoia in the United States and elsewhere just as new geopolitical arrangements, ideological investments, and shifts of populations and capital come to fill the vacancy, left by the end of the cold war."[14] He finds this paradoxical since the end of the Cold War should have eased paranoid anxieties all around. Instead:

> It now appears that cold war paranoia may have actually played the role of a collective psychological defence mechanism against a far more disturbing pathology that is only now beginning to find avenues of public expression. Nostalgia for the more ordered world of cold war anxieties would appear to be *a nostalgia for a paranoia in which the persecutor had a more or less recognizable face and a clear geographical location* ... my work is informed by a concern that where there is a culture of paranoia fascism of one kind or another may not be far behind.[15]

Post-9/11 it seems that what Santner calls the (U.S.'s) 'nostalgia' for an enemy with a 'recognizable face' as the object of its paranoia became fulfilled by Islam. At the same time, without detracting in any way from Santner's incisive critique of (post)modernity via Schreber and Freud, had Santner cast even a cursory glance beyond the U.S., he may have noted a parallel, emergent paranoia within the Muslim world regarding Western perceptions of a steadily demonized Islam. Not to mention a long existing, almost global paranoia about the U.S. in much of the non-Western world, including the Muslim world. Similarly, as noted at the start of this chapter, paranoia was evident in Europe around the same time as George Bush's proclamation of the New World Order. These trends were becoming globally evident by the late 80's when the Soviet Union collapsed and when Muslim paranoia about American paranoia about Islam had impelled certain scholars to explore this issue already in the early 90's.[16]

Whereas Santner reacts to paranoia in the U.S. in political and economic terms about the New World Order during this period (early 90's), others analyzed the more socio-cultural trends, such as a boom in the proliferating service industry of 'private investigators' specializing in spying on spouses or a prospective mate. Apart from the increasingly evident 'victim syndrome' particularly as encouraged by psychology/psychiatry, there were other, less publicized reports indicating the widespread nature of paranoia among ordinary citizens and their experience of the Trickster archetype. For example, there is a record of a correspondence between a certain Sally Fox, her Congress representative and the FBI in which she had complained that the comedian "Bob Hope's insanity was violating (her) civil rights" by "interfering in her normal thinking".[17] It transpired that the FBI had actually been receiving "Eight hundred to nine hundred complaints *a day* from people all around the country saying the same thing: Bob Hope is crazy, and interferes with their normal thinking."[18]

On a more serious note, it has also been examined how the paranoia within US academia during the 80's regarding feminist spirituality went in tandem with a new found involvement with religion in the male academy. Textual analysis of the latter revealed close similarities to the language used when a gay person decides to come out of the closet. That is, barring one's professional interest in theology, being drawn to religion seemed to elicit the same anxieties associated with admitting one was gay. Simultaneously, feminist engagement with religion, unless within the traditional malestream, was dismissed by leading academics as 'New Age Nonsense'.[19]

Seen in its wider historical context, Schreber's breakdown was precipitated by what Santner calls a "crisis of investiture" that is, when rites and procedures through which an individual is endowed with a new social status, cease to transform a person's self-understanding. In Jungian and anthropological terms this is similar to the idea that rites of passage while enacted ritually (literally) are primarily symbolic in purpose, aiming to transform (self)consciousness/awareness. This transformation can only occur if the symbolic Imagination is valued and is in turn grounded in human psychological development realities. As has been made clear, the erosion/denial/loss of the symbolic is of course one of the main features of modernity and I referred to speeded up rites of passage in individuals such as Mohamed Atta or young males generally today, including Pakistanis.

According to Santner, when acts of symbolic investiture no longer usefully transform the subject's self-understanding, the performative force of these rites may assume the shape of a demonic persecutor, some 'other' who threatens our borders and our treasures. Libido must go somewhere as Freud said, which in Jungian terms means that the psychospiritual energy of these rites either in terms of absence or displacement, recoils on itself to create a pathology which is a sort of negative theology in terms of creating a mental state of 'God Almightiness'. The heroic ego becomes even more inflated, deluded and even more paranoid. Incidentally, Santner provides evidence that it was Jung who first alerted Freud to the Schreber text through one of his studies but Freud chose not to acknowledge this. Santner sees this intellectual 'lapse' as part of Freud's own incipient paranoia which made him "compromise the originality and integrity of his own authorial voice."[20]

Whether political, cultural or academic, it was evident that the end of the cold war simultaneously witnessed a global resurgence of religion and different types of socio-political paranoia. Fin-de-siecle Europe at the turn of the last century seems a mildly unpleasant dream compared to the present nightmare unfolding in the Middle East and now gradually involving the whole world, including the West.

Roosters, Pea-Cocks and Cultural Paranoia

The (post)Jungian critique of modernity shows that it is psychologically strongly anchored in a Cartesian-Christianist ethos which is intolerant, exclusivist, violent, literal and misogynist; regarding the world in absolute, black and white, monolithic terms. Modern Islamism presents a similar face, and in their totalizing, masculinized ideals of self and God, both find all manner of moral justification for violent actions, opposing anything that is different, including that which is inward, ambiguous, metaphoric, feminine. This is the psychology of modern fanaticism whether Western, Muslim, 'secular' or religious. And this is partly why the U.S. and al-Qaeda/Daesh seem to be echoes of each other, what Bruce Lincoln calls "symmetric dualism,"[21] mirror images of what is actually in many ways a similar (un)consciousness. Between them, in more ways than one, they alert to us the invisible realities of the symbolic creative imagination.

When a person or nation's beliefs breakdown, there is a general disorder. Instead of regarding the disorder as a rebellion against itself, the heroic state/ego's response is paranoid violence against what is sees as 'other(s)', to which it is in reality inextricably related. Post Cold War and 9/11, the USA as an analogue of the ego continues to deny its historical contributions to the present. In the process of denial its own, equally heroic and violent shadow rises from different places. Whether individuals or nations, we are all in, and yet not in the mirror of the other. Which is why there is this dizzying sense of unreality. Swept along by the momentum of the Hero-Shadow of modernity and his notion(s) of God, wherever one is located on the globe, the fear is inescapable as we sleepwalk through events that we think we 'see through' and yet cannot stop the dream-nightmare.

To the extent that the Al-Qaeda/Daesh and American rhetoric mirror each other's paranoia, both exhibit what has been earlier referred to as the Rooster or Pea-Cock factor in modern modes of thought. That is, rivalry between purportedly incommensurable perspectives is often only an illusion caused by *rivalry between men*. It is an illusion since it is based within a purely male imaginary, only one sex, which constitutes a given psycho-political, academic, philosophical arena. As Teichmann puts it:

> The creative ethnographic-reading imagination tells us, surely, that these dogmas represent nothing more or less than the tribal mores of teenage human males. ... Why do philosophers elevate the temporary instinctual behavior patterns of the male teenager, into (allegedly) self-evident truths? The creative imagination readily suggests an answer, but it is not a very polite one.[22]

While Teichmann takes shelter in feminine propriety, one impolite answer is that the paranoid discourse of our Islamist and American/European protagonists has to do with the sexual/religious syndrome delineated in our case studies and exemplified by Schreber and Freud. Catalyzed by (post)-modernity, the syndrome has to do with a crisis in masculinity and its spirituality, or lack thereof.

As many of the studies on Schreber show, his delusions could be linked to different currents in modernity, such as a steady disembodiment in the study of 'mind', which in turn attempted to control the body (women, nature) through ascending technoscience. Other studies bolster and amplify this connection showing how in the 19th Century there was a proliferation of research programs which aimed to maximize the productivity of the 'human motor' and to minimize what Santner sees as "the body's stubborn subversion of modernity."[23]

This tendency towards disembodiment has only gained momentum over the last century and so have the body's attempts to cope with it. As was already mentioned, 'hysteria' in women, literally 'the wandering uterus' and widespread during the 19th and early 20th Century in the West, has given way to the more serious *anorexia nervosa* which has become a visually graphic symbol of the state of the Feminine in the human soul/psyche. But to return to our primary subject, males/masculinity, another part of the impolite answer to Teichmann's observation can be discerned in Santner's rhetorical question emerging from his study of Schreber: "In a certain sense, Schreber's *Memoirs* could be seen as an attempt to answer the question ... *what remains of virility at the end of the nineteenth and beginning of the 20th century?*"[24] A century down the road, the short, impolite answer is: not much. Except in war. But then again, given the reliance on drones etc., the question still remains.

*

Teichmann's observations about modern philosophy and academic discourse reflecting the mores of teenage males, can be linked up to an even more impolite answer to the question

Santner poses on behalf of Schreber.

A cursory glance at the temporary instinctual tribal mores of teenage males indicates that they sexually tend to swing from one self-absorbed extreme to another, such is the nature of testosteronal awakening. Additionally, since most societies still frown upon heterosexual sex at an early age the overwhelmingly hormonally driven energy of that stage frequently finds a 'safe' outlet of an intrasexual nature. Frequently this is disguised in competitive games which ensure intimate bodily contact, e.g. wrestling, an anxious preoccupation with relative size and 'performance', hand-to-hand combat, so to speak; or then, the homosexual act itself. Not necessarily as a precursor of being gay but simply as a stress release mechanism for what, at that age, can only be a literalized *eros and* phallic *logos*.

Given that we inhabit the Age of the Literal, one does not have to resort to any depth analysis of symbols to come up with an answer to Santner's question about modern virility. That is, since symbols are transpersonal they are still present but almost entirely reduced to literalisms. At one level, the situation is similar to Baudrillard's analysis of late capitalist society in which all distinction between image and reality, depth and surface have vanished creating a hyper-reality internal only to the media. In a media-ted world, instead of signs having real life referents there is an endless stream of autonomous signifiers of self-referent images/imitations.[25]

However, from the perspective of the Imagination this hyper-reality is no less 'real'. Given that symbols are the language and substance of the Imagination that is indelible and only partially 'dependent' on the human psyche in its capacity to 'read'/'see' them, the literal level of the symbol will retain and reflect this indelible quality. Put another way, in the absence/waning of the sense of the sacred/symbolic connection we are literally confronted by symbol(s). They are what they say, literally. Thus, the question about what remains of virility today has an obvious, literal answer: between Roosters and Pea-Cocks, and the enormous global sales of Viagra, not to mention dropping sperm counts in the North, the literal answer self-evidently points to a handicapped virility diminished in scope and expression.

As the physical manifestation of a psycho-spiritual condition, positive virility has also to do with chivalry, controlled power, a respect and devotion to the feminine and all it represents, and a recognition that this is the only way life can flourish. In the absence of these, however rational and strong, virility becomes paranoid sterility; literal violence, hostile and ultimately destructive of self and others.

Libido must go somewhere. Beyond 'going' violently at women's bodies, unable to reconcile and distinguish between desire and 'fellow feeling', it is repressed, transformed into paranoid homophobia and projected onto other males. Not always as sexual desire of course but in delusions of Grandiosity or Persecution, bound together by the glue of fear and insecurity about the intentions of the other, including the 'Feminine Other'.

The Bottom Line

Contemporary cultural paranoia has as much to do with homophobic diminished virility as with a fear and horror of the feminine. Social historians have shown how in heteronormative contexts, sodomy becomes a form of punishment. Crimes such as theft are treated to a regime of 'penetrative penalty' utilizing sodomy as a form of humiliation through establishing the 'penetrated' as the inferior male.[26] Post-9/11, two images encapsulate this male behavior. The first was a cartoon of Osama bin Laden being sodomized by a U.S. bomb, with the 'penetrated'/'penetrating' twin towers in the background. The second was a news shot of a bomb headed for Afghanistan and the words "High Jack this fags" written on it.[27] These images make explicit the nature of Teichmann's demurral about the real nature of "teenage male mores" as the psychodynamics dominating the present historical moment, and how the protagonists identify themselves and the other(s): He did it to 'us'; now we are going to do it to him. The disclosures of Abu Ghraib and other atrocities by U.S. troops in Iraq provide, yet again, the literal confirmation of this impulse.

In a different context, Jonathan Goldberg's *Sodometries* examines the preoccupation with sodomy by Europeans encountering the New World.[28] Cortez, the leader of the Conquistadors, noted in his first letter to Spain that "they are all sodomites!" Goldberg analyzes this preoccupation as aiming to make the victim of conquest inherently preposterous and thereby rationalize the discourse of conquest. Simultaneously, this logic masks the conquerors' own desire to colon-ize which becomes nothing more than a euphemism for violation/rape/humiliation/dominance.

As Freccero point out, looking at sodomy from within such a frame is problematic only in the context of Western modernity's struggles in understanding gay identity. Particularly in the U.S., constructions of homosexuality do not distinguish between the 'old discourse' of penetrated/penetrator. Given the heroic either/or, black/white approach, you are 'homosexual' irrespective of the position you assume, 'active/passive'. But the seemingly dead metaphor 'fag' on the bomb suggests otherwise, at least in the subjectivity of the U.S. military, not to mention how militarized masculinity conceives of sexuality as lethal penetration.[29]

One has already detailed the links of all stripes of Islamists with the motif of homosexuality and an outward machismo which valorizes violence and demeans women. Even in civilian contexts in Pakistan, politicians tell each other to 'go and put on bangles' which is meant as an insult to an opponent who is perceived as 'weak'. In both instances, Islamist or American, this game—of teenage male mores—continues, in which both sides continue on a path of overt or covert 'penetrative penalty'. Given the unacknowledged and fearful psychological underpinnings (fear of the feminine and being penetrated-as-inferior/woman), both continue to generate global paranoia.

Within modernity these psycho-sexual politics are also vividly present in the idea of the nation state and international discourse. The following extracts about paranoid symptoms from some standard clinical manuals/texts in psychology, vividly describes the present situation, whether of nations, for example the United States or Pakistan, or the Islamists, or the countries of the 'international community':

> "Pervasive and unwarranted suspiciousness and mistrust." "Individuals are hypervigilant and take precautions against perceived threat". "Perceive an unusually wide range of stimuli". "Tend to avoid blame even when it is warranted". "Avoidance of depression". "Question loyalty of others". "Insist on secrecy". "Severe and critical with others". "Tendency to counter-attack". "Unwilling to comprise". "Intense but suppressed anger". "Driving ambitions, aggressive and unusually hostile and destructive". "Generate uneasiness and fear among others". "Often interested in mechanical devices, electronics and automation". "Avoid surprise by virtually anticipating it". "Dread ... passive surrender". "Inordinate fear of losing power to shape events in accordance with their own wishes". "Transformation of internal tension into external tensions". "Continuous state of total mobilization". "Giving into external domination and giving into internal pressure involve a threat". "Fear of being tricked into surrendering some elements of self-determination". "Generally uninterested in art and

aesthetics". "Friends are constantly tested...until they withdraw or actually become antagonistic". "rarely laugh". "Lack of true sense of humor". "Keenly aware of who is superior or inferior". "what looks like comfortable familiarity...is not friendly, only designed to look friendly". "Disdain people seen as weak, soft ... very sensitive to criticism and have an excessive need for autonomy."[30]

Post-9/11, Western analyses of Bin Laden/Al-Qaeda were surfeit with 'expert' opinions of the same syndrome. Given Western psychology's own unconsciousness, it actually offers precious little other than the most facile observations which are then absorbed into perspectives on international affairs. Just to give one example from Benjamin Orbach in the *Middle East Review of International Affairs*: The individuals of Al-Qaeda are "angry lost souls ... a mishmash of disgruntled poor', looking for "a ticket out of their empty, routine existence ... to become a hero,"[31] which can just as well describe the motivation for joining the army in any country and otherwise also the majority of young males on the planet. Similarly, modernity is simply about video games and alcohol, not a shared psychology. Thus the terrorists were "placed perilously close to modernity, but could not partake of it."[32] Yet, oddly, they could reflect an "extraordinary amount of patience and planning and intelligence."[33] Textual analysis of a poem by Bin Laden shows a "clear picture of his perception of the world into exactly defined and opposing spheres..."[34] Similarly, militants like Atta were inspired basically by guilt for indulging in alcohol, video games, etc. and they did what they did in order to be redeemed! Towards the end, the author concludes that actually bin Laden has been transformed into a myth and hero by the U.S. and the media. The real threat is not him but of a "radical ideology that has ... no interest in negotiation with the West."[35] Another expert writing on 'Terrorist Psycho-Logic' offers this gem of psychological insight into the question of why people turn to terrorism. "Individuals become terrorists in order to join terrorist groups and commit acts of terrorism."[36]

CHAPTER 12:
BEYOND PARANOIA

Behind every fanaticism lurks a secret doubt.
(C.G. Jung¹)

Revelation and Paranoia

We have yet to answer the question as to who decides what is the (in)correct meaning in revelation and paranoia.

Today, it seems that the criteria of the former belong to theology and the latter to psychology. The pro-fessor (psychology) and con-fessor (religion) have become the arbiters of the pros and cons of paranoia and theology. Between them, meaning has been monopolized. Whereas earlier it was only women, today all those who disagree with the official malestream narratives are either mad or bad.

The clinical criteria of paranoid insanity are mostly social or rather used to be so. That is, if more than a few individuals hold a similar belief, it cannot be paranoia. At the same time, as the Nazi's or Jonestown suggest, not to mention the millions waiting for the Apocalypse today, social criteria are inadequate for differentiating delusion from revelation. The problem remains, in what is by now a 'post-truth' world, as to who decides how to discern the meaning of events or texts, sacred or secular.

Perhaps the problem is in the modern way of posing the question. Typically, it is to separate, categorize, and then search for explanations. To see, for example, delusion and revelation as different categories of experience, or to separate the individual from society. Whereas, the meaning may actually be in their interconnection. "...psychiatry cannot reach the endemic paranoia, the delusional potential in individuals without addressing its source in the collective: the doctrinal need for a hidden God whose revelations cannot be clearly distinguished from delusions."[2]

The primary issue has to do with the transpersonal dimension of the individual, whether we locate this connection in 'society' or other equally large concepts like 'God'. The point is that paranoia has to do with both the personal and transpersonal. It becomes particularly evident when the latter is conceived, as it is by religious fundamentalists, as wholly Other and utterly Unknowable. And whatever little is known about It, is invariably Male. Meaning follows accordingly in what is foremost, a *dis-ease* about other invisible (to you and me) connections.

A most significant *disconnection* in history is, of course, Cartesianism's separation of (meta) mind and (physical) body. The impact of scientism has already been discussed at many levels, on both the Western and/or 'high' Islamist mind. As evident in dominant secular and religious ideologies, it includes the repression of the feminine in both (hu)man consciousness and its conception of the Divine. While both secular and religious fundamentalisms may be seen as a last resort for clinging to meaning, their paranoia nevertheless remains; hence a continued sense of suspicion about the 'other'. As the three cases of paranoia reveal, this 'other' can also be a transpersonal 'Other' with which all protagonists remain unconsciously connected. Given that our theological dictionary states that there could be no 'dealing, let alone fellowship' with a permanently hidden God, and more importantly, that 'it belongs to the *nature* of deity to manifest itself', can these suspicions/paranoia have to do with this 'Nature'?

In the *Gift of Death*, Derrida discusses the figure of Abraham and the sacrifice demanded of him by this 'Other', i.e. the God of Judaism, Christianity and Islam. The internecine strife between these religions can be seen as an endless enactment of the original sacrifice in which "I can respond only to the one (or to the One), that is, to the other, by sacrificing the other to that one." At one level, this seems to be self-evidently and existentially correct. However, it is so only when God is regarded to begin with, as implied by Derrida, to be wholly Other. Then indeed each (human) 'other' is also perceived in similar terms. Interestingly, in recounting the sacrifice of Abraham, Derrida is "struck by the absence of woman" in a story of masculine figures, of hierarchies among men (God the father, Abraham and his son). Derrida does not consider the most obvious possibility, that is, can this Other also be the Feminine?

If it is in the 'nature' of Deity to reveal itself, then between modernity and religious fundamentalism, paranoia can be considered as a combination of fear, denial and refusal to *acknowledge* the Immutable Feminine other and which insists on being known. This is what Jung partly meant when he said that religion is a defense against a religious experience: "Religion means dependence on and submission to the irrational facts of experience."[3]

The misogyny of all fundamentalisms, thus (self-)creates a self-perpetuating paranoia. As became evident through our case studies, it is a misogyny that is not only religious but also intellectual/secular, one which cannot readily bear mystery, ambiguity and blurred concepts of consciousness (or gender). It assumes that the hidden (Feminine) is either utterly unknowable or harmful. Literalized in attitudes to women in the Muslim world, the hidden must either remain out of (in)sight, or then, in modern Western terms, like women's bodies, scientifically 'fully exposed'. Either way, there is a reluctance to respect It and live on *Its* terms and take responsibility for what this entails.

Beyond Heroic Solutions

The preceding exploration of paranoia and homosexuality was located in the encounter with not only sameness, but also difference. Insofar as both men and women are similar and different, the same can be said for their religious experiences. If the focus in this book has been on males/masculinity, it is partly because it is the dominant available material. This is not said in rancor or dismay but simply as statement of fact about the Hidden Feminine. Similarly, the focus on the negative masculine is neither to deny its positive dimensions nor to deny the negative aspects of the feminine. Again, it is a question of what perspectives need to be highlighted against existing dominant ones. Put another way, if modernity creates a dominant exclusivist and hyper-masculine notion of self (ego), it does so by repressing inner psychological diversity, not only regarding alternate masculinities vis-à-vis the heroic ego, but especially all that is feminine.

According to Freud, in situations of stress, the dominant mass of ideas constituting the ego are challenged by the return of the repressed and the ensuing conflict becomes the core of symptom formation when "what was abolished internally returns from without."[4] Whereas Freud was looking at things in terms of literal homosexual desire, his statement can be read at an entirely symbolic level. That is, paranoia can be seen as a defense against the return of the repressed feminine/Feminine which, in our case studies, and the present global climate of violence, indicates that the Feminine is not just about life, love and art. That is, one is not suggesting that since the problem can be summed up as 'masculine', salutary solutions are to be found in the 'feminine'.

Seeking and suggesting facile solutions is to be sentimentally hijacked by the masculinist ego which *needs* (creates) problems in order to solve them thus validating itself through power and reason, and this syndrome of creating/solving 'problems' eventually leads to Final Solutions. From our archetypal view, the problem is not posed in order to provide solutions. Rather, it is to open the questions of life to transpersonal and culturally imaginative reflection.

Viewing global paranoia from this lens, the return of the repressed Feminine alerts us to the totality which is life, that is (Mother) Nature itself. The great Hindu goddesses graphically portray this Totality of life, death, rebirth. As the matrix from which all life emerges, the Feminine is also the place of death and dis-solution, engendering in us the antithesis of the heroic: a sense of the small, limitation, decay, humble insignificance, fear, doubt, yielding, surrender. Resisting the return of these not-so-nice realizations within the psyche ensures Her return is with a vengeance and one has noted the consequences of heroic resistance to it in Schreber's case. In this context, Shakespeare's enduring insight into human nature and the power of images that grip the public imagination, telescoped the Return/Revenge of the Repressed when he wrote 'Hell hath no fury like a woman scorned'. The film *Fatal Attraction* is a vivid contemporary rendering of the same syndrome. At a different, more salutary level, the return of the forgotten feminine in Christianity is evident in global bestsellers such as *The Da Vinci Code*; played out, let us remember, in an arena of males murdering each other in a Cartesian-Christianist milieu.

*

Having males as the thematic focus of this book is not to imply that women are unaffected by the problematics of modernity. In spite of feminism, one really still has scant knowledge of these matters vis-à-vis women, that is, the nature of women's spiritualities and sexualities outside of the male imaginary. As a whole, this area remains to be further explored and documented. While there are many self-accounts of women and mental illness, there is nothing to parallel Boisen, Perceval and Schreber in terms of a genre or thematic coherence.

Interestingly, till the mid 60's, textbooks were quite categorical that paranoia occurred more in males.[5] Today, it seems it is "slightly more common in women than in men."[6] Depending where one locates oneself in the feminist spectrum, this can be construed as 'progress', one more step ahead in the demand for equality. However, given the dominance of the male imaginary especially within psychiatry/psychology, it indicates yet again the plight of women and the feminine in modern consciousness, not to mention the 'tricky' ideas of delusion and paranoia.

The Masters and Johnson syndrome about women's multiple orgasm(s) finds its counterpart in this 'official' increase in women with paranoid delusions. It is reminiscent of a story in which a paranoid keeps proclaiming he is dead. The doctor fails in persuading him. Finally, he asks the patient if dead men bleed? 'Of course not' is the reply. At which point the doctor pricks the finger of the patient and then asks him if he is dead. On seeing the blood flowing, the patient responds "whaddya know doc, dead men *do* bleed!"[7] It seems the male imaginary is incorrigible when it comes to women who, in turn, are unable to resist what they experience as a 'fatal attraction' towards desiring equality on the basis of no difference between the sexes.

Nevertheless, thanks to modernity, for the first time in history, literacy is becoming available to women on a vast scale and eventually one hopes that other ways of looking at paranoia will emerge. Meanwhile, in both the Western and Islamic world, more and more women are getting involved in a spectrum of conservative religious movements, paranoia and all. At the same time, apart from conservative movements, emerging research indicates some interesting features showing how women's attitudes to spirituality and religion can be radically different from men's attitudes. Outside of fundamentalism, women seem to have a general predisposition to mysticism and hence, towards a more inclusive, 'heretical' relationship with a given religion (Which leads of course to intra religious paranoia). Another feature has to do with a marked presence of humor about life, themselves, even God.[8]

*

Written more than a century ago when the modernity-project was in the process of consolidation and expansion, Perceval's observations remain startlingly relevant to understanding not only the impact of modernity on the human psyche, but also the contemporary dominant face(s) of religion. Initially a voice from within the Christian West, his words can be contemplated also by those who today see themselves as both Muslims and modern intellectuals:

> I conceive therefore that lunacy is also a state of confusion of *understanding* by which the mind mistakes the commands of the spirit of humor, or of irony, or of drollery ... that many minds are in this state...that perhaps this is the state of every human mind. ... I mean in the operations of the human intellect, the Deity ... often intimates his will by thus jesting ... if I may be allowed to call it so ... making false every future

deliberation and conception, and action. Hence, I imagine, it is, that those who profess religion are often so hypocritical.[9]

Beyond paranoia, Perceval's observations about multiple possibilities of meaning within the Word are relevant to all types of oral/written secular/sacred discourse and anticipate deconstruction by a hundred years. His words regarding hypocrisy also hold up a mirror to ethical issues within post-structuralism regarding individual and political responsibility and questions of justice. Without these dimensions, post-structuralism becomes the collective intellectual equivalent of the psychopathology of paranoia. Apart from the 'initiated', no wonder many find academic post-structuralism nihilistic, bewildering in its jargon and a subject of derision. An Islamic deconstruction of post-structuralist deconstruction could lead to the conclusion that the latter's quest is akin to the archetypal madman, Majnun and his quest for Laila.[10] Given that Majnun's madness/quest was for the Feminine, the analysis must distinguish between those who deconstruct linguistically for its own sake and those who are in search of something that is both within *and* outside the Text.

The Last Word

Shadows & shit

The Quran itself becomes the penultimate postmodern (i.e. ancient) expression—elliptical, parabolic, baffling, challenging—one can say today, even playing with, the compulsively defining modern mind. As this mind turns to religion, and it seems many well educated Muslims are doing so, it needs to be aware that the extent of God's (un)knowability, in some measure, is related to ignorance/knowledge of oneself.

To repeat once more: Knowledge of oneself (soul) comes

before knowledge of God, says the *hadith*. To which one can add that the capacity for seeing difference/diversity (*ijtehad*) *within* oneself will be reflected accordingly in one's conceptions of Divinity. The Quran takes diversity as a given; among God's signs "is the creation of the heavens and the earth, and the diversity of your tongues and colors. In that surely are signs for those who possess knowledge/learning." (30:22) elsewhere it says "...We have created you, male and female, and have made you peoples and tribes that you may *know* one another..." (49:13).

All knowledge, including self-knowledge is based on contrast. As stated earlier, perceptual contrast is both a biophysical law and a cognitive one. (see p. 167 and following) "To understand himself man needs to be understood by another. To be understood by another, he needs to understand another."[11] The Quranic affirmation of human diversity implies the need to recognize not only how we are similar but also the deeper significance of our difference(s). Thus, the Quran speaks of how it is simply not in the scheme of things that humanity should all be of a single faith/religion. "Unto every one of you have we appointed a (different) law and way of life. And if God had so willed, He could surly have made you all one single community but He willed it otherwise in order to test you by means of what he has vouchsafed unto you. Vie then, with one another in doing good works" (5:48). This translation by Asad is a common one namely, of a trial or test, regarding religious conduct.[12] Similar translations also assume that what has been given to each is simply a religious/dogmatic path and therein lies the test.

However, given the ultimately ambiguous (linguistic) bedrock of the Text, it has also been translated/interpreted with other nuances, for example, a relatively less well known translation puts it thus: "For each one of you did We prescribe a spiritual law and a well-defined way (a code in secular matters). And if Allah had so willed He might have made you one community (by force) but He wishes to show your perfection (the capacities and capabilities) that He has endowed you with. Therefore vie with each in doing good."[13] The word 'test' is not used. We are not (meant to be) the same because of the varied nature of our 'capacities and capabilities' we have been endowed with. It is these which (potentially) develop in the encounter with difference hence 'vie with each in doing good'.

The implication here is that what we *share* is our flaws and failures, and what sets us *apart*, makes us distinct(ive), is our positive potentialities and capacities in the service of the pursuit of 'the good'. In Jungian terms it is to acknowledge the dark side, the shadow in all of us. In more human terms, to put it bluntly, when it comes to our shit, we are all the same.

Ironically, while there is a growing respect for the laws of Nature and a general 'return' to it, modern ideas of human nature remains quite unnatural. Either there is no such thing, only genetics; or then culturally relativized to such an extent that, in either case it cannot be discussed substantively. Both suggest a defense mechanism of a heroic ego in denial of not only its inner diversity but especially its shadow, that is, the more shitty side(s) to us which we would rather not acknowledge to oneself or others.

Yet, as a natural phenomenon shit/shadows accompanies us as long as we are alive and becomes a vital part in the regeneration of life. An excellent natural fertilizer, the more polite word 'humus' is also linked to 'humility'—which may come when we deal with our (psychological) shit(s). This process of facing/seeing one's malodorous side(s), has, in today's worlds, become literally difficult. In the West, thanks to modern plumbing and efficient methods of garbage disposal it is invisible. Out of sight out of mind. Given its overwhelmingly public presence in the Muslim world, and in the absence of contrast, it is also rendered 'invisible'. Like a fish in water or the air we breathe, it is out of our daily awareness. Individual or collective, our shit, this (un)acknowledged fact of life, will not disappear through naive attempts at interfaith or other types of dialogue. Rather, as our unconscious shadow, it will simply be projected onto others.

Like individuals, religions share similar features but each has a unique 'mix' in which certain aspects are emphasized and others less; for example, fear, love and knowledge of God are common to the three monotheisms. Studies in comparative religion suggest that these qualities are emphasized differently, giving each monotheism a unique identifying profile.[14] Christianity, for example, talks of fear and knowledge but its most prominent feature is love. Similarly, while fear and love are urged in the Quran, its main emphasis is on knowledge. Judaism too contains all these dimensions but the most prominent has to do with fear. All these are different *styles* of relationships to the Divine and today of course, are completely inverted in their expressions. Thus, today instead of love there is hatred, instead of knowledge there is ignorance and instead of fear a fearless-ness expressed at all levels of social and political life. As an American president once put it: "The only thing to fear is fear itself."

It is forgotten that fear teaches one a sense of limits, of not crossing certain lines. As the Bible tells us, fear of the Lord is the beginning of Wisdom. The environmental crisis can be linked to the valorization of fearlessness in modernity's approach to nature, which, until recently, was seen as something to be conquered and controlled like women's bodies.

However, as was mentioned before, it is an axiom in depth-psychology that what we vehemently deny from within, will sooner or later confront us from without. As such, in our quest for fearlessness today, wherever we are on the globe, we are haunted by fear—in fact in its extreme form of terror.

Thus, before any of the monotheisms can reclaim the positive aspects of fear, love and knowledge of God, they too must confront their own shadow(s)/shit. Not only as it has accumulated over millennia, but especially in their denial and denigration of the Feminine.

Fear

Earlier I have explained how Theos or 'God', as the archetype of meaning, concerns a manner of existence, a set of ideas and attitudes to life. Its universally appearing forms suggest an eternal connection and the invitation implicit in religion, re-*ligio*: to re-link/connect. At the heart of every religion there is an intransigent core which will not yield to education, argument, logic and 'common sense'. This is because its function is to simply reflect that which is Immutable. As the presence of paranoia suggests, the immutable connection remains. Immutability implies sight, and thus, the first task of the Muslim intellectual is to simply *bear witness* to what s/he 'sees'.

As our own lives should attest, there are situations when it is difficult to get by only on faith, or for that matter, love. Among the numerous elements of styles of relationship with the Divine—faith, fear, love, beauty, bewilderment, friendship, knowledge—it seems that hatred, ignorance and an adolescent fearlessness/ machismo will continue to dominate political and religious discourse. Given the ego's defenses against the forgotten 'Other', fear is unconsciously projected onto all sorts of enemies, which, of course, have to be dealt with fear-less-ly.

If the dominant conception of the Transcendent is of an invisible, invincible Masculine force hurling thunderbolts at us at the drop of a hat (or hijab), then some will continue to be haunted by the specter of a bearded man hiding in a cave in Pakistan/Afghanistan, orchestrating trans-continental terrorist attacks on them. Simultaneously, others will continue to be haunted by the terror of aerial armadas dropping the modern equivalent of thunderbolts from the sky. Given the dominance of masculine literalism and the tendency of paranoids to make self-fulfilling prophecies, escalating violence seems to be the hallmark of the New World Order. Simultaneously, in the worldwide rise of fundamentalism in all religions, there is an implicit global attack on feminism and the Feminine.[15] While the Quran does not mention the Resurrection of Christ, many Muslims have nevertheless been swept up by similar apocalyptic scenarios fed by the media.

The frightening thing is that a literal Resurrection first requires a literal Apocalypse. The global paranoia created by the global war on terror has obscured the basic anti-environmental stance of the protagonists. Propelled by the rapture awaiting them in heaven, every natural disaster on Earth confirms their belief(s). Ecocide is good news. The commentator Bill Moyers claims that in the U.S. today the delusional is no longer marginal. One third of Americans believe the Bible is literally true. "For them a war with Islam in the Middle East is to be welcomed, an essential conflagration on the road to redemption ... millions of Christian fundamentalists believe that environmental destruction is not only to be disregarded but hastened as a sign of the coming apocalypse."[16] While many may see this ecocide as the 'revenge of the sacred' unleashed on modernity, surely many more have had enough of a singular and relentless focus on the Vengeful 'face' of God. For them, other Divine Attributes, particularly Graciousness and Mercy are primary in terms of Divine Self declaration.[17]

The coming flood of fear—of the 'other', in all its numerous guises of racism, xenophobia, fundamentalism—will test to the extreme, the religious ideals of 'blind' faith *and* love. In the same way that love is not just sex or pill-induced ecstasy, God is not just ritual devotion and the born again enthusiasm of faith. In such a scenario, the Muslim intellectual will carry a considerable responsibility.

Muslim intellectuals

My clinical and social experience suggests that a major problem among Muslims today, is the constant conflation of the sociological/political with the psychological. The internalization of various socio/political/economic discourses constituting 'identity' have overwhelmed one of the main reasons why religion exists, namely, not just 'how to live' but more so, given the mystery of death, 'how to die'. This is something we will all experience and know nothing about. Death is a uniquely *individual* experience, it has to be faced alone, there are no experts on the matter—hence, the psychological primacy of the individual's subjectivity and religion.

Personally, I doubt that the posthumous interrogation of the self will have much to do with nationalism, ethnicity, gender, geopolitics, even education. Rather, it will be the *body* and its limbs, tongue, skin which will 'testify';[18] not what was in our 'mind' but what was in our 'heart', which we frequently link to 'soul' when conveying subjective depth ('heart and soul'). Today heart dis-ease is the leading global illness and a preferred method of treatment is to 'by pass' it (surgically).

According to Jung, most highly educated people remain profoundly ignorant of their self(s), their unconsciousness is "incredible ... not to mention their prejudices and irresponsible way of dealing, rather not dealing, with them."[19] One dimension of dealing with one's prejudices and shadow means a re-valuing of *mythos*, a re-visioning of *logos*, and a re-negotiation of a cognitively complicated nexus of one's personal, religious, cultural and intellectual history. That is, a re-visioning of *logos* beyond adolescent Cartesianism into its widest sense of the application of vast knowledge resources which are the gift of modernity. A wide range of insights from psychological, cultural, linguistic and historical sources need to be interfaced with religion to construct subjective architectures of meaning.

This difficult and complex process precludes any substantive engagement with the body which remains, for many people, particularly women, a mystery, which does not require to be 'solved' but rather experienced as mediated by the imagination. Similarly, for many Muslims, especially women, re-configuring the 'mind' and re-connecting it with the body is a daunting task. It will necessarily, eventually involve at some level, an active engagement with the politics of meaning and interpretation, thereby risking the accusation of academic and/or religious 'heresy'. However, it is useful to bear in mind that prior to its meaning in post-Nicene Christianity, the word 'heresy' in Greek simply meant 'to *choose* for oneself'. Depending on our choices, the de-colonization of the Muslim religious imagination, and particularly women's, remains post-colonialism's final frontier.[20]

The disquieting border

One can note that Schreber addressed his memoirs *not* to psychiatrists but to theologians and philosophers.[21] A detailed reading of the *Memoirs* via the Islamic philosophy of the Imagination and an examination of pathological-paranoid Islamism can prove to be a useful prophylactic exercise in understanding what Lifton has called, in another context, the "disquieting border area of theology and psychopathology."[22]

Beyond bearing witness to the times, knowledge, of oneself and other religions is required to cope with what in many ways seems to be a fearful future. There is really no way of knowing what the future holds and perhaps I'm being paranoid for no reason. Which simply confirms my initial (self)diagnosis in the light of 'expert opinion' that "to date there are no confirmed demonstrations that any form of treatment can significantly improve paranoid personality disorder."[23] The situation is hopeless but not serious. Because when all is said and done, according to other experts in the field, paranoia is quite "a rare condition".[24]

Notes

Introduction

[1] Jung, Carl Gustav; 'The Spiritual Problem of Modern Man' in Jung, Carl Gustav, *The Collected Works of C.G. Jung..* Vol. 10., p.153.Princeton University Press. Princeton, NJ (Original work published 1948) Any further reference to the collected works of Jung will be abbreviated to C.W.

[2] In Pakistan, this view is evident in Hoodbhoy Pervez; *Muslims and Science: Religious Orthodoxy and the Struggle for Rationality.* Vanguard. Lahore. 1991.

[3] See for example, Cahoone, Lawrence; *Cultural Revolutions: Reason versus Culture in Philosophy, Politics and Jihad.* University of Pennsylvania Press. Philadelphia. 2005. / Menleman, Johan H. (ed.); *Islam in the Era of Globalization: Muslim Attitudes to Modernity.* Routledge. New York/London. 2002. / Ali, Tariq; *Clash of Fundamentalisms: Crusader, Jihads and Modernity.* London. Verso. 2002. / Armstrong, Karen; *The Battle for God.* Knopf. New York. 2000. / Enben, Roxanne Leslie; *Enemy in the Mirror: Islamic fundamentalism and the Limits of Modern Rationalism.* Princeton University Press. Princeton, NJ. 1999. / Tibi Bassom; *The Challenge of Fundamentalism: Political Islam and the New World Disorder.* University of California Press. Berkeley. 1998. / Moaddel, M. and Talatoff, K.; *Modernist and Fundamentalists Debates in Islam: A Reader.* Palgrave Macmillan. New York. 2000.

[4] Marty, Martin E. & Appleby, Scott R.; *Fundamentalism Comprehended.* University of Chicago Press. Chicago. 1995. See also Armstrong,Karen; *The Battle for God.* op. cit.

[5] Habermas, Jurgen; 'Faith and Knowledge ... an Opening'. Speech given at acceptance of the Peace Prize of the German Publishers and Booksellers Association. Paulskirche. Frankfurt. 14.01.2001. Translation by Kermit Suelson. See Habermas, Jurgen; *The Philosophical Discourse of Modernity: Twelve Lectures.* Polity Press. Cambridge, UK. 2002.

[6] Gellner, Ernest; *Postmodernism, Reason and Religion.* Routledge. London. 1992.

[7] Armstrong, Karen; *The Battle for God.* op. cit. p.xii.

[8] For a black humored recounting of prominent situationist theorists who committed suicide see Hussey Andrew; 'Au Revoir, Cruel World' in *The Modern Review.* London. 1995. Reprinted as 'Esprit de Mort' in *Harper's Magazine* September 1995.

[9] To name just a few: Harding, Sandra; *Is Science Multicultural? Postcolonialisms, Feminism and Epistemologies.* Bloomington, Indiana University. Press. 1998. / Martin, Emily; 'The Egg and the Sperm: How Science has constructed a Romance Based on Stereotypical Male-Female Roles' in Keller, Evelyn F. & Longino, Helen (eds.); *Feminism and Science.* Oxford University Press. Oxford, New York. 1996. / Bem, Sandra; *The Lenses of Gender.* Yale University Press. New Haven. 1993.

[10] See Adams, Carol (ed); *Ecofeminism and the Sacred.* Continuum. New York. 1994. / Merchant, Carolyn; *Radical Ecology.* Routledge. New York. 1992. / Spretnak, Charlene; *States of Grace: The Recovery of Meaning in the Postmodern Age.* Harper. San Francisco. 1991. / Reeves, Peggy; *Female Power and Male Dominance.* Cambridge University Press. Cambridge, 1981. / Plumwood, Val; 'Nature, Self and Gender: Feminism, Environmental Philosophy and the Critique of Rationalism' in *Hypatia: A Journal of Feminist Philosophy.* Vol. 6 No.1. Spring 1991. pp.1-7. / Kheel, Marti; 'Ecofeminism and Deep Ecology: Reflections on Identity and Difference' in Robb, Card S. & Casebolt, C.J. (eds); *Covenant for a New Creation: Ethics, Religion and Public Policy.* Mary, Knoll. Orbis Books. New York. 1991. / For a comprehensive bibliography on these subjects see Spretnak, Charlene; 'Ecofeminism: Our Roots and Flowering' in Diamond Irene & Ornstein Gloria (eds). *Reweaving the World: The Emergence of Ecofeminism.* Sierra Club Books. San Francisco. 1990.

[11] Spretnak, Charlene; *States of Grace.* op. cit.

[12] King, Ursula; 'Book review of Gendering the Spirit: Women, Religion and the Postcolonial Response' in *Feminist Theology.* Volume 13. Issue 3. Sage Publication. London. 2005. pp.399-404.

[13] Smith, Huston, 'Postmodernism's Impact on the Study of Religion' in *Journal of the American Academy of Religion.* Vol. 58. Issue 4. Winter 1990. pp.653-670. See also, Heelas Paul, Marti David & Morris Paul; *Religion, Modernity and Postmodernity.* Blackwell Publishing. Oxford. 1998.

[14] *Newsweek,* 'A Postmodern President'. 16-01-1994.

[15] Fisk, Robert; 'Who is Copying Who in War of Words' in *The Independent.* London. 11-10-2001. See also: Ali, Tariq, *The Clash of Fundamentalisms.* op. cit.

[16] See for example: Castells, Manuel; *The Information Age: Economy, Society and Culture.* Vol. II. Blackwell Publishing. Oxford. 2004.

[17] Nandy, Ashis: 'A New Cosmopolitism' in Chen, Kuan-Hsing (ed.); *Trajectories: Inter-Asia Cultural Studies;* Routledge. London/New York. 1998. pp.146-147.

[18] See, for example: Mckibben, Bill; *Enough: Staying Human in an Engineered Age.* Times

Books. New York. 2003. / Mckibben, Bill; *The End of Nature*. Anchor Books. New York. 1997. / Tiles, Mary & Oberdiek, Hans; *Living a Technological Culture: Human Tools and Human Values*. Routledge. London/New York. 1995. / Kroker, Arthur; *The Possessed Individual: Technology and Postmodernity*. MacMillan. London. 1992.

[19] See for example: Schussler, Fiorenza Elizabeth; *In Memory of Her: A Feminist Exploration of Christian Origins*. 1983. / Wilson A.N.; 'Christianity and Modernity' in *The Guardian*. 5-12-2000. / Selvidge, Marla; *Notorious Voices: Feminist Biblical Interpretation, 1500-1920*. Continuum. 1996. / Ostriker, Susan; *Feminist Revision and the Bible*. Blackwell Publishing. Oxford. 1993. / Ilana, Pardes; *Countertraditions in the Bible: A Feminist Approach*. Harvard University Press. Cambridge. 1992. Schussler, Fiorenza Elizabeth; *But She Said: Feminist Practices of Biblical Interpretation*. Beacon Press. Boston. 1992. / Trible, Phyllis; *Texts of Terror: Literary and Feminist Reading of Biblical Narratives*. Fortress Press. Philadelphia. 1984. / Reuther, Rosemary; *Sexism and God Talk*. Beacon Press. Boston 1983. / Pagels, Elaine; *The Gnostic Gospels*. New York. Vintage Books. 1988.

[20] See for example: Noble, David F.; *A World without Women: The Christian Clerical Culture of Western Science*. Knopf. New York. 1992. / Primavese, Anna; *From Apocalypse to Genesis: Ecology, Feminism and Christianity*. Burns and Dates. Kent. 1991. / Scherer, Glenn; 'The Road to Environmental Apocalypse' in *Grist Magazine*. 27-10-2004. Also published on *Grist.org* as 'Christian-right views are swaying politicians and threatening the environment'. 28-10-2004. http://grist.org/article/scherer-christian/ (last visited 17-10-2015) / White, Jr. Lynn; 'The Historical Roots of our Ecological Crisis' in Nash, James (ed.); *Loving Nature*. Abington Press. Nashville. 1991. / In contrast Ganchet, Marcel; *The Disenchantment of the World: A Political History of Religion*. Princeton University Press. 1998.

[21] Hillman, James ; *Re-Visioning Psychology*. Harper and Row. New York. (1975) 1977.

[22] Jung, Carl Gustav; 'Civilization in Transition' in *C.W.* Vol. 10.

[23] Jung, Carl Gustav; 'The Spiritual Problem of Modern Man' in *C.W.* Vol. 10. p.151.

[24] Jung, Carl Gustav; 'After the Catastrophe; in *C.W.* Vol. 10.p.437.

[25] Jung, Carl Gustav; 'The Spiritual Problem of Modern Man' in *C.W.* Vol. 10. p.163.

[26] ibid.

[27] ibid. p.171.

[28] ibid. p.196.

[29] ibid. pp.193 & 185.

[30] Ahmed, Durre S.; 'Islam and the West: A Psychological Analysis' in *Journal of the Henry Martyn Institute*, 19/1, 2000. Republished as 'Islam and the West: An Analysis of C.G. Jung's Understanding of Islam', in *Iqbal Review*. Lahore 2004.

[31] See for example in the work of Judith Butler.

[32] See for example: Lauter, Estella & Schreir, Ruppereht Carol; *Feminist Archetypal Theory: Interdisciplinary Re-Visions of Jungian Thought*. University of Tennessee Press. Knoxville, Tennessee. 1985. / Samuels Andrew; *Politics and the Couch: Citizenship and the Internal Life*. Profile Books. London. 2001. / Barnaby, Karin and D'Acierno, Pelligrino (eds.); *C.G. Jung and the Humanities: Towards a Hermenentics of Culture*. London. Routledge. 1990. / Goldenberg, Naomi; 'A Feminist Critique of Jung' in Moore R.C. & Meckel D. (eds.); *Jung, Christianity in Dialogue: Faith, Feminism, Hermeneutics*. Paulist Press. New York. 1990.

[33] Bly, Robert; Iron, John & Tacey, David; *Remarking Men: Jung, Spirituality and Social Change*. Routledge. London. 1997.

[34] Connors, W.R.; 'Why Were We Surprised' in *The American Scholar*. Spring 1991.

[35] The Wilson Quarterly; *Editorial*. Spring 1991.

[36] Campbell, Jan; *Arguing with the Phallus: Feminist, Queer and Postcolonial Theory. A Psychoanalytic Contribution*. Zed books. London. 2003. p.3.

[37] *The Economist*; 'The Next War, They Say'. 04-08-1994.

CHAPTER 1:
THEORETICAL BACKGROUND

[1] Jung, Carl Gustav;'The Spiritual Problem of Modern Man' in *C.W.* Vol 10.p.153.

[2] Hillman, James; *Archetypal Psychology*. op. cit. p.54.

[3] For details and bibliography see: Myers, Diana; 'Feminist Perspectives on the Self' in *Stanford Encyclopedia of Philosophy*. 2004. http://plato.stanford.edu/entries/feminism-self/ (last visited 15-10-2015)

[4] ibid.

[5] ibid.

[6] ibid.

[7] Lloyd, Genevieve; 'Madeness, Metaphor, and the 'Crisis' of 'Reason' in Antony, Louise & Wih, Charlotte (eds.); *A Mind of One's Own*. Boulder: West view Press. 1992.

[8] Freud, Sigmund; *The Future of an Illusion*. Hogarth Press. London. 1962.

[9] See, for example, *TIME* magazine's special issue 'The Century's Greatest Minds' on the leading thinkers and scientists of the 20th Century. 29-03-99. Or *Newsweek's* cover story 'Freud's Enduring Legacy: How His Ideas Still Shape Psychotherapy'. 4-07-1988.

[10] Hillman, James; *Archetypal Psychology: A Brief Account*. Spring Publications. Dallas. 1985.

[11] Armstrong, Karen; *The Battle for God*. op. cit.

[12] Slok, Johannes; *Devotional Language*. Translated by Henrik Mossin. Walter De Gruyter

Incorporated. Danbury. 1996.

[13] Metzger, Bruce & Coogan, Michael (eds.); *The Oxford Companion to the Bible*. Oxford University Press. New York/Oxford. 1993. pp.463-464.

[14] Joyce, James; *A Portrait of the Artist as a Young Man*. 1916.

[15] Corbin, Henry; *Creative Imagination in the Sufism of Ibn-i-Arabi*. Bollingen series. Princeton. 1975.

[16] In a response to Herbert Marcuse in Brown, Norman O.; *Negations*. Allen Lane. London. 1968. p.244.

[17] Hillman, James; *Re-visioning Psychology*. op. cit. p.xi.

[18] Morny, Joy; 'Images and Imagination' in *Encyclopedia of Religion*. MacMillan. New York. 1987.

[19] Jung, Carl Gustav; *C.W.* Vol. 14. p.634.

[20] Jung, Carl Gustav; 'Answer to Job' in *C.W.* Vol. 11. pp.610-616.

[21] Jung, Carl Gustav; *C.W.* Vol 5, p.183 / Vol. 9. p.357 / Vol. 10. p.638.

[22] Jung, Carl Gustav; 'The Role of the Unconscious' in *C.W.* Vol. 10. p.5.

[23] Papini, Giovanni; 'A Visit to Freud'. Colosseum. s.l. 1934. Reprinted in *Review of Existential Psychology and Psychiatry*. IX. 1969. pp.130–134.

[24] Whitford, Margaret (ed.); *The Irigaray Reader*. Blackwell Publishing. Oxford. 1991.

[25] Irigaray, Luce in Whitford, Margaret (ed.); *The Irigaray Reader*. op. cit. 1991.

[26] Armstrong, Karen; *A Short History of Myth*. op. cit. p.117.

[27] Campbell, Joseph; *The Hero with a Thousand Faces*. Bollingen Series. Princeton University Press. Princeton, NJ.1978.

[28] Neumann, Erich; *The Origins and History of Consciousness*. Princeton University Press. Princeton, NJ.1971.

[29] Hillman, James; *Inter views*. Harper and Row. New York. 1983.

[30] Hillman, James; 'Loose Ends: Primary Papers' in *Archetypal Psychology*. Spring Publications. Dallas. 1975. p.94.

[31] Jung, Carl Gustav; *C.W.* Vol. 10. p.507

[32] Jung, Carl Gustav; 'Commentary on 'The Secret of the Golden Flower'. Alchemical Studies' in *C.W.* Vol. 13. p.51.

CHAPTER 2:
RELIGION AND MODERNITY

[1] Jung, Carl Gustav; 'The Spiritual Problem of Modern Man' in *C.W.* Vol. 10 p.52.

[2] Jung, Carl Gustav; 'Self-Knowledge 'in *C.W.* Vol. 10 pp.565-581. Subsequently part of the book *The Undiscovered Self.* See also, Vol. 9ii. p.77 and Vol. 9ii. p.521.

[3] Jung, Carl Gustav; 'Answer to Job' in *C.W.* Vol. 11 pp.610-616.

[4] Hillman, James; *Archetypal Psychology.* op. cit.

[5] Lewis, Bernard; *Islam and the West.* Oxford University Press. New York. 1983. p.83.

[6] See for example: Cantwell, Smith Wilfred; *Faith and Belief.* Princeton University Press. Princeton, NJ. 1979. / Smith, Jonathan; *Map is Not the Territory: Studies in the History of Religions.* Leiden University Press. 1978. / Cooey, Paula; *Religious Imagination and the Body: A Feminist Analysis.* Oxford University Press. New York. 1994 / Asad, Talal; 'Genealogies of Religion: Discipline and Reasons of Power' in *Christianity and Islam.* John Hopkins Press. Baltimore. 1993.

[7] Lincoln, Bruce; *Holy Terrors: Thinking about Religion after September 11.* University of Chicago Press. Chicago. 2003. p.1-2.

[8] See: Tambiah, Stanley J; *Magic, Science, Religion, and the Scope of Rationality.* Cambridge University Press. 1991.

[9] ibid.

[10] For extensive sources and details, see Hillman, James; *The Myth of Analysis: Three Essays in Archetypal Psychology.* Northwestern University Press. Harper and Row. New York. (1972) 1978. See also Hillman; *Re-visioning Psychology.* op. cit.

[11] See: Barlow, David (ed.); *Clinical Handbook of Psychological Disorders. A Step-by-Step Treatment Manual.* Fourth Edition. Guilford Press. New York. 2007.

[12] Jung, Carl Gustav; *C.W.* Vol.13:54

[13] Freud, Sigmund; *New Introductory Lectures on Psychoanalysis.* Hogarth Press. London. 1933. p.106.

[14] WHO; *Gender and Women's Mental Health.* http://www.who.int/mental_health/prevention/genderwomen/en/ (last visited 15-10-2015)

[15] Matteo, S; 'The Risk of Multiple Addictions: Guidelines for Assessing a Woman's Drug and Alcohol Use' in *The Western Journal of Medicine.* Vol. 149(6). 1988. P.742. See also Nellis, Muriel; *The Female Fix.* Penguin Books. New York. 1988.

[16] See Chapter 1, endnote 9.

[17] See for example: Bordo, Susan; *The Flight of Objectivity: Essays on Cartesianism and Culture.* State University of New York Press. 1987. / Bordo, Susan; 'The Cartesian Masculinization of Thought' in *Signs: Journal of Women and Culture in Society.* Vol II Issue3. University of Chicago Press. Chicago 1986. / Lloyd, Geneviere; 'The Man of 'Reason': 'Male' and 'Female'' in *Western Philosophy.* University of Minnesota Press. Minneapolis. 1993.

[18] Hillman, James; *Inter Views.* op cit. p.82. See especially, Chapter 5, 'A Running Engagement with Christianity'.

[19] Lewontin, R.C.; 'Women Versus the Biologists' in *The New York Review of Books.* 7-04-1994. Lewontin is a Harvard biologist

[20] Jung, Carl Gustav; *C.W.* Vol.12. p.16.

[21] Jung, Carl Gustav; *C.W.* Vol.10. p.210.

[22] Asad, Muhammad; *The Message of the Quran.* The Book Foundation. 2003.

[23] McClain, Ernest; *Meditations Through the Quran.* Nicholas-Hays. Maine. 1981.

[24] ibid.

[25] Hillman, James; *Inter Views.* op. cit. pp.78-84.

[26] *TIME;* 'Evil: Does it exist—or do bad things just happen?' 10-6-1991.

[27] Jung, Carl Gustav; *C.W.* Vol.10. p.572.

[28] Hillman, James; *Inter Views.* op. cit. pp.78-84.

[29] ibid. pp.140-143.

[30] ibid. p.29.

[31] ibid. pp.81-82.

[32] ibid. pp.78-79.

[33] Weber, Max; *The Protestant Ethic and the Spirit of Capitalism.* Translated by Parsons Talcott. George Allen & Unwin Ltd. London. 1930.

[34] Hillman, James; *Inter Views.* op. cit. p.92.

[35] Jung, Carl Gustav ; *C.W.* Vol. 10. pp.554-555.

[36] Warner, Maria; 'Fantasy's Power and Peril' in *The New York Times Book Review.* 16-12-2001.

[37] Hillman, James; *Re-Visioning Psychology.* op. cit. p.33.

[38] Armstrong, Karen; *The Battle for God.* op. cit. p.200.

[39] Jung, Carl Gustav; *C.W.* Vol. 10. p.457.

[40] ibid.

[41] Jung, Carl Gustav; 'After the Catastrophe' in *C.W.* Vol. 10. pp440-443. See also Jung, 'The Fight with the Shadow' in *C.W.* Vol. 10. pp444-457.

[42] Kristeva, Julia; *New Maladies of the Soul.* Columbia University Press. New York. 2001.

[43] Armstrong, Karen; *The Battle for God.* op. cit. p.200.

[44] O'Kane, Maggie; 'Hunting Radovan' in *The Guardian.* 20-02-2001.

[45] Hillman, James; *Inter Views.* op. cit. pp.140-143. (My emphasis)

[46] Quoted in, Van der Post Laurens; *Jung and the Story of Our Time*. Penguin Books. 1978. p.234.

[47] Armstrong, Karen; *A Short History of Myth*. Penguin. 2005. p.103.

[48] ibid. pp.88-89.

[49] See for example, Primavese; *From Apocalypse to Genesis*. op. cit. / Scherer; op. cit. / White; *The Historical Roots of our Ecological Crisis*. op. cit. / Reuther, Rosemary R.; *Gaia and God: An Ecofeminist Theology of Earth Healing*. Harper Collins. New York. 1992. / Santmire Paul; *The Travail of Nature: The Ambiguous Ecological Promise of Christianity*. Fortress Press. Philadelphia. 1985. / Hessel, D.T. & Reuther, R.R.; *Christianity and Ecology: Seeking the Well Being of Earth and Humans*. Harvard University Press. Cambridge. 2000.

[50] See for example, Elaine Pagels, Elizabeth Schussler Fiorenza, Grace Jantzen among many others. For more details see Boyce-Tillman June; 'Unconventional Wisdom-Theologizing the Margins' in *Feminist Theology*. Vol 13. Issue 3. 2005. pp.317-341.

[51] Long, Eugene Thomas; 'Twentieth Century Philosophy of Religion 1900-2000' in *Handbook of Contemporary Philosophy of Religion*. Vol. 1. Kluwer Publications. Dordrech. 2000. For more bibliographic details see Frankenberry, Nancy; 'Feminist Philosophy of Religioni in *Stanford Encyclopedia of Philosophy*. Online. 2004. http://plato.stanford.edu/entries/feminist-religion

[52] Newton, Judith; 'White Guys'. in *Feminist Studies*.Vol.24. Issue 3. 1998.

[53] Connell, R.W.; *Masculinities*. University of California Press. Berkeley. 1995.

[54] Pfeil, Fred; *White Guys: Studies in Postmodern Domination and Difference*. Verso. London. 1995.

[55] See Kimmel, Michael; *Manhood in America: a Cultural History*. Free Press. New York. 1996. / Beneke, Timothy; *Proving Manhood: Reflections on Men and Sexism*. University of California Press. Berkeley. 1997. / Edwards, Tim; *Cultures of Masculinity*. Routledge. New York. 2006.

[56] Lockhart, William; '"We are One Life" But Not of One Gender Ideology: Unity, Ambiguity and Promise Keepers' in *Sociology of Religion*. Spring 2000.

[57] ibid.

[58] Jung; Carl Gustav; *C.W.* Vol. 10. p.574.

[59] Derrida, Jacques; *Acts of Religion*. Routledge. London. 2002. p.63.

[60] Nandy, Ashis; *The Intimate Enemy: Loss and Recovery of Self under Colonialism*. Oxford University Press. Delhi. 1983. p.xi.

[61] Hillman, James; *Inter-Views*. op. cit. p.143.

CHAPTER 3:
CARTESIAN-CHRISTIANIST-ISLAMISM

[1] Jung, Carl Gustav; 'Man And His Symbols' *C.W.* Vol. 9ii.p.424.

[2] Berry, Philippa & Werncik, Andrew (eds.); *Shadow of Spirit: Postmodernism and Religion.* Routledge. New York. 1992.

[3] ibid. p.3 & 57.

[4] Bryld, M & Lykke, N; *Cosmodolphins: Feminist Cultural Studies of Technology, Animals and the Sacred.* Zed Books. London. 2000.

[5] Wilson, Catherine; 'Modern Western Philosophy' in Nasr, S. Hossein (ed.); *History of Islamic Philosophy.* Routledge. London/New York. 1996. pp.1013-1016.

[6] See references in Introduction and Part I.

[7] See, for example, Hoodbhoy; op. cit.

[8] Ahmed, Durre S.; *Masculinity, Rationality and Religion: A Feminist Perspective.* 2nd edition. ASR. Lahore. (1994) 2001.

[9] For example, vis-à-vis modernity, see Banuri, Tariq; 'Modernization and its Discontents' in Marglin and Marglin (eds.); *Dominating Knowledge.* Clarendon Press. Oxford. 1990.

[10] Armstrong, Karen; *Islam: A Short History.* Random House. New York. 2000. p.16.

[11] Ong, Walter J.; *Orality and Literacy: The Technologizing of the Word.* Methuen. New York. 1982.

[12] As cited in Brown, Norman O.; 'The Apocalypse of Islam' in Andrews, V; Bosnak R. & K. Goddwin (eds.); *Facing Apocalypse,* Spring Publications. Dallas. 1987. p.149.

[13] Jung, Carl Gustav; 'A Study in the Process of Individuation' in *C.W.* Vol. 9.

[14] As cited in Brown, Norman O; *The Apocalypse of Islam.* op. cit. p.138.

[15] Eco, Umberto; *The Role of the Reader: Explorations in the Semiotics of Texts.* Bloomington. 1979. p.63.

[16] Wilson, Edmund; *Axels Castle.* Collins/Fantana Library. London. 1961. p.178.

[17] Eco, Umberto; *The Role of the Reader.* op. cit. pp.54-65. (My emphasis.)

[18] Hodgson, M.G.S.; 'A Comparison of Islam and Christianity as Framework of Religious Life' in *Diogenes.* Vol. 3. 1960.

[19] Atherton, J.S.; *The Books at the Wake.* Carbondale and Edwardsville. 1974. Chapter 12.

[20] Brown, Norman O; *The Apocalypse of Islam.* op. cit.

[21] As cited in ibid.

[22] ibid. pp.154-155.

[23] Steward, Desmond; *Mecca.* W.W. Norton. New York. 1980.

[24] Ahmed, Durre; *Masculinity, Rationality and Religion.* op. cit.

[25] Abul el Fadl, Khaled; 'Islam and the Theory of Power' in *Islam: Images, Politics Paradox.* Middle East Report. 221. Winter 2001. http://www.merip.org/mer/mer221/islam-theology-power

[26] Bruce, Lawrence; *Defenders of God: The fundamentalist revolt against the modern age.* University of South Carolina Press. 1989.

[27] Jung, Carl Gustav; 'The Fight with the Shadow' in *C.W.* Vol. 10. pp.455-456.

[28] ibid.

[29] Qadir, Ali; 'The University on the Edge'. Unpublished M. Phil. Thesis. NCA. Lahore. 2007.

[30] Asad, Muhammad; *Islam at the Crossroads.* Sheikh M. Ashraf. Lahore. 1934. Reprinted 1991. p.48. This is a typical example: "… the world of Islam urgently needs today not a new philosophical outlook but only up to date scientific and technical equipment."

[31] Abul el Fadl, Khaled; op. cit.

[32] ibid. (My emphasis.)

[33] Armstrong, Karen; *Muhammad: A Biography of the Prophet.* Harper Collins. New York. 1992.

[34] The term was first used by Chandra Muzaffer, editor *JUST.* Malaysia.

[35] Burckhardt, Titus; *Art of Islam: Language and Meaning.* World of Islam Festival Trust. London. 1976.

[36] See for example: Howden, Daniel; 'The Destruction of Mecca: Saudi Hardliners are wiping out their own Heritage' in *The Independent.* 6-8-2005. / Pope, Hugh; 'Iconic Clash: Saudi Fights to End Demolition Driven by Islamic Dictate… A Mall Goes up in Mecca' in *The Wall Street Journal.* 18-8-2004.

[37] For details, see Wheelan, Simon; 'Saudi Government Demolishes Historic Ottoman Castle'. *www.wsws.org.* 28-01-2002 / *Newsweek;* 'Another Cultural Massacre'. 19-02-2002.

[38] See: *Dawn* of 16-11-2002 and *Daily Times* of 29-08-2006.

[39] See Hillman, James; *Inter Views.* op. cit. p.142.

[40] Nasr, Vali. *The Vanguard of the Islamic Revolution: The Jamaati-Islami of Pakistan.* U.C.L.A. Press. 1994.

[41] Nasr, S. Hossein; *Knowledge and the Sacred.* Edinburgh University Press. 1981.

[42] *The Economist;* 'In the Beginning'. 21-04-2007.

[43] Kepel, Gilles; *The Revenge of God: The Resurgence of Islam, Christianity and Judaism in the Modern World.* Oxford. 1994.

[44] Munir Report; *Report of the Court of Inquiry into the Punjab disturbances of 1953.*

Lahore. 1954.

[45] Ewing, Katherine; *Arguing Sainthood: Modernity, Psychoanalysis and Islam.* Duke University Press. Durham. 1997. p.252.

[46] Wilson, Catherine; 'Modern Western Philosophy'. op. cit. p.1015.

[47] Chambers Twentieth Century Dictionary.

[48] See: *The Economist*; 'Worst Outbreak of Civil Violence'. 15-06-1974. / *TIME*; 31-05-75. p.12.

[49] The Nobel Foundation; 'Abdus Salam – Biographical'. On *Nobelprize.org.* http://www.nobelprize.org/nobel_prizes/physics/laureates/1979/salam-bio.html. (Last visited 17/10/2015).

[50] Ahmed, Durre S.; 'Violence and the Feminine in Islam: A Case Study of the Zikris' in Durre Ahmed (ed.); *Gendering the Spirit: Women, Religion and the postcolonial Response.* ZED Books. London. 2002.

[51] Friedmann, Yohanan; *Prophecy Continuous: Aspects of Ahmadi Religious Thought and Its Medieval Background.* Berkeley. University of California Press. 1989. p.43. The transcript of the proceedings of 1974 at the National Assembly of Pakistan, entitled 'Proceedings of The Special Committee of the Whole House Held in Camera To Consider the Qadiani Issue' were eventually declassified on legal petition in 2010. They can be found on the internet archive at https://ia801506.us.archive.org/9/items/NAProceedings1974/NA-Proceeding-1974.pdf

[52] ibid. (My emphasis.)

[53] National Assembly's verdict on finality of prophethood of Hazrat Muhammad (peace be upon him). Islamabad. 1974. As cited in Friedmann, Yohanan; *Prophecy Continuous.* op. cit.

[54] Human Rights Commission of Pakistan; *The Annual Report of the Human Rights Commission of Pakistan.* 2004. / Human Rights Commission of Pakistan; *The Annual Report of the Human Rights Commission of Pakistan.* 2005.

[55] On the Ahmadi view of *jihad* see Friedmann, Yohanan; *Prophecy Continuous.* op. cit. pp.184-185. For further analyses on the Ahmadiyya case, see also Qadir, Ali; 'When Heterodoxy Becomes Heresy: Using Bourdieu's Concept of Doxa to Describe State-Sanctioned Exclusion in Pakistan' in *Sociology of Religion.* 76/2. DOI: 10.1093. Socrel/srv015. 2015 / Qadir, Ali; 'Parliamentary hereticization of the Ahmadiyya: The modern world implicated in Islamic crises' in Ganiel, G.; Monnot C. & Winkel H. (eds.), *Religion in Times of Crisis.*; Swatos W. (ed.). The ASR Book Series: Religion and the Social Order. Brill. Leiden. 2014. pp.135-152 / Gosset, Sherrie; *Muslim vs. Muslim: The Untold Story.* 4-1-2005.

CHAPTER 4:
CARTESIAN-CHRISTIANISM
& CARTESIAN-CHRISTIANIST ISLAMISM

[1] Jung, Carl Gustav; 'The Spiritual Problem of Modern Man' in *C.W.* Vol. 10. p195.

[2] *The Economist*; editorial on euthanasia. 20-07-1999.

[3] Hillman, James; *Inter Views*. op. cit.

[4] Freud, Sigmund; *New Introductory Lectures on Psychoanalysis*. op. cit. p.106. (My emphasis.)

[5] Kabbani, Raana; *Imperial Fictions. Europe's Myths of the Orient*. Harper Collins. London. 1986.

[6] Armstrong, Karen; *Muhammad*. op. cit. p.239.

[7] McDermott, Terry; *Perfect Soldiers*. Harper Collins. New York. 2005.

[8] Schuon, Frithjof; *Sufism: Veil and Quintessence*. World Wisdom Books. Bloomington, Indiana. 1979.

[9] See, for example, Simmer, Brown Judith; *Daikini's Warm Breath. The Feminine Principle in Tibetan Buddhism*. Shambhala. Boston. 2001.

[10] Jung, Carl Gustav; *Seminar on Dream Analysis 1928-1930*. William McGuire (ed.) Princeton University Press. Bollingen Series XC/X. p.335.

[11] Jung, Carl Gustav; 'Aion: Researches into the Phenomenology of the Self' in *C.W.* Vol. 9ii p519.

[12] Ahmed, Durre; *Islam and the West*. op. cit.

[13] Armstrong, Karen; *Muhammad*. op. cit.

[14] Jung, Carl Gustav; 'The Spiritual Problem of Modern Man' in *C.W.* Vol. 10.pp93-94.

[15] *The Economist*; 'Islam and the Vatican: An Invitation to Talk Business'. 21-10-06.

[16] Roy, Olivier; 'What is the driving force behind jihadist terrorism? – A scientific perspective on the causes/circumstances of joining the scene' Speech delivered at BKA Autumn Conference *International Terrorism: How can prevention and repression keep pace?*, 18 - 19 November 2015. https://life.eui.eu/wp-content/uploads/2015/11/OLIVIER-ROY-what-is-a-radical-islamist.pdf

[17] Malik, Kenan; 'Europe's Dangerous Multiculturalim'. in *Foreign Affairs*. 8-12-2015.

CHAPTER 5:
THE UPHEAVAL OF OUR WORLD

[1] Jung, Carl Gustav; 'The Spiritual Problem of Modern Man' in *C.W.* Vol. 10. p.177.

[2] Jung, Carl Gustav; 'Modern Man in Search of a Soul'. op. cit.

[3] McDermott, Terry; 'A Perfect Soldier' in Los *Angeles Times*. 27-1-2002. Subsequently, see his book *Perfect Soldiers*. op. cit.

[4] ibid. All following quotes will come from this source and all emphases are mine.

[5] See Dowd, Maureen; 'Liberties: Cleopatra and Osama'. in *New York Times*. 18-11-2001. Dowd is quoting history professor, Robert McElvaine.

[6] Jung, Carl Gustav; *C.W.* Vol. 5. p.3.

[7] Corbin, Henry; *Alone with the Alone: Creative Imagination in the Sufism of Ibn-i-Arabi*. Bollingen series XCI. Translated by Manheim Ralph. Princeton University Press. Princeton. 1975. p.38.

[8] Jung, Carl Gustav; *C.W.* Vol. 10:164.

[9] Hillman, James; *Re-visioning Psychology*. op. cit. / Hillman; *Inter Views*. op. cit.

[10] See Gitlin, Todd; 'With God on Our Side. Reading the State of Union.' Opendemocracy.net. 30-1-2003. www.opendemocracy.net.

[11] Campbell, Joseph; *The Power of Myth*. Doubleday. 1988.p. 71.

[12] Corbin, Henry, *Alone with the Alone*. op. cit. p.80

[13] Ahmed, Durre; *Masculinity, Rationality and Religion*. op. cit. p.106.

[14] Ahmed, Durre; 'Changing Faces of Tradition' in Edith Sizoo (ed.); *Women's Lifeworlds: Women's Narratives on Shaping their Realities*. Routledge. London. 1977.

[15] Smith, Huston; *Beyond the Postmodern Mind*. 2nd ed. Harper Collins. (1991) 2002.

INTERLUDE:
ISLAM'S FEMININE DIMENSION

[1] Eliot T.S.; *Four Quartets*, Harcourt, 1943.

[2] *The Economist*; 16-11-91

[3] Hillman, James; *The Myth of Analysis*. op. cit. p.218.

[4] Quran 23: 12-14. Translation by Abdullah Yusuf Ali. My emphasis

[5] Quran 23:14.

[6] Quran 39:6. Common translation by Abdullah Yusuf Ali.

[7] Quran 39:6. My emphasis

[8] Quran 20:115-122.

[9] Schuon, Frithjof; *Understanding Islam*. 2nd edition. George Allen and Unwin. London. (1963) 1986. p.13.

[10] Kabbani, Rana; *Imperial Fictions*. op. cit.

[11] ibid. p.84-85.

[12] ibid. p.x.

[13] Armstrong, Karen; *Muhammad*. op cit.

[14] Armstrong, Karen; *Holy War: The Crusades and Their Impact on Today's World*. Macmillan. London. 1991.

[15] Armstrong, Karen; *Muhammad*. Op. cit. p.27.

[16] ibid. p.145.

[17] ibid.

[18] Schuon, Frithjof; *Understanding Islam*. op. cit. p.404.

[19] See Bouhdiba, Abdulwahab; *Islam and Sexuality*. Routledge & Kegan Paul.. London. 1985.

[20] Burckhardt, Titus; *Fusus al-Hikam [Translation of Muhi-ud-din Ibn 'Arabi's] The Wisdom of the Prophets*. Arabic to French translation by Burckhardt. French to English by Seymour Angela. Beshara. Gloucestershire. 1975. p.120.

[21] See for example Wilson, Peter L. & Pourjavady Nasrollah; *The Drunken Universe: An Anthology of Sufi Poetry*. Phanes Press. Michigan. 1987; Wilson Peter L., *Scandal: Essays in Islamic Heresy*. Autonomedia Press. New York. 1988.

[22] Bouhdiba, Abdulwahab; op. cit.

[23] Bouhdiba, Abdulwahab; op. cit.

[24] Schuon, Frithjof; *Islam and Perennial Philosophy*. London. World of Islam Publishing. Lahore. 1986. p.11.

[25] Schuon, Frithjof; *Understanding Islam*. op. cit. p.37.

[26] Murata, Sachiko; *The Tao of Islam: A Sourcebook on Gender Relationships in Islamic Thought*. State University of New York Press. 1992. p.7.

[27] ibid. p.23.

[28] Murata, Sachiko; *The Tao of Islam*. Op. cit. p.18.

[29] Nasr, S. Hossein; 'The Male and Female in the Islamic Perspective' in *Studies in Comparative Religion*. Vol. 14. Issue 1 and 2. Winter-Spring 1980. pp.67-75.

[30] ibid.

[31] See Glossary in Burckhardt, Titus; *Fusus al-Hikam*. op. cit.

[32] See Quran 17:110.

[33] Rumi; *Mathnawi*. V. 37II. As translated in Chittick, William C.; *The Sufi Path of Love: The Spiritual Teachings of Rumi*. State University of New York Press. 1983. p.166.

[34] "... the interaction of parts of mind is triggered by contrast ... information is a difference that makes a difference". Bateson, Gregory; *Mind and Nature: A Necessary*

Unity. Dutton. New York. 1979. pp.94-100. This book of Bateson is probably one of the best books on the mind/body 'problem'. See also his discussion on the significance of the image in human perception. pp.32-38.

[35] Corbin, Henry; *Alone with the Alone.* op. cit. pp.159-160.

CHAPTER 6:
ACADEMIC RELIGION AND MYSTICAL ISLAM

[1] Asad, Talal; *Genealogies of Religion.* op. cit. p.29.

[2] Lincoln, Bruce; *Holy Terrors.* op. cit. pp.1-2.

[3] Cooey, Paula; *Religious Imagination and the Body.* op cit. See also: Berry, Philippa & Werncik, Andrew (eds.); *Shadow of Spirit: Postmodernism and Religion.* Routledge. New York. 1992.

[4] Tambiah, Stanley; op. cit. p.32.

[5] Asad, Talal; *Genealogies of Religion.* op. cit. See also: Cooey; *Religious Imagination and the Body.* op. cit. p.123.

[6] Cooey, Paula; *Religious Imagination and the Body.* op. cit. p.5.

[7] Interview given by Frank Vogel in 1993 to National Public Radio (NPR). As cited in Foer Franklin; ''Moral Hazard': Interview with Khaled Abou El Fadl.' in *New Republic.* Vol. 227. Issue 21. 11-18-2002.

[8] Foer, Franklin; 'Moral Hazard'. op. cit.

[9] See for example on his personal website: www.frankevogel.net.

[10] Martyn Kramer, Washington Institute for Near East Policy cited in Foer, Franklin; 'Moral Hazard' op. cit.

[11] Asad, Talal; *Genealogies of Religion.* op. cit. p.29.

[12] de Riencourt, Amaury; *Sex and Power in History.* Dell Publishing. 1974.

[13] Nasr, S. Hossein; *Living Sufism.* Mandala. 1980.

[14] Winters, Michael; 'Islamic Attitudes towards the Human Body' in Jane Marie Law (ed.); *Religious Reflections on the Human Body.* Indiana University Press. Bloomington. 1995. p.41.

[15] Armstrong, Karen; *A Short History of Myth.* op. cit. p.101.

[16] Bouhdiba, Abdulwahab; *Islam and Sexuality.* op. cit.

[17] Said, Edward W.; Impossible Histories: Why the Many Islams Cannot Be Simplified' *Harper's Magazine.* July 2002. http://harpers.org/archive/2002/07/impossible-histories/ (last visited 13-06-2002).

[18] Hillman, James; *The Myth of Analysis: Three Essays in Archetypal Psychology.*

Northwestern University Press. Harper and Row. New York. (1972) 1978.

[19] See for example: King, Ursula; *Religion and Gender*. Blackwell Publishers. Oxford. 1995. / Cooey, Farmer & Ross; *Embodied Love: Sensuality and Relationship as Feminist Value*. Harper and Row. San Francisco. 1987. / Irigaray, Luce; *This Sex Which Is Not One* Translated by Poter Catherine with Burke Carolyn; Cornell University Press. Ithaca. 1985. / Irigaray, Luce; *An Ethics of Sexual Difference*, Cornell University Press. Ithaca. 1993. / Jardine, Alice; *Gynesis: Configurations of Women and Modernity*. Cornell University Press. Ithaca. 1985. / Jones Ann Rosalind; 'Writing the Body: Towards an Understanding of l'Ecriture Feminine' in Showalter, Elaine (ed.); *The New Feminist Criticism: Essays on Women, Literature and Theory*. Pantheon, New York. 1985. pp.361-377. / Scarry Elaine; *The Body in Pain: The Makings and Unmaking of the World*. Oxford University Press. New York. 1985. / Sheets-Johnstone, Maxine; *Give the Body its Due*. SUNY. Albany. 1992. / Rubin, Suleiman Susan; '(Re)writing the Body: The Politics and Poetics of Female Eroticism' in *Poetics today: International Journal for Theory and Analysis of Literature and Communication* Vol. 6. Issue 1-2. 1985. pp.43-65. / Sullivan, Lawrence; 'Body Works: Knowledge of the Body in the Study of Religion' in *History of Religion* Vol. 30. Issue 1. August 1990. pp.86-99.

[20] Cooey, Paula; *Religious Imagination and the Body*. op. cit. p.5.

[21] Jung, Carl Gustav; 'Analytical Psychology and Weltanschauung' in *C.W.* Vol. 8. p.370.

[22] de Reincourt, Amaury; *Woman and Power in History*. Sterling Publishers. Delhi. (1983) 1989.

[23] Ong, Walter J.; *Fighting for Life: Contest, Sexuality and Consciousness*. Cornell University Press. 1981.

[24] Hillman, James; *In Search: Psychology and Religion*. Charles Scribner and Sons. New York. 1967.

[25] Ewing, Katherine; *Arguing Sainthood: Modernity, Psychoanalysis and Islam*. Duke University Press. Durham. 1997.

[26] Soelle, Dorothee; *The Silent Cry: Mysticism and Resistance*. Fortress Press. New York. 2001.

[27] Jung, Carl Gustav; *Seminar on Dream Analysis*. op. cit. p.336.

[28] Schimmel, Annemarie; *Mystical Dimensions of Islam*. University of North Carolina Press. 1975. p.435.

CHAPTER 7:
THE DESTRUCTION OF ISLAM'S FEMINIST DIMENSION

[1] Rumi, Jelaluddin; Taken from different Ghazals, as translated by William C. Chittick in *The Sufi Path of Love: The Spiritual Teachings of Rumi*. State University of New York Press. Albany. 1983. p.340 & p.226.

[2] Hillman, James; *The Myth of Analysis*, op. cit. p.255.

[3] ibid. p.254.

[4] ibid. p.257.

[5] See Hillman, James; *The Myth of Analysis*. op cit. p.260.

[6] Freud, Sigmund & Breuer, Josef; *Studies in Hysteria*. In S.E. Vol. II. Pelican Books. London. 1974. p.57.

[7] See 'The Qalandar as Trope' in Ewing Katherine; *Arguing Saint Hood*. op. cit.

[8] Michael, Dols; *Majnun: The Madman in Medieval Islamic Society*. Clarendon. Oxford. p.32.

[9] ibid.

[10] Jalal, Ayesha; *Self and Sovereignty*. Routledge. London/New York. 2002.

[11] Ahmed, Durre; *Masculinity, Rationality and Religion*. op. cit.

[12] Ewing, Katherine; *Arguing Sainthood*. op. cit.

[13] Said, Edward; *Impossible Histories*. op. cit.

[14] See Ahmed, Durre; *Violence and the Feminine in Islam*. op. cit.

[15] See Ahmed, Durre; *The Final Frontier*. op. cit.

[16] Wilson,Peter L; *Scandal*. op. cit.

[17] ibid, p.30.

[18] Pagels, Elaine; *The Gnostic Gospels*. op. cit.7.

CHAPTER 8:
THE TERROR WITHIN

[1] Jung, Carl Gustav; 'Civilization in Transition' in *C.W*. Vol. 10. p.325.

[2] Ashraf, Nasim; 'The Islamization of Pakistan's Educational System: 1979-1989' in *Viewpoints: The Islamization of Pakistan: 1979-2009*. Middle East Institute; Washington D.C. s.d.

[3] Shehzad, Mohammad; 'School Books That Teach Children To Hate' in *The Friday Times*. 14-2-2003.

[4] For details of the social conditions and the genesis of the Taliban, see Rashid, Ahmed; *Taliban: Militant Islam, Oil and Fundamentalism in Central Asia*. I.B. Tauris & Co. Ltd. 2000.

[5] Erikson, E.H.; *Childhood and Society*. Revised ed. Norton. New York. 1980.

[6] See for example: Freedman, A. & Kaplan ,H.; *Comprehensive Text Book of Psychiatry*. 2nd edition. Williams and Wilkins. Baltimore. 1967. pp.665-675. / Davison G.C. &

Neale J.M.; *Abnormal Psychology.* 6th edition. John Wiley. New York. 1994. p.265.

[7] Freedman, A & Kaplan, H (eds.); 'Paranoid Reactions' in *Comprehensive Text Book of Psychiatry.* op. cit. p.674.

[8] ibid.

[9] Shehzad, Mohammad; 'School Books That Teach Children To Hate' op. cit. See also, Nayyar A.H.; 'Pakistan: Islamisation of Curricula' in *South Asian Journal.* Vol. 2. 2003.

[10] Freedman & Kaplan (eds.); 'Paranoid Reactions' in *Comprehensive Text Book of Psychiatry.* op. cit.

[11] Miller Alice; 'Political Consequences of Child 'Abuse' in *The Journal of Psycho History.* Vol 26 Issue 2. Fall 1998.

[12] *TIME;* 'The Science of Happiness' 17-01-2005. Incidentally, it seems happiness has little to do with poverty and education.

[13] For details of the case see: *Dawn.* 1-2-2002.

[14] See: *The Herald.* December 1999 - January 2000.

[15] Transparency Market Research; *Erectile Dysfunction Drugs Market is expected to reach an estimated value of US$3.4 billion in2019.* Nasdaq Globe Newswire. 16-04-2015. http://globenewswire.com/news-release/2015/04/16/725113/10129251/en/Erectile-Dysfunction-Drugs-Market-is-expected-to-reach-an-estimated-value-of-US-3-4-billion-in-2019-Transparency-Market-Research.html

[16] The images of these advertisements and their detailed analysis appeared in Ahmed, Durre; 'Heroes and Zeroes' in Zaidi, Saima; *Mazaar, Bazaar. Design and Visual Culture in Pakistan.* Oxford University Press. Oxford. 2009.

PART III
(TITLE PAGE)

[1] Hofstadter, Richard; 'The Paranoid Style in American Politics' in *Harper's Magazine.* November, 1964.

CHAPTER 9:
INTELLECTUALS (HOMO)SEXUALITY,
RELIGION AND PARANOIA

[1] Jung, Carl Gustav; *C.W.* Vol. 18. p.585.

[2] Hofstadter, Richard; *The Paranoid Style in American Politics.* op. cit.

[3] Ibid.

[4] Hillman, James; *Archetypal Psychology*. op. cit.

[5] Hofstadter, Richard; *The Paranoid Style in American Politics*. op. cit.

[6] Ibid.

[7] Ibid.

[8] *New York Times*; 'The High Cost of Xenophobia' 27-1-1992; which opens with the sentence: "Japan bashing has suddenly become a frenzy."

[9] *The Economist*; 'From There to Intolerance' 20-7-1991.

[10] *The Economist*; 'Sam, Sam, the Paranoid Man' 18-2-1992.

[11] Morrow, Lance; 'A Nation of Finger Pointers' in *TIME*. 12-8-1991.

[12] *Newsweek*; 27-4-1992.

[13] See also Hofstadter, Richard J.; 'The Paranoid Style' in *American Politics: And Other Essays*. Vintage Books. New York. (1952) 2008.

[14] As cited in Freedman & Kaplan; *Comprehensive Textbook of Psychiatry*. Op. cit. p.660.

[15] The American Psychiatric Association; *Diagnostic and Statistical Manual of Mental Disorders (DSM IV)*. 1994.

[16] Freedman & Kaplan (eds.); *Comprehensive Textbook of Psychiatry*. op. cit.

[17] WebMD; *Delusional Disorders*. http://www.webmd.com/schizophrenia/guide/delusional-disorder (last visited 16-10-2015)

[18] Jaspers Karl; *General Psychopathology*. Chicago University Press. 1963. p.99.

[19] Freud, Sigmund; 'Psycho-analytical Notes upon an Autobiographical Account of a Case of Paranoia (Dementia Paranides) (1911)'. *iCollected Papers*. 3rd ed. Vol. III. Hogarth. London. 1946. / See also: Freud, Sigmund; 'A Case of Paranoia running counter to the Psycho-analytical theory of the Disease (1915)' in *Collected Papers*. 3rd ed. Vol. II. Hogarth. London. 1946.

[20] *TIME*; 'The Century's Greatest Minds'. 29-03-99.

[21] Gay, Peter; 'Psychoanalyst Sigmund Freud' in *TIME* 29-03-99; *Newsweek*; 'Freud's Enduring Legacy: How His Ideas Still Shape Psychotherapy.' 4-07-1988.

[22] Davison & Neale; *Abnormal Psychology*. op. cit. p.398.

[23] For example, the work of Luce Irigaray and Julia Kristeva. See: Whitford (ed.); *The Irigaray Reader*. op. cit. 1991.

[24] Hillman, James; *The Myth of Analysis*. op. cit. p.218.

[25] Steinem, Gloria; *Ms*. 4/5. 1994.

[26] See: Masters, Virginia & Johnson, William; *Human Sexual Response*; Little Brown. Boston. 1966. / Masters, Virginia & Johnson, William; *Human Sexual Inadequacy*;

Little Brown. Boston. 1970.

[27] See: Kinsey, Pomerey, Martin & Geehard; *Sexual Behaviour in the Human Male*. W.B. Sanders. Philadelphia. 1948. / Kinsey, Pomerey, Martin & Geehard; *Sexual Behaviour in the Human Female*. W.B. Sanders. Philadelphia. 1953.

[28] Hillman, James; *The Myth of Analysis*. op. cit. pp.220-249

[29] ibid.

[30] Foucault, Michel; *The History of Sexuality*. Vintage Books. New York. Vol. 1. 1980. / Foucault Michel; *The History of Sexuality*. Vintage Books. New York. Vol. 2. 1986. / Foucault Michel; *The History of Sexuality*. Vintage Books. New York. Vol. 3. 1988.

[31] Hillman, James; *The Myth of Analysis*. op. cit. p.218

[32] Irigaray, Luce; 'The Bodily Encounter with Mother' in Whitford (ed.); *The Irigaray Reader*. op. cit.

[33] Irigaray, Luce; 'Sexual Difference' in Toril Moi (ed.); *French Feminist Thought: A Reader*. Wiley-Blackwel. 1987. p.118.

[34] Ong; Walter; *Fighting for Life: Contest, Sexuality and Consciousness*. Ithaca. Cornell U. Press. 1981. p. 90

[35] Cooey, Paula; *Religious Imagination and the Human Body*. op. cit. p.9.

[36] Hillman James; *On Paranoia*. Spring Publications. Dallas. 1986. p.1.

[37] James, William; *The Varieties of Religious Experience*. Longman Green. London. 1902.

[38] Kittel, G. (ed.); *Theological Dictionary of the Old Testament*. Vol. 3. Grand Rapids. 1965.

[39] Santner, Eric; *My Own Private Germany: Daniel Paul Schreber's Secret History of Modernity*. Princeton University Press. 1998. p.20.

[40] Schreber, Daniel Paul; *Memoirs of my Nervous Illness*. Translated by MacAlpine Ida and Hunter Richard. Dawson. London. 1955. Republished by Harvard University Press. Cambridge. 1988.

[41] Boisen, Anton T.; *Out of Depth: An Autobiographical Study of Mental Disorder and Religious Experience*. Harpers. New York. 1960.

[42] ibid. p.83.

[43] ibid. pp.81-85.

[44] ibid. p.107.

[45] ibid. pp.81-107.

[46] ibid. p.95.

[47] ibid. p.100.

[48] ibid. pp.100-120.

[49] ibid. p.119.

[50] ibid. p.107.

[51] ibid. p.200.

[52] ibid. p.120.

[53] Bateson, Gregory; *Perceval's Narrative: A Patient's Account of his Psychosis*. William Morrow. New York. 1974.

[54] Originally published in 1838 – 1840. 2 vols. *A Narrative of the Treatment Experiences by a Gentleman during a State of Mental Derangement, Designed to Explain the Causes and the Nature of Insanity*. By John Perceval.

[55] Bateson, Gregory; *Perceval's Narrative*. op. cit. pp.27-28.

[56] ibid. p.29.

[57] ibid. p.30.

[58] ibid. p.11.

[59] ibid. p.152.

[60] ibid. p.308.

[61] Cameron, Norman; 'Psychotic Disorders II: Paranoid Reactions' Freedman & Kaplan (eds.); in *Comprehensive Text Book of Psychiatry*. 3rd edition. Williams and Wilkins. Baltimore. (1967) 1980. pp.665-667.

[62] Schreber; *Memoirs of my Nervous Illness*. op. cit. p.146.

[63] ibid. p.252.

[64] ibid. p.352.

[65] ibid. p.30

[66] See Hillman, James; *On Paranoia*, op. cit. p.19. See also Santner, Eric; *My Own Private Germany*. op. cit.

[67] As cited in Hillman, James, *On Paranoia*, op. cit. p.336.

[68] Schreber; *Memoirs of my Nervous Illness*. op. cit. p.322.

[69] ibid. p.337.

[70] ibid. p.148.

[71] See Hillman, James; *On Paranoia*. op. cit. p.19.

[72] Hillman, James; *Archetypal Psychology*. op. cit. 1981.

[73] Hillman, James James; *Loose Ends: Primary Papers in Archetypal Psychology*. Spring Publications. Dallas. 1975. p.xx.

[74] Hillman James; *Suicide and the Soul*. Harper and Row. New York. 1973.

[75] Corbin, Henry; *Alone with the Alone*. op. cit. p.297.

[76] Asad, Mohammad; *The Message of the Quran*. op. cit. Although Asad's translation is excellent, by and large I will be using the translation of Allamah Nooruddin, Amatul Rahman Omar & Abdul Mannan Omar, *The Holy Quran*. Noor Foundation. Delaware. 2001.

[77] Allamah Nooruddin, Amatul Rahman Omar & Abdul Mannan Omar, *The Holy Quran*. Noor Foundation. Delaware. 2001.

[78] For details see Chittick, William; *The Sufi Path of Love*. op. cit. p.352-353.

[79] Murata, Sachiko; *The Tao of Islam*. op. cit.

[80] Hillman, James; *In Search*. 1967, p.42.

[81] Wilson, Catherine; 'Modern Western Philosophy' in *Encyclopedia of Islamic Philosophy*. Part II. S Hossein Nasr (ed). 2002. pp.1013-1029.

[82] Corbin, Henry; *Avicenna and the Visionary Recital*. 1960. / Corbin; *Alone with the Alone*. op. cit. / Corbin; *Cyclical Time and Ismaili Gnosis*. s.d. /See also, Chittick, William *Sufi Path of Love*. op. cit. and *Sufi Path of Knowledge* op. cit. Also Chittick, William; *Imaginal Worlds: Ibn al Arabi and the Problem of Religious Diversity*. 1994.

[83] Chittick, William; 'Ibn 'Arabi' in *The Encyclopedia of Islamic Philosophy*. op. cit. pp.497-523.

[84] Chittick, William; *Sufi Path of Love*. op. cit. pp.248-249.

[85] From Corbin's *Spiritual Body and Celestial Earth*. Cited by Harold Bloom in his Preface to 6th edition of *Alone with the Alone*. op. cit. p.xvi.

[86] Bloom, Harold; ibid. Bloom claims being deeply influenced by Corbin's work and this is in fact clearly evident in his more recent books. For example, see Bloom, Harold; *Omens of Millennium: The Gnosis of Angels, Dreams, and Resurrection*. Riverhead Books. New York. 1996.

[87] ibid.

[88] ibid.

[89] Jung, Carl Gustav; *CW*, Vol. 13. p.75

[90] Hillman, James; *Archetypal Psychology*. op. cit. p.6.

[91] Casey, Edward S.; 'Towards an Archetypal Imagination'. In *Spring: An Annual of Archetypal Pscychology and Jungian Thought*, Spring Publications. 1974: pp.1-32.

[92] Hillman, James; *On Paranoia*, op. cit. p.30.

[93] ibid. p.336.

[94] ibid. p.330.

CHAPTER 10:
PARANOIA RE-VIEWED

[1] As cited in Hillman, James, *On Paranoia*. op. cit. p.20.

[2] Hillman, James; *The Myth of Analysis*, op. cit. p.64.

[3] ibid.

[4] Eliade, Mircea; *Shamanism: Archaic Techniques of Ecstasy*. Bollingen Series LXXVI. Princeton Press University. s.l. (1951) 1974.

[5] Hillman, James; *In Search*. op. cit. pp.105-108.

[6] Hillman, James; *On Paranoia*. op. cit. p.10.

[7] Freud, Sigmund; *Collected Papers*. 1946. p.447.

[8] ibid. p.448.

[9] Perlmutter, Richard; *A Family Approach to Psychiatric Disorders*. 1996. p.80.

[10] Jung, Carl Gustav; 'The Undiscovered Self' in *C.W.* Vol. 10. p.554.

[11] Campbell, Jan; 'For Esme with Love and Squalor' in *Psychopolitics and Cultural Desires*. UCC Press. London. 1998.

[12] Jung, Carl Gustav ;'The Undiscovered Self' n *C.W.* Vol. 10:554.

[13] Huston, Smith; *Brilliant Answers to the Wrong Question: Postmodernism and the Worlds Religions*. 2005.

[14] Caputo, John; *Good News about Alterity: Derrida and Theology*. 1993. p.453.

[15] For more on this see Hillman, James; *Revisioning Psychology*. 1977. p.8.

[16] Campbell, Jan; *Arguing with the Phallus*. 2000.

[17] Boisen, Anton; *Out of Depth*. 1960. p.111.

[18] Bateson, Gregory; *Perceval's Narrative: A Patient's Account of his Psychosis*. William Morrow. New York. 1974. p.270-271.

[19] Hillman, James; *The Myth of Analysis*. 1978.

[20] Boisen, Anton; *Out of Depth*. 1960. p.99.

[21] Boisen, Anton; *Out of Depth*. 1960. p.101.

[22] Cited in Santner, Eric; *My Own Private Germany*. 1998. p.121.

[23] Eilberg-Schwartz, Howard; *God's Phallus: And Other Problems for Men and Monotheism*. Boston Beacon Press. 1994.

[24] Santner, Eric; *My Own Private Germany*. 1998.

[25] Boyarin, Daniel; 'Jewish Masochism: Couvade, Castration, and Rabbis in Pain' in *American Imago*. 51. Spring 1994. p.3-36.

[26] Hillman, James; *On Paranoia*. 1986. p.27.

[27] Ong, Walter; *Fighting for Life*. 1981. p.77.

[28] Nasr, Hossein; *Male and Female in the Islamic Perspective*. 1980.

[29] Schuon, Frithjof; *Understanding Islam*. op. cit. p.37.

[30] Schuon, Frithjof; *From the Divine to the Human Indiana*. op. cit.

[31] Corbin, Henry; *Creative Imagination in the Sufism of Ibn-i-Arabi*. 1975. pp.159-160.

[32] Hillman, James; *In Search*. 1967. p.107.

[33] Boisen, Anton; *Out of Depth*. 1960. p.281.

[34] For more about this archetype in the context of Pakistan, see Ahmed, Durre; *Masculinity, Rationality and Religion*. 2001.

[35] Levinson & Ember (ed). *The Encyclopedia of Cultural Anthropology*. 1996. pp.618-621.

[36] Ahmed, Durre S; 'The Last Frontier' in Durre Ahmed (ed.); *Gendering the Spirit: Women, Religion and the postcolonial Response*. ZED Books. London. 2002.

[37] Chittick, William; *The Sufi Path of Love*. op. cit. p.99.

[38] Bateson, Gregory; *Perceval's Narrative*. op. cit. p.125.

[39] Freud, Sigmund; *Collected Papers*. op. cit.. pp.354-356.

[40] Hillman, James; *On Paranoia*. op. cit. pp.50-56.

[41] Bateson, Gregory; *Perceval's Narrative*. op. cit. p.311

[42] ibid. p.37

CHAPTER 11:
MODERNITY AND PARANOIA

[1] Jung, Carl Gustav; 'After the Catastrophe' in *C.W.* Vol. 10.

[2] Canetti, Elias; *Crowds and Power*. Farrar Strarss. New York. 1984.

[3] Deleuze, Gilles & Guatarri, Feliz; *Anti-Oedipus: Capitalism and Schizophrenia*. Minneapolis University Press. 1983.

[4] Foucault, Michel; *Discipline and Punish*. Pantheon Books. 1977.

[5] Niederland, William; *The Schreber Case: Psychoanalytic Profile of a Paranoid Personality*. N.J. Analytic Press. Hillsdale. 1984.

[6] Lothane, Zvi; *In Defense of Schreber: Soul Murder and Psychiatry*. N.J. Analytic Press. Hillsdale. 1992.

[7] Schatzman, Morton; *Soul Murder: Persecution in the Family*. Random House. New York. 1973.

[8] Chabot, Barry; *Freud on Schreber*. Amherst University of Massachusetts Press. 1982.

[9] Santner, Eric; *My Own Private Germany*. op. cit. p.9.

[10] ibid. p.xii.

[11] ibid.

[12] ibid.

[13] ibid. p.xiii.

[14] ibid.

[15] ibid. p.xiii-xiv. (My emphasis)

[16] See for example Ahmed; *Islam and the West*. op. cit. / Ahmed; *Masculinity, Rationality and Religion*. op. cit.

[17] *Harper's Magazine*. December 1991.

[18] *Harper's Magazine*. December 1991. Also see: Rieff David; *Victims All? Recovery Co-dependency and the Art of Blaming Someone Else. Harper's. Magazine* Oct. 1991.

[19] Ahmed, Durre S.; 'Foolish Questions, Impolite Answers: Intellectuals and Religion' in Ralte Lalrinawmi & Faria Stella (eds.); *Waging Peace: Building a World in which Life Matters*. Indian Women in Theology/ISPCK. Delhi. 2004.

[20] Santner, Eric; *My Own Private Germany*. op. cit. p.23.

[21] Lincoln, Bruce; *Holy Terrors*. op. cit. p.19.

[22] Teichmann, Jenny; 'Don't be Cruel or Unreasonable': a review of Richard Rorty's 'Contingency, Irony and Solidarity'. *New York Times* 23-4-89.

[23] Santner, Eric; *My Own Private Germany*, op. cit. p.8.

[24] Santner, Eric; *My Own Private Germany*, op. cit. p.9. (My emphasis.)

[25] Bandrillard, J.; *Simulaera and Simulation*. Translation by Sheila Faria Glaser. University of Michigan Press. 1994.

[26] Trexler, Richard; *Sex and Conquest: Gendered Violence, Political Order and the European Conquest of the Americas*. Cornell University Press. Ithaca. 1995.

[27] Frecco, Carla; 'They are all Sodomites!' Gender and September 11: A roundtable. In *Signs: Journal of Women, Culture and Society*. Vol. 28, No. 11. 2002.

[28] Goldberg, Jonathan; *Sodometries: Renaissance Texts, Modern Sexualities*. Stanford University Press. Stanford. 1992.

[29] Frecco, Carla; 'They are all Sodomites!' op. cit.

[30] The American Psychiatric Association; *Diagnostic and Statistical Manual of Mental Disorders (DSM III)*. 1980. / Durand M. & Barlow H.; *Essentials of Abnormal*

Psychology. Wadsworth. 3ᵈ edition. 2003. pp.412-413. / Additional material as cited in Hillman; *On Paranoia*. op. cit. pp.49-50.

[31] Orbach, Benjamin; *Usama Bin Laden and Al-Qaida*. In *Middle East Review of International Affairs*. MERIA. Vol. 5. No. 4. December 2001.

[32] Ibid.

[33] Ibid.

[34] Ibid.

[35] Ibid.

[36] Post, J.; 'Terrorist Psycho-Logic' in Walter Reich (ed.); *Origins of Terrorism*. The Woodrow Wilson Press. Washington D.C. 1990. p.35.

CHAPTER 12:
BEYOND PARANOIA

[1] Jung, Carl Gustav; *Civilization in Transition* in C.W. Vol. 10:1375

[2] Derrida, Jacques; *The Gift of Death*. Translated by David Wills. University of Chicago Press. 1995. pp.70-87.

[3] Jung, Carl Gustav; *C.W*. Vol. 10:505.

[4] Freud, Sigmund; *Collected Papers*. op. cit. p.71.

[5] Freedman & Kaplan (eds.); *Comprehensive Textbook of Psychiatry*. op. cit. p.666.

[6] WebMD; *Delusional Disorders*. op. cit.

[7] Hillman, James; *On Paranoia*. op. cit.

[8] Ahmed, Durre S.; *The Last Frontier*. op. cit.

[9] Bateson, Gregory; *Perceval's Narrative*. op. cit. p.281.

[10] Dols, Michael; *Majnun: The Madman in Medieval Islamic Society*. Clarendon. Oxford. 1992.

[11] Hora ,Thomas; 'Tao, Zen and Existential Psychotherapy' in *Psychologia*. 2:236–42. 1959.

[12] Asad, Muhammad; *The Message of the Quran*. op. cit.

[13] Nooruddin, Amatul Rahman & Abdul Mannan, *The Holy Quran*. op. cit..

[14] Schuon, Fritjhof; *Spiritual Perspectives and Human Facts*. Faber and Faber. London. 1985.

[15] Morgan, Robin; 'Our Bodies Our Souls' in *MS*. September & October 1997.

[16] Moyers, Bill; 'Battlefield Earth' on *Alternet* 08-12-2004. http://www.alternet.org/story/20666/battlefield_earth (last visited 2015). See also:

Scherer; *The Road to Environmental Apocalypse.* op. cit. / McKibben; *Enough.* op. cit.

[17] Quran 6:12, 7:156 and 17:110

[18] Quran 24:24 and 41:21.

[19] Jung, Carl Gustav; *C.W.* Vol. 18:611.

[20] For a further elaboration on this theme, see: Ahmed, Durre S.; *The Last Frontier.* op. cit.

[21] Santner, Eric; *My Own Private Germany.* op. cit. p.82.

[22] Lifton, Robert J.; 'The Image of the 'End of the World': A Psychohistorical View' in Friedlander, Holton, Marx & Skolnikoff (eds.); *Visions of Apocalypse: End or Rebirth?* New York. Holmes and Meier. 1985.

[23] WebMD; *Delusional Disorders.* op. cit.

[24] Durand & Barlow; *Essentials of Abnormal Psychology.* op. cit. p.413.

INDEX

BIBLIOGRAPHY

Abul, el Fadl Khaled; 'Islam and the Theory of Power' in *Islam: Images, Politics Paradox. Middle East Report*. Winter 2001..

Adams, Carol (ed); *Ecofeminism and the Sacred*. New York. Continuum. 1994.

Ahmed, Durre S.; 'Changing Faces of Tradition' in Edith Sizoo (ed.); *Women's Lifeworlds: Women's Narratives on Shaping their Realities*. Routledge. London. 1977.

Ahmed, Durre S.; 'Foolish Questions, Impolite Answers: Intellectuals and Religion' in Ralte Lalrinawmi & Faria Stella (eds.); *Waging Peace: Building a World in which Life Matters*. Indian Women in Theology/ISPCK. Delhi. 2004.

Ahmed, Durre S.; 'Heroes and Zeroes' in Zaidi, Saima; *Mazaar Bazaar. Design and Visual Culture in Pakistan*. Oxford University Press. Oxford. 2009.

Ahmed, Durre S.; 'Islam and the West: A Psychological Analysis'. in *Journal of the Henry Martyn Institute*, Vol.19. Issue1, 2000. Republished as 'Islam and the West: An Analysis of C.G. Jung's Understanding of Islam' in *Iqbal Review*. Lahore 2004.

Ahmed, Durre S.; 'Violence and the Feminine in Islam: A Case Study of the Zikris' in Durre Ahmed (ed.); *Gendering the Spirit: Women, Religion and the postcolonial Response*. ZED Books. London. 2002.

Ahmed, Durre S.; *Masculinity, Rationality and Religion: A Feminist Perspective*. 2nd edition. ASR. Lahore. (1994) 2001.

Ahmed, Durre S; 'The Last Frontier' in Durre Ahmed (ed.); *Gendering the Spirit: Women, Religion and the postcolonial Response*. ZED Books. London. 2002.

Ali, Tariq; *Clash of Fundamentalisms: Crusader, Jihads and Modernity*. London. Verso. 2002.

Armstrong, Karen; *A Short History of Myth*. Penguin. New York. 2005.

Armstrong, Karen; *Holy War: The Crusades and Their Impact on Today's World*. Macmillan. London. 1991.

Armstrong, Karen; *Islam: A Short History*. Random House. New York. 2000.

Armstrong, Karen; *Muhammad: A Biography of the Prophet*. Harper Collins. New York. 1992.

Armstrong, Karen; *The Battle for God.* Knopf. New York. 2000.

Asad, Muhammad; *Islam at the Crossroads.* Sheikh M. Ashraf. Lahore. 1934. Reprinted 1991.

Asad, Muhammad; *The Message of the Quran.* The Book Foundation. 2003.

Asad, Talal; *Genealogies of Religion: Discipline and Reason of Power in Christianity and Islam.* John Hopkins Press. Baltimore. 1993.

Ashraf, Nasim; *The Islamization of Pakistan's Educational System: 1979-1989.* In Middle East Institute; *Viewpoints: The Islamization of Pakistan: 1979-2009.* Washington D.C. s.d.

Atherton, J.S.; *The Books at the Wake.* Carbondale and Edwardsville. 1974.

Bandrillard, J.; *Simulaera and Simulation.* Translation by Sheila Faria Glaser. University of Michigan Press. 1994.

Banuri, Tariq; *Modernization and its Discontents.* In Marglin and Marglin (eds.); *Dominating Knowledge.* Clarendon Press. Oxford. 1990.

Barlow, David (ed.); *Clinical Handbook of Psychological Disorders. A Step-by-Step Treatment Manual.* Fourth Edition. Guilford Press. New York. 2007.

Barnaby, Karin and D'Acierno, Pelligrino (eds.); *C.G. Jung and the Humanities: Towards a Hermenentics of Culture.* London. Routledge. 1990.

Bateson, Gregory; *Mind and Nature: A Necessary Unity.* Dutton. New York. 1979.

Bateson, Gregory; *Perceval's Narrative: A Patient's Account of his Psychosis.* William Morrow. New York. 1974.

Bem, Sandra; *The Lenses of Gender.* Yale University Press. New Haven. 1993.

Beneke, Timothy; *Proving Manhood: Reflections on Men and Sexism.* University of California Press. Berkeley. 1997.

Berry, Philippa & Werncik, Andrew (eds.); *Shadow of Spirit: Postmodernism and Religion.* Routledge. New York. 1992.

Bloom, Harold; *Omens of Millennium: The Gnosis of Angels, Dreams, and Resurrection.* Riverhead Books. New York. 1996.

Bly, Robert; Iron, John & Tacey, David; *Remarking Men: Jung, Spirituality and Social Change.* Routledge. London. 1997.

Boisen, Anton T.; *Out of Depth: An Autobiographical Study of Mental Disorder and Religious Experience.* Harpers. New York. 1960.

Bordo, Susan; 'The Cartesian Masculinization of Thought' in *Signs: Journal of Women and Culture in Society.* Vol.II. Issue 3 University of Chicago Press. 1986.

Bordo, Susan; *The Flight of Objectivity: Essays on Cartesianism and Culture.* State University of New York Press. 1987.

Boyarin, Daniel; 'Jewish Masochism: Couvade, Castration, and Rabbis in Pain'. in *American Imago.* Vol.51. Spring 1994.

Boyce-Tillman, June; 'Unconventional Wisdom-Theologizing the Margins' in *Feminist Theology.* Vol.13. Issue3. 2005..

Brown, Norman O.; 'The Apocalypse of Islam' in Andrews, V.; Bosnak R. & K. Goddwin (eds.); *Facing Apocalypse,* Spring Publications. Dallas. 1987.

Brown, Norman O.; *Negations.* Allen Lane. London. 1968.

Bruce, Lawrence; *Defenders of God: The fundamentalist revolt against the modern age.* University of South Carolina Press. 1989.

Bryld, M. & Lykke, N.; *Cosmodolphins: Feminist Cultural Studies of Technology, Animals and the Sacred.* Zed Books. London. 2000.

Burckhardt, Titus; *Art of Islam: Language and Meaning.* World of Islam Festival Trust. London. 1976.

Burckhardt, Titus; *Fusus al-Hikam [Translation of Muhi-ud-din Ibn 'Arabi's] The Wisdom of the Prophets.* Arabic to French translation by Burckhardt. French to English by Seymour Angela. Beshara. Gloucestershire. 1975.

Cahoone, Lawrence; *Cultural Revolutions: Reason versus Culture in Philosophy, Politics and Jihad.* University of Pennsylvania Press. 2005.

Cameron, Norman; 'Psychotic Disorders II: Paranoid Reactions' in Freedman & Kaplan (eds.) *Comprehensive Text Book of Psychiatry.* 3rd edition. Williams and Wilkins. Baltimore. (1967) 1980..

Campbell, Jan; 'For Esme with Love and Squalor' in *Psychopolitics and Cultural Desires.* UCC Press. London. 1998.

Campbell, Jan; *Arguing with the Phallus: Feminist, Queer and Postcolonial Theory. A Psychoanalytic Contribution.* Zed books. London. 2003.

Campbell, Joseph; *The Hero with a Thousand Faces.* Bollingen Series. Princeton University Press. 1978.

Campbell, Joseph; *The Power of Myth.* Doubleday. 1988.

Canetti, Elias; *Crowds and Power.* Farrar, Straus and Giroux New York. 1984.

Caputo, John; 'Good News about Alterity: Derrida and Theology' in *Faith and Philosophy*, Vol.10. Issue4. October 1993.

Casey, Edward S.; 'Towards an Archetypal Imagination' in *Spring: An Annual of Archetypal Psychology and Jungian Thought.* Spring Publications. 1974.

Castells, Manuel; *The Information Age: Economy, Society and Culture.* Vol. II. Blackwell Publishing. 2004.

Chabot, Barry; *Freud on Schreber.* Amherst University of Massachusetts Press. 1982.

Chittick, William .; 'Ibn 'Arabi' in *The Encyclopedia of Islamic Philosophy.* 497-523. London. Routledge. 1996.

Chittick, William .; *Imaginal Worlds: Ibn al Arabi and the Problem of Religious Diversity.* SUNY. Press. Albany 1994.

Chittick, William .; *The Sufi Path of Love: The Spiritual Teachings of Rumi.* State University of New York Press. 1983.

Coningham, Rotin & Lewer, Nick; *Archaeology and Identity in South Asia: Interpretations and Consequences.* Antiquity 74: 664-667. 2000.

Connel,l R.W.; *Masculinities*. University of California Press. Berkeley. 1995.

Connors ,W.R.; 'Why Were We Surprised' in *The American Scholar*. Spring 1991.

Cooey, Paula; *Religious Imagination and the Body: A Feminist Analysis*. Oxford University Press. New York. 1994.

Cooey; Farmer & Ross; *Embodied Love: Sensuality and Relationship as Feminist Value*. Harper and Row. San Francisco. 1987.

Corbin Henry; *Alone with the Alone: Creative Imagination in the Sufism of Ibn-i-Arabi*. Bollingen series XCI. Translated by Manheim Ralph. Princeton University Press. Princeton. 1975.

Corbin Henry; *Avicenna and the Visionary Recital*. Bollingen Series. New York. 1960.

Corbin Henry; *Cyclical Time and Ismaili Gnosis*. Kegan & Paul International. London. s.d. available at http://www.imagomundi.com.br/espiritualidade/corbin_cyclical_time.pdf

Davison, G.C. & Neale J.M.; *Abnormal Psychology*. 6th edition. John Wiley. New York. 1994.

de Reincourt, Amaury; *Woman and Power in History*. Sterling Publishers. Delhi. (1983) 1989.

de Riencourt Amaury; *Sex and Power in History*. Dell Publishing. 1974.

Deboer, Fredrik, *America's Suicide Epidemic is a National Security Crisis*, Foreign Policy, 04/28/2016. http://foreignpolicy.com/2016/04/28/americas-suicide-epidemic-is-a-national-security-crisis (Last visited 06/12/2016)

Deleuze ,Gilles & Guatarri, Feliz; *Anti-Oedipus: Capitalism and Schizophrenia*. Minneapolis University Press. 1983.

Derrida, Jacques; *Acts of Religion*. Routledge. London. 2002.

Derrida, Jacques; *The Gift of Death*. Translated by David Wills. University of Chicago Press. 1995.

Dols, Michael; *Majnun: The Madman in Medieval Islamic Society*. Clarendon. Oxford. 1992.

Dowd, Maureen; 'Liberties: Cleopatra and Osama' in *New York Times*. 18-11-2001.

Durand, M. & Barlow, H.; *Essentials of Abnormal Psychology*. Wadsworth. 3d edition. 2003.

Eco, Umberto; *The Role of the Reader: Explorations in the Semiotics of Texts*. Bloomington. 1979.

Edwards, Tim; *Cultures of Masculinity*. Routledge. New York. 2006.

Eilberg-Schwartz, Howard; *God's Phallus: And Other Problems for Men and Monotheism*. Beacon Press. Boston. 1994.

Eliade, Mircea; *Shamanism: Archaic Techniques of Ecstasy*. Bollingen Series LXXVI. Princeton Press University. s.l. (1951) 1974.

Enben, Roxanne Leslie; *Enemy in the Mirror: Islamic fundamentalism and the Limits of Modern Rationalism*. Princeton University Press. 1999.

Erikson, E.H.; *Childhood and Society*. Revised ed. Norton. New York. 1980.

Ewing, Katherine; *Arguing Sainthood: Modernity, Psychoanalysis and Islam*. Duke University Press. Durham. 1997.

Fisk, Robert; 'Who is Copying Who in War of Words' in *The Independent*. London. 11-10-2001.

Foer, Franklin; 'Moral Hazard': Interview with Khaled Abou El Fadl. In *New Republic*. Vol. 227. Issue 21. 11-18-2002.

Foucault, Michel; *Discipline and Punish*. Pantheon Books. 1977.

Foucault, Michel; *The History of Sexuality*. Vintage Books. New York. Vol. 1. 1980.

Foucault, Michel; *The History of Sexuality*. Vintage Books. New York. Vol. 2. 1986.

Foucault, Michel; *The History of Sexuality*. Vintage Books. New York. Vol. 3. 1988.

Frankenberry, Nancy; 'Feminist Philosophy of Religion' in *Stanford Encyclopedia of Philosophy*. Online. 2004. http://plato.stanford.edu/entries/feminist-religion

Frecco, Carla; 'They are all Sodomites!' Gender and September 11: A roundtable' in *Signs: Journal of Women, Culture and Society*. Vol. 28, No. 11. 2002.

Freedman, A. & Kaplan H.; *Comprehensive Text Book of Psychiatry*. 2nd edition. Williams and Wilkins. Baltimore. 1967. pp. 665-675.

Freud, Sigmund; 'A Case of Paranoia running counter to the Psycho-analytical theory of the Disease (1915)' in *Collected Papers*. 3rd ed. Vol. II. Hogarth. London. 1946.

Freud, Sigmund; 'Psycho-analytical Notes upon an Autobiographical Account of a Case of Paranoia (Dementia Paranides) (1911)' in *Collected Papers*. 3rd ed. Vol. III. Hogarth. London. 1946.

Freud, Sigmund; *Collected Papers*. 3rd ed. Hogarth Press. London. 1946.

Freud, Sigmund; *New Introductory Lectures on Psychoanalysis*. Hogarth Press. London. 1933.

Freud, Sigmund; *The Future of an Illusion*. Hogarth Press. London. 1962.

Freud, Sigmund; *The Standard Edition of the Complete Psychological Works of Sigmund Freud*. Translated by Strachy, James & Strachey Alix. Hogarth Press. London. 1955.

Friedmann, Yohanan; *Prophecy Continuous: Aspects of Ahmadi Religious Thought and Its Medieval Background*. Berkeley. University of California Press. 1989.

Ganchet, Marcel; *The Disenchantment of the World: A Political History of Religion*. Princeton University Press. 1998.

Gay, Peter; 'Psychoanalyst Sigmund Freud' in *TIME* 29-03-99.

Gellner, Ernest; *Postmodernism, Reason and Religion*. Routledge. London. 1992.

Gitlin, Todd; *With God on Our Side. Reading the State of Union*. Opendemocracy.net. 30-1-2003. www.opendemocracy.net.

Goldberg, Jonathan; *Sodometries: Renaissance Texts, Modern Sexualities*. Stanford University Press. Stanford. 1992.

Goldenberg, Naomi; 'A Feminist Critique of Jung' in Moore R.C. & Meckel D. (eds.);

Jung, Christianity in Dialogue: Faith, Feminism, Hermeneutics. Paulist Press. New York. 1990.

Gosset Sherrie; *Muslim vs. Muslim: The Untold Story*. AIM. 4-1-2005. http://www.aim-org/aim_column_print/2482_0_3_01. (last visited 2010)

Habermas, Jurgen; 'Faith and Knowledge' an opening speech given at acceptance of the Peace Prize of the German Publishers and Booksellers Association. Paulskirche. Frankfurt. 14.01.2001. Translation by Kermit Suelson.

Habermas, Jurgen; *The Philosophical Discourse of Modernity: Twelve Lectures*. Polity Press. 2002.

Harding, Sandra; 'Is Gender a Variable in conceptions of Reality'. Paper delivered at the Fifth International Colloquium on Rationality. Vienna. 1981

Harding, Sandra; *Is Science Multicultural? Postcolonialisms, Feminism and Epistemologies*. Bloomington, Indiana University. Press. 1998.

Heelas, Paul, Marti David & Morris, Paul; *Religion, Modernity and Postmodernity*. London. Blackwell. 1998.

Herper, Matthew; *The World's Best-Selling Drugs*. Forbes.com. 16-3-2004. http://www.forbes.com/2004/03/16/cx_mh_0316bestselling.html

Hessel, D.T. & Reuther R.R.; *Christianity and Ecology: Seeking the Well Being of Earth and Humans*. Harvard University Press. Cambridge. 2000.

Hillman, James; *Archetypal Psychology: A Brief Account*. Spring Publications. Dallas. 1985.

Hillman, James; *In Search: Psychology and Religion*. Charles Scribner and Sons. New York. 1967.

Hillman, James; *Inter views*. Harper and Row. New York. 1983.

Hillman, James; *Loose Ends: Primary Papers in Archetypal Psychology*. Spring Publications. Dallas. 1975.

Hillman, James; *Loose Ends: Primary Papers in Archetypal Psychology*. Spring Publications. New York/Zurich. 1975.

Hillman, James; *On Paranoia*. Spring Publications. Dallas. 1986.

Hillman, James; *Re-Visioning Psychology*. Harper and Row. New York. (1975) 1977.

Hillman, James; *Suicide and the Soul*. Harper and Row. New York. 1973.

Hillman, James; *The Myth of Analysis: Three Essays in Archetypal Psychology*. Northwestern University Press. Harper and Row. New York. (1972) 1978.

Hodgson, M.G.S.; 'A Comparison of Islam and Christianity as Framework of Religious Life' in *Diogenes*. 3. 1960.

Hofstadter, Richard J.; *The Paranoid Style in American Politics: And Other Essays*. Vintage Books. New York. (1952) 2008.

Hofstadter, Richard; 'The Paranoid Style in American Politics' in *Harper's Magazine*. November, 1964. Can be downloaded at: http://harpers.org/archive/1964/11/the-paranoid-style-in-american-politics

Hoodbhoy, Pervez; *Muslims and Science: Religious Orthodoxy and the Struggle for Rationality*. Vanguard. Lahore. 1991.

Hora, Thomas; *Tao, Zen and Existential Psychotherapy*. In *Psychologia*. 2:236—42. 1959.

Howden, Daniel; 'The Destruction of Mecca: Saudi Hardliners are wiping out their own Heritage'. in *The Independent*. 6-8-2005.

Human Rights Commission of Pakistan; *The Annual Report of the Human Rights Commission of Pakistan*. 2004.

Human Rights Commission of Pakistan; *The Annual Report of the Human Rights Commission of Pakistan*. 2005.

Hussey, Anderw; 'Au Revoir, Cruel World' in *The Modern Review*. Reprinted as 'Esprit de Mort' in *Harper's* Magazine. September 1995.

Ilana, Pardes; *Countertraditions in the Bible: A Feminist Approach*. Cambridge. Mass Harvard University. Press. 1992.

Irigaray, Luce; 'Sexual Difference' in Toril Moi (ed.); *French Feminist Thought: A Reader*. Wiley-Blackwel. 1987.

Irigaray, Luce; *An Ethics of Sexual Difference,* Cornell University Press. Ithaca. 1993.

Irigaray, Luce; *This Sex Which Is Not One* Translated by Poter Catherine & Burke Carolyn (eds.); Cornell University Press. Ithaca. 1985.

Jalal, Ayesha; *Self and Sovereignty*. Routledge. London/New York. 2002.

James, William; *The Varieties of Religious Experience*. Longman Green. London. 1902.

Jardine, Alice; *Gynesis: Configurations of Women and Modernity*. Cornell University Press. Ithaca. 1985.

Jaspers, Karl; *General Psychopathology*. Chicago University Press. 1963.

Jones, Ann Rosalind; 'Writing the Body: Towards an Understanding of l'Ecriture Feminine' in Showalter, Elaine (ed.); *The New Feminist Criticism: Essays on Women, Literature and Theory*. Pantheon, New York. 1985.

Joyce, James; *A Portrait of the Artist as a Young Man*. 1916.

Jung, Carl Gustav; *Modern Man in Search of a Soul*. Routledge, Kegan & Paul. London. 1966.

Jung, Carl Gustav; *Seminar on Dream Analysis 1928-1930*. William McGuire (ed.) Princeton University Press. Bollingen Series XC/X. p..

Jung, Carl Gustav; *The Collected Works of C.G. Jung*. H. Read, M. Fordham and G. Adler (eds). Translated by RFC Hull. Routledge and Kegan Paul. London. 1967.

Kabbani, Raana; *Imperial Fictions. Europe's Myths of the Orient*. Harper Collins. London. 1986.

Keller, Evelyn F. & Longino Helen (eds.); *Feminism & Science*. Oxford University Press. Oxford. 1996.

Kepel, Gilles; *The Revenge of God: The Resurgence of Islam, Christianity and Judaism in the Modern World*. Penn State University Press; 1 edition (December 13, 1993). 1993.

Khan, Muhammad Zafarullah; *The Quran*. Curzon Press. London. 1970.

Kheel, Marti; 'Ecofeminism and Deep Ecology: Reflections on Identity and Difference' in Robb, Card S. & Casebolt, C.J. (eds); *Covenant for a New Creation: Ethics, Religion and Public Policy*. Mary Knoll. Orbis Books. New York. 1991.

Kimmel, Michael; *Manhood in America: a Cultural History*. Free Press. New York. 1996.

King, Ursula; Book review of Gendering the Spirit: Women, Religion and the Postcolonial Response. In *Feminist Theology*. 13/3. 2005.

Kinsey, Pomerey, Martin & Geehard; *Sexual Behaviour in the Human Male*. W.B. Sanders. Philadelphia. 1948.

King, Ursula; *Religion and Gender*. Blackwell Publishers. Oxford. 1995.

Kinsey, Pomerey, Martin & Geehard; *Sexual Behaviour in the Human Female*. W.B. Sanders. Philadelphia. 1953.

Kittel, Gerhard. (ed.); *Theological Dictionary of the Old Testament*. Vol. 3. Grand Rapids. 1965.

Kristeva, Julia; *New Maladies of the Soul*. Columbia University Press. New York. 2001.

Kroker, Arthur; *The Possessed Individual: Technology and Postmodernity*. MacMillan. London. 1992.

Lakoff, George; *Metaphors We Live By*. University of Chicago Press. Chicago. 1980.

Lakoff, George; *Moral Politics: How Liberals and Conservatives Think*. University of Chicago Press. Chicago. 1987.

Lauter, Estella & Schreir Ruppereht Carol; *Feminist Archetypal Theory: Interdisciplinary Re-Visions of Jungian Thought*. University of Tennessee Press. Knoxville, Tennessee. 1985.

Levinson & Ember (ed.); *The Encyclopedia of Cultural Anthropology*. Vol. II. Henry Holt. New York. 1996.

Lewis, Bernard. *Islam and the West*. Oxford University Press. New York. 1983.

Lewontin, R.C.; 'Women Versus the Biologists' in *The New York Review of Books*. 7-04-1994.

Lifton, Robert J.; 'The Image of the 'End of the World': A Psychohistorical View' in Friedlander, Holton, Marx & Skolnikoff (eds.); *Visions of Apocalypse: End or Rebirth?* New York. Holmes and Meier. 1985.

Lincoln, Bruce; *Holy Terrors: Thinking about Religion after September 11*. University of Chicago Press. Chicago. 2003.

Lloyd, Geneviere; *The Man of 'Reason': 'Male' and 'Female' in Western Philosophy*. University of Minnesota Press. Minneapolis. 1993.

Lloyd, Genevieve; *Madeess, Metaphor, and the 'Crisis' of 'Reason'*. In Antony Louise & Wih Charlotte (eds.); *A Mind of One's Own*. Boulder: West view Press. 1992.

Lockhart, William; '"We are One Life" But Not of One Gender Ideology: Unity, Ambiguity and Promise Keepers' in *Sociology of Religion*. Spring 2000.

Long, Eugene Thomas; 'Twentieth Century Philosophy of Religion 1900-2000' in

Handbook of Contemporary Philosophy of Religion. Vol. 1. Kluwer Publications. Dordrech. 2000.

Lothane, Zvi; *In Defense of Schreber: Soul Murder and Psychiatry.* N.J. Analytic Press. Hillsdale. 1992.

Manadal, D.; 'Ayodhya Archaeology after Demolition'. 1993. http://www.resurgenceonline.com/pictures/issues.htm. (last visited 2010)

Mann, A. and Jane, Lyle; *Sacred Sexuality.* Element Books. Shaftesbury. 1995.

Martin, Emily; 'The Egg and the Sperm: How Science has constructed a Romance Based on Stereotypical Male-Female Roles' in Keller, Evelyn F. & Longino, Helen (eds.); *Feminism and Science.* Oxford University Press. Oxford. 1996.

Marty, Martin E. & Appleby, Scott R.; *Fundamentalism Comprehended.* University of Chicago Press. Chicago. 1995.

Masters, Virginia & Johnson, William; *Human Sexual Inadequacy;* Little Brown. Boston. 1970.

Masters, Virginia & Johnson, William; *Human Sexual Response;* Little Brown. Boston. 1966.

Matteo S.; 'The Risk of Multiple Addictions: guidelines for Assessing a Woman's Drug and Alcohol Use' in *The Western Journal of Medicine.* . 1988.

McClain, Ernest; *Meditations Through the Quran.* Nicholas-Hays. Maine. 1981.

McDermott, Terry; 'A Perfect Soldier' In *The Los Angeles Times.* 27-1-2002

McDermott, Terry; *Perfect Soldiers.* Harper Collins. New York. 2005.

Mckibben, Bill; *Enough: Staying Human in an Engineered Age.* Times Books. New York. 2003.

Mckibben, Bill; *The End of Nature.* Anchor Books. New York. 1997.

Menleman, Johan H. (ed.); *Islam in the Era of Globalization: Muslim Attitudes to Modernity.* Routledge. New York/London. 2002.

Merchant, Carolyn; *Radical Ecology.* New York Routledge. 1992.

Metzger, Bruce & Coogan, Michael (eds.); *The Oxford Companion to the Bible.* Oxford University Press. New York/Oxford. 1993.

Miller, Alice; 'Political Consequences of Child 'Abuse'' in *The Journal of Psycho History.* 26/2. Fall 1998.

Moaddel, M. and Talatoff K.; *Modernist and Fundamentalists Debates in Islam: A Reader.* Palgrave Macmillan. New York. 2000.

Morgan, Robin; 'Our Bodies Our Souls' in *MS.* September & October 1997.

Morny, Joy; 'Images and Imagination' in *Encyclopedia of Religion.* MacMillan. New York. 1987.

Morrow, Lance; 'A Nation of Finger Pointers' in *TIME* 12-8-1991.

Moyers, Bill; 'Battlefield Earth' on *Alternet* . 08-12-2004. http://www.alternet.org/story/20666/battlefield_earth (last visited 2015)

Munir Report; *Report of the Court of Inquiry into the Punjab disturbances of 1953.* Lahore. 1954.

Murata, Sachiko; *The Tao of Islam: A Sourcebook on Gender Relationships in Islamic Thought.* State University of New York Press. 1992.

Murphy, Peter (ed.); *Feminism and Masculinities.* Oxford University Press. New York/London. 2004.

Myers, Diana; 'Feminist Perspectives on the Self' in *Stanford Encyclopedia of Philosophy.* 2004. http://plato.stanford.edu/entries/feminism-self/ (last visited 15-10-2015)

Nandy, Ashis: 'A New Cosmopolitism' in Chen, Kuan-Hsing (ed.); *Trajectories: Inter-Asia Cultural Studies;* Routledge. London/New York. 1998.

Nandy, Ashis; *The Intimate Enemy: Loss and Recovery of Self under Colonialism.* Oxford University Press. Delhi. 1983.

Nasr, S. Hossein; 'The Male and Female in the Islamic Perspective'. in *Studies in Comparative Religion.* Vol. 14. Issue 1 and 2. Winter-Spring 1980.

Nasr, S. Hossein; *Knowledge and the Sacred.* Edinburgh University Press. Edinburgh. 1981.

Nasr, S. Hossein; *Living Sufism.* Mandala. 1980.

Nasr, Vali. *The Vanguard of the Islamic Revolution: The Jamaati-Islami of Pakistan.* U.C.L.A. Press. 1994.

National Assembly of Pakistan. *Proceedings of The Special Committee of the Whole House Held in Camera To Consider the Qadiani Issue.* Pakistan Press, Islamabad. 1974. https://ia801506.us.archive.org/9/items/NAProceedings1974/NA-Proceeding-1974.pdf (last visited 10-12-2015)

Nayyar, A.H.; Pakistan: 'Islamisation of Curricula' in *South Asian Journal.* Vol. 2. 2003.

Nellis, Muriel; *The Female Fix.* Penguin Books. New York. 1988.

Neumann, Erich; *The Origins and History of Consciousness.* Princeton University Press. 1971.

New Scientist; An Interview with Dr. Abdus Salam. 26-08-1976.

New York Times; 'The High Cost of Xenophobia'. 27-1-1992.

Newsweek; 'A Postmodern President'. 16-01-1994. (see also: http://www.newsweek.com/postmodern-president-187498)

Newsweek; 'Another Cultural Massacre' 19-02-2002.

Newsweek; 'Freud's Enduring Legacy: How His Ideas Still Shape Psychotherapy'. 4-07-1988.

Newton, Judith; 'White Guys' in *Feminist Studies.* Vol.3. 1998.

Niederland, William; *The Schreber Case: Psychoanalytic Profile of a Paranoid Personality.* N.J. Analytic Press. Hillsdale. 1984.

Noble, David F.; *A World without Women: The Christian Clerical Culture of Western Science.* Knopf. New York. 1992.

Nooruddin, Allamah, Amatul Rahman Omar & Abdul Mannan Omar, *The Holy Quran.*

Noor Foundation. Delaware. 2001.

Northrop, Frye, *Myth and Metaphor: Selected Essays. 1974-1988*. Robert Denham (ed.). University of Virginia. 1991.

O'Kane, Maggie; 'Hunting Radovan' in *The Guardian*. 20-02-2001.

Ong, Walter J.; *Fighting for Life: Contest, Sexuality and Consciousness*. Cornell University Press. 1981.

Ong, Walter J.; *Orality and Literacy: The Technologizing of the Word*. Methuen. New York. 1982.

Orbach, Benjamin; 'Usama Bin Laden and Al-Qaida' In *Middle East Review of International Affairs*. MERIA. Vol. 5. No. 4. December 2001.

Ostriker, Susan; *Feminist Revision and the Bible*. Blackwell. Oxford. 1993.

Pagels ,Elaine; *The Gnostic Gospels*. New York. Vintage Books. 1988.

Papini, Giovanni; 'A Visit to Freud'. Colosseum. s.l. 1934. Reprinted in *Review of Existential Psychology and Psychiatry*. IX. 1969.

Perlmutter, R.A.; *A Family Approach to Psychiatric Disorders*. American Psychiatric Press. Washington DC. 1996.

Pfeil, Fred; *White Guys: Studies in Postmodern Domination and Difference*. Verso. London. 1995.

Plumwood, Val; 'Nature, Self and Gender: Feminism, Environmental Philosophy and the Critique of Rationalism' in *Hypatia: A Journal of Feminist Philosophy*. Vol. 6 Issue 6. 1991.

Pope, Hugh; 'Iconic Clash: Saudi Fights to End Demolition Driven by Islamic Dictate… A Mall Goes up in Mecca' in *The Wall Street Journal*. 18-8-2004.

Post, J.; 'Terrorist Psycho-Logic' in Walter Reich (ed.); *Origins of Terrorism*. The Woodrow Wilson Press. Washington D.C. 1990.

Primavese, Anna; *From Apocalypse to Genesis: Ecology, Feminism and Christianity*. Burns and Dates. Kent. 1991.

Qadir, Ali; 'Parliamentary hereticization of the Ahmadiyya: The modern world implicated in Islamic crises' in Ganiel G., Monnot C. & Winkel H. (eds.), *Religion in Times of Crisis* in Swatos W. (ed.). The ASR Book Series: Religion and the Social Order. Brill. Leiden. 2014.

Qadir, Ali; 'The University on the Edge' Unpublished M. Phil. Thesis. NCA. Lahore. 2007.

Qadir, Ali; 'When Heterodoxy Becomes Heresy: Using Bourdieu's Concept of Doxa to Describe State-Sanctioned Exclusion in Pakistan'. in *Sociology of Religion*. 76/2. DOI: 10.1093. Socrel/srv015. 2015.

Rashid, Ahmed; *Taliban: Militant Islam, Oil and Fundamentalism in Central Asia*. I.B. Tauris & Co. Ltd. 2000.

Reeves, Peggy; *Female Power and Male Dominance*. Cambridge University Press. Cambridge. 1981.

Reuther ,Rosemary; *Sexism and God Talk*. Beacon Press. Boston 1983.

Reuther, Rosemary R.; *Gaia and God: An Ecofeminist Theology of Earth Healing*. Harper Collins. New York. 1992.

Rieff, David; 'Victims All? Recovery Co-dependency and the Art of Blaming Someone Else'. *Harper's Magazine*. Oct. 1991.

Roy, Olivier; 'What is the driving force behind jihadist terrorism?—A scientific perspective on the causes/circumstances of joining the scene'. Speech delivered at BKA Autumn Conference International Terrorism: How can prevention and repression keep pace?, 18 - 19 November 2015. https://life.eui.eu/wp-content/uploads/2015/11/OLIVIER-ROY-what-is-a-radical-islamist.pdf

Rubin, Suleiman Susan;' (Re)writing the Body: The Politics and Poetics of Female Eroticism' in *Poetics today: International Journal for Theory and Analysis of Literature and Communication*. Vol.6 Issue1-2. 1985

Said, Edward W.; 'Impossible Histories: Why the Many Islams Cannot Be Simplified' *Harper's Magazine*. July 2002. http://harpers.org/archive/2002/07/impossible-histories/ (last visited 13-06-2002).

Samuels, Andrew; *Politics and the Couch: Citizenship and the Internal Life*. Profile Books. London. 2001.

Santmire, Paul; *The Travail of Nature: The Ambiguous Ecological Promise of Christianity*. Fortress Press. Philadelphia. 1985.

Santner, Eric; *My Own Private Germany: Daniel Paul Schreber's Secret History of Modernity*. Princeton University Press. 1998.

Scarry, Elaine; *The Body in Pain: The Makings and Unmaking of the World*. Oxford University Press. New York. 1985.

Schatzman, Morton; *Soul Murder: Persecution in the Family*. Random House. New York. 1973.

Scherer, Glenn;' The Road to Environmental Apocalypse' in *Grist Magazine*. 27-10-2004. Also published on *Grist* as 'Christian-right views are swaying politicians and threatening the environment'. 28-10-2004. http://grist.org/article/scherer-christian/ (last visited 17-10-2015)

Schimmel, Annemarie; *My Soul is a Woman: The Feminine in Islam*. The Continuum Publishing Company. New York. 2003.

Schimmel, Annemarie; *Mystical Dimensions of Islam*. University of North Carolina Press. 1975.

Schreber, Daniel Paul; *Memoirs of my Nervous Illness*. Translated by MacAlpine Ida and Hunter Richard. Dawson. London. 1955. Republished by Harvard University Press. Cambridge. 1988.

Schuon, Frithjof; *From the Divine to the Human Indiana*. World Wisdom Books. 1980.

Schuon, Frithjof; *Islam and Perennial Philosophy*. Scorpion, Cavendish. 1976.

Schuon, Frithjof; *Sufism: Veil and Quintessence*. World Wisdom Books. Bloomington, Indiana. 1979.

Schuon, Frithjof; *Understanding Islam*. 2nd edition. George Allen and Unwin. London. (1963) 1986.

Schuon, Fritjhof; *Spiritual Perspectives and Human Facts*. Faber and Faber. London. 1985.

Schussler, Fiorenza Elizabeth; *But She Said: Feminist Practices of Biblical Interpretation*. Beacon Press. Boston. 1992.

Schussler, Fiorenza Elizabeth; *In Memory of Her: A Feminist Exploration of Christian Origins*. 1983.

Selvidge, Marla; *Notorious Voices: Feminist Biblical Interpretation, 1500-1920*. Continuum. 1996.

Sheets-Johnstone, Maxine; *Give the Body its Due*. SUNY. Albany. 1992.

Shehzad, Mohammad; 'School Books That Teach Children To Hate' in *The Friday Times*. 14-2-2003.

Sigmund, Freud & Josef, Breuer; 'Studies in Hysteria'. In S.E. Vol. II. Pelican Books. London. 1974.

Simmer, Brown Judith; *Daikini's Warm Breath. The Feminine Principle in Tibetan Buddhism*. Shambhala. Boston. 2001.

Sisk, John P.; *The Georgia Review*. Fall 1989.

Slok, Johannes; *Devotional Language*. Translated by Henrik Mossin. Walter De Gruyter Incorporated. Danbury. 1996.

Smith, Huston, 'Postmodernism's Impact on the Study of Religion' in *Journal of the American Academy of Religion*. Vol.58Issue4. 1990.

Smith, Huston; 'Brilliant Answers to the Wrong Question: Postmodernism and the Worlds Religions' in Suheyl Umar Muhammad; *Iqbal Review: Journal of the Iqbal Academy Pakistan*, Vol. 46 Issue2&4, April & October 2005.

Smith, Huston; *Beyond the Postmodern Mind*. 2nd ed. Harper Collins. (1991) 2002.

Smith, Jonathan; *Map is Not the Territory: Studies in the History of Religions*. Leiden University Press. 1978.

Smith, Wilfred C,; *Faith and Belief*. Princeton University Press. 1979.

Soelle, Dorothee; *The Silent Cry: Mysticism and Resistance*. Fortress Press. New York. 2001.

Spretnak, Charlene; 'Ecofeminism: Our Roots and Flowering' in Diamond, Irene & Ornstein, Gloria (eds). *Reweaving the World: The Emergence of Ecofeminism*. Sierra Club Books. San Francisco. 1990.

Spretnak, Charlene; *States of Grace: The Recovery of Meaning in the Postmodern Age*. Harper. San Francisco. 1991.

Steinem, Gloria; *Ms*. 4/5. 1994.

Steward, Desmond; *Mecca*. W.W. Norton. New York. 1980.

Sullivan, Lawrence; 'Body Works: Knowledge of the Body in the Study of Religion' In *History of Religion* Vol.30 Issue1. August 1990..

Tambiah, Stanley J.; *Magic, Science, Religion and the Scope of Rationality*. Cambridge University Press. 1991.

Teichmann, Jenny; 'Don't be Cruel or Unreasonable': a review of Richard Rorty's Contingency, Irony and Solidarity'. *New York Times*. 23-4-89.

The American Psychiatric Association; *Diagnostic and Statistical Manual of Mental Disorders (DSM III)*. 1980.

The American Psychiatric Association; *Diagnostic and Statistical Manual of Mental Disorders (DSM IV)*. 1994.

The Economist; 'From There to Intolerance'. 20-7-1991.

The Economist; 'In the Beginning'. 21-04-2007.

The Economist; 'Islam and the Vatican: An Invitation to Talk Business'. 21-10-06.

The Economist; 'Sam, Sam, the Paranoid Man'. 18-2-1992.

The Economist; 'The Next War, They Say'. 04-08-1994.

The Economist; 'Worst Outbreak of Civil Violence'. 15-06-1974.

The Economist; editorial on euthanasia. 20-07-1999.

The Herald; 'On Powerlessness'. 1996.

The Nobel Foundation; 'Abdus Salam—Biographical' on *Nobelprize.org*. http://www.nobelprize.org/nobel_prizes/physics/laureates/1979/salam-bio.html. (Last visited 17/10/2015).

The Wilson Quarterly; *Editorial*. Spring 1991.

Tibi, Bassom; *The Challenge of Fundamentalism: Political Islam and the New World Disorder*. University of California Press. Berkeley. 1998.

Tiles, Mary & Oberdiek, Hans; *Living a Technological Culture: Human Tools and Human Values*. Routledge. London/New York. 1995.

TIME; 'Evil: Does it exist—or do bad things just happen?'. 10-6-1991.

TIME; 'The Century's Greatest Minds'. 29-03-99

TIMEe; 'The Science of Happiness'. 17-01-2005.

Transparency Market Research; Erectile Dysfunction Drugs Market is expected to reach an estimated value of US$3.4 billion in 2019. *Nasdaq Globe Newswire*. 16-04-2015. http://globenewswire.com/news-release/2015/04/16/725113/10129251/en/Erectile-Dysfunction-Drugs-Market-is-expected-to-reach-an-estimated-value-of-US-3-4-billion-in-2019-Transparency-Market-Research.html

Trexler, Richard; *Sex and Conquest: Gendered Violence, Political Order and the European Conquest of the Americans*. Cornell University Press. Ithaca. 1995.

Trible, Phyllis; *Texts of Terror: Literary and Feminist Reading of Biblical Narratives*. Fortress Press. Philadelphia. 1984.

Van der, Post Laurens; *Jung and the Story of Our Time*. Penguin Books. 1978.

Warner, Maria; 'Fantasy's Power and Peril' in *The New York Times*. 16-12-2001.

Weber, Max; *The Protestant Ethic and the Spirit of Capitalism*. Translated by Parsons

Talcott. George Allen & Unwin Ltd. London. 1930.

WebMD; *Delusional Disorders.*
http://www.webmd.com/schizophrenia/guide/delusional-disorder (last visited 16-10-2015)

Wheelan Simon; 'Saudi Government Demolishes Historic Ottoman Castle'.
www.wsws.org. 28-01-2002.

White, Jr. Lynn; 'The Historical Roots of our Ecological Crisis' in Nash, James (ed.);
Loving Nature. Abington Press. Nashville. 1991.

Whitford, Margaret (ed.); *The Irigaray Reader.* Blackwell. Oxford. 1991.

WHO; 'Gender and Women's Mental Health'.
http://www.who.int/mental_health/prevention/genderwomen/en/ (last visited 15-10-2015)

Wilson A.N.; 'Christianity and Modernity' in *The Guardian.* 5-12-2000.

Wilson, Catherine; 'Modern Western Philosophy' in Nasr S. Hossein (ed.); *History of Islamic Philosophy.* Routledge. London/New York. 1996..

Wilson, Edmund; *Axels Castle.* Collins/Fantana Library. London. 1961.

Wilson, Peter L. & Pourjavady Nasrollah; *The Drunken Universe: An Anthology of Sufi Poetry.* Phanes Press. Michigan. 1987.

Wilson, Peter; *Scandal: Essays in Islamic Heresy.* Automedia Press. New York. 1988.

Winters, Michael; 'Islamic Attitudes towards the Human Body' in Jane Marie Law (ed.);
Religious Reflections on the Human Body. Indiana University Press. Bloomington. 1995.

World Archaeological Congress; *A Closer Look at Ayodhya Issue.* Papers in Session7'
http://www.wac.uct.ac.za/croatia/7.htm. (last visited 2010)

About Yunus Publishing

Yunus Publishing produces web and print projects on religion, politics and mysticism. Its publications and projects include(d) *Halal Monk: A Christian on a Journey through Islam*, a collection of conversations with important Muslim scholars, activists and artists; *thoughtsofgandhi.org*, a webtool that allows people to receive weekly Gandhi quotes; and *Punkademics*, a series of thorough research works that breach the boundaries of mainstream academia.

To be informed of future releases
If you would like to be informed of our new publications, please subscribe to the newsletter on *yunuspublishing.org*. You will only be contacted when a new book or web project is launched; your address will never be shared and you can unsubscribe at any time.

A kind request
Word-of-mouth is, of course, crucial for a small and independent publishing endeavour such as ours. So, if you enjoyed this book, please consider leaving a review at the website of the retailer where you purchased it. Even if it's only a line or two, it can be a huge help.

Contact
For any comments, questions or requests, you're always welcome to send an e-mail to: *mail@yunuspublishing.org*.

www.yunuspublishing.org

www.ingramcontent.com/pod-product-compliance
Lightning Source LLC
Chambersburg PA
CBHW031143270326
41931CB00006B/126